Face of A Man *(Ink on paper)*

The English Writings of Rabindranath Tagore

The English Writings of Rabindranath Tagore

Volume Three

Plays
Stories

Introduction by

Mohit K. Ray

ATLANTIC
PUBLISHERS & DISTRIBUTORS (P) LTD

Published by
ATLANTIC
PUBLISHERS & DISTRIBUTORS (P) LTD
B-2, Vishal Enclave, Opp. Rajouri Garden,
New Delhi-110027
Phones : 25413460, 25429987, 25466842

Sales Office
7/22, Ansari Road, Darya Ganj,
New Delhi-110002
Phones : 23273880, 23275880, 23280451
Fax : 91-11-23285873
web : www.atlanticbooks.com
e-mail : info@atlanticbooks.com

ISBN 81-269-0756-8 (Vol. III)
ISBN 81-269-0666-9 (Set)

Printed in India
at Syndicate Binders, NOIDA (U.P.)

CONTENTS

VOLUME IV

ESSAYS

INTRODUCTION

Tagore's English writings—originals and translations—have not received the attention that they deserve. The purpose of this edition is to make the English writings of Tagore available to the widest possible range of readers interested in the writings of Tagore all over the world with just the bare, minimum information necessary for appreciating the writings, and leave the critical assessment to the readers themselves.

There may be two possible reasons for the neglect of Tagore's English writings. First is Tagore's prolific output, Shakespearean felicity and protean plasticity as a Bengali poet, who, though well-versed in English, chose to write in the medium of his mother tongue, and there is hardly any literary form that he did not touch upon and turn into gold. His creative genius found expression in poems, plays, novels, essays, short stories, satirical pieces, textbooks for children, and songs of all kinds. The only literary form that he did not try is epic. But in his long, eventful and creative eighty years of life he virtually 'lived' an epic.

Tagore was both a nationalist and an internationalist, a man of action and contemplation, a pioneer in cooperative farming and a writer of profound philosophical essays. As a writer he always kept his antennae out and registered every intellectual movement that was taking place in the West and yet always remaining deeply embedded in Upanishadic thoughts. Profoundly oriented in Indian classical thoughts, he was equally a modernist in his sensibility. He was a man who touched the kindred points of heaven and earth, and harmonized in himself the best of the East and the West. It is largely due to his mighty stature as a Bengali poet who practically wrote only in Bengali for nearly the first fifty years of his life, that nobody really bothered about his English writings and his own translations of his own writings.

The second possible reason is the supposedly 'poor' quality of his translations subsequent to the translation of *Gitanjali*. Incidentally, while requesting André Gide to translate Tagore's *Gitanjali*, St. John Perse wrote: "The English translation of Tagore's which he himself made ... is the only really poetic English language work to have appeared in a long time." After Tagore received the Nobel Prize for literature in 1913 there was a growing demand for his writings in the West, and as Tagore was not apparently satisfied by the translations others—mainly his admirers—made, he began to translate his writings himself. But the tremendous hurry if not 'the wicked speed' with which he began to translate, seriously affected the quality of the translations. Many scholars feel that one reason of the waning reputation of Tagore in the West is the poor quality of his translations. But there are others who feel that the translations—particularly the translations of his poems are not as bad as they are said to be. On the contrary, they argue, in keeping with Tagore's own view that translation of a poem is essentially a reincarnation, the soul of the source language poem assuming a new body in the target language poem. It is worth recalling in this connection what Tagore said in an interview given to *Portland Press* in Washington on 23 October 1916:

> My English translations are not the same. Each country has its symbols of expression. So when I translate my work I find new images and presently new thought and finally it is something almost entirely new. The fundamental idea is the same but the vision changes. A poem cannot be translated, it can only be relived in a different atmosphere.

And again, in an interview given to *Evening Post* in New York on 9 December 1916 he reiterated:

> The English versions of my poems are not literal translations. When poems are changed from one

> language into another, they acquire a new quality and a new spirit, the ideas get new birth and are reincarnated.

Even earlier, on 13 March 1913, Tagore had written to Ajit Kumar Chakrabarti: "What I try to capture in my English translation is the heart and core of my original Bengali. That is bound to make for a fairly wide deviation. If I were not there to help you out, you might probably find it impossible to identify the original in the translation." And in another letter written two months later on 12 May 1913 he admits that "the forms and features of the original become different in my translations—the way I do them these days. My translations are more a reflection than an exact replica of the original image".

Rilke had a similar experience. In a letter to Lou Andreas-Salomé Rilke mused: "*einige Mal nahm ich sogar das gleiche Thema französisch und deutsch vor, das sich dann, von jeder Sprache aus, zu meiner Überraschung, anders entwickelte: was sehr gegen die Naturlichkeit des Übersetzen spräche*" ("... a few times I even set myself the same theme in French and in German, which then, to my surprise, developed differently from each language: which would speak very strongly against the naturalness of translation"). Come what may, the point is whether Tagore's English translations are good or bad, whether the translation furthered his reputation or damaged it, is immaterial. The fact of the matter is that they are his, and his own translation of whatever quality it may be is more valuable to a Tagore lover than the best translation made by somebody else, as Van Gogh's one original single scratch is more valuable than the best possible copy by some other artist.

The value of Tagore's English writings lies here: they constitute an important part of his total *oeuvre,* add a new magnificent dimension to it and offer us a glimpse into the mystique of the creative anxiety that could have haunted even this greatest writer of the twentieth century—about his possible reception in an alien culture.

I express my indebtedness to late Professor Sisir K. Das, an eminent Tagore scholar, who had done commendable pioneering work in this direction.

My special thanks go to my colleague Professor Rama Kundu for valuable assistance in readying the volume.

I am grateful to Dr K.R. Gupta, Chairman of M/s Atlantic Publishers and Distributors (P) Ltd., New Delhi, for the confidence evinced in me and for seeing the book through the press.

MOHIT K. RAY

PREFACE

In the present set of volumes, Volume III contains Tagore's plays and stories, while Volume IV contains essays and talks in English or English translations.

Chitra, with which the Volume III begins was first published by the India Society, London, in 1913. It is the English translation of *Citrāngadā,* a Bengali play published in 1892. But there are many changes in the dramatic structure of the play.

Sacrifice and Other Plays was published by Macmillan, New York, in 1917. The other plays referred to in the title are *Sanyasi, Malini,* and *The King and the Queen.* Thus altogether there are four plays. *Sanyasi* (The Ascetic) is based on Tagore's Bengali play *Prakṛtir Pratiśodh*. There are so many changes in the structure, characterization etc., that it is virtually a new play. *Malini* is based on Tagore's Bengali play *Mālinī.* The translation is fairly faithful, but there are some cuts and condensations. *Sacrifice* is based on Tagore's Bengali play *Bisarjan.* It is also drastically revised and condensed, so much so that in place of the five acts of the original Bengali play it has only one act. *The King and the Queen* is based on Tagore's Bengali play *Rāja O Rānī.* In place of the five acts of the original Bengali play the English version has only two acts and many parts of the original play have been left out. Even then many scholars think that the play comes very close to the Shakespearean model.

Autumn Festival is the English version of Tagore's Bengali play *Sarodotsav*. The translation was first published in *The Modern Review* in 1919, and later in book form by A.C. Sarkar from the Brahmo Mission Press the same year.

The Trial is the English prose translation of Tagore's verse play, *Lakshmīr Parīkshā* (The Test of Lakhsmi) and was published in *The Modern Review* in 1920.

The Waterfall, an English translation of *Muktadhārā* (Free Current), was published in *The Modern Review* in 1922. Tagore's note on the play is produced as 'A Note on the Play', prefacing the text in *The Modern Review.*

Red Oleanders, an English translation of Tagore's Bengali play *Raktakarabī,* was first published by Macmillan, London, in 1925.

The Crown, the English translation by Tagore of his Bengali play *Mukut*, was first printed in *Rabindra Biksha* in 1983.

King and Rebel, an original work in English, was first printed in *Rabindra Biksha* in 1977.

Of the four stories reprinted in this Volume, *Victory* is the translation of *Jay Parājay*, and was published in 1892 and was later included in *Hungry Stones and Other Stories.*

Giribala is the English translation of Tagore's Bengali story *Man Bhanjan*, which was first published in *The Modern Review* in 1917 and was later included in *Broken Ties and Other Stories,* published in 1925.

The Patriot, the English rendering of Tagore's Bengali story *Samskar*, was published in *The Modern Review* in 1928.

The Parrot's Training, Tagore's translation of *Tota Kahini* was published by Thacker, Spink and Co., Calcutta and Simla, in 1918. It was later included in *The Parrot's Training and Other Stories,* published by Visva-Bharati in 1944.

Preface to Sadhana

Sadhanā (The Realization of Life) was first published by Macmillan, London in 1913. The book contains eight essays with a Preface by Tagore. In the Preface Tagore wrote: "I should add perhaps that these papers embody in a connected form, suited to this publication, ideas which have been culled from several of the Bengali discourses which I am in the habit of giving to my students in my school at Bolpur (in Bengal); and I have used here and there translations of passages from these

(Tagore's Bengali discourse) done by my friends, Babu Satish Chandra Roy and Babu Ajit Kumar Chakravarti and the last paper of the series, 'Realization in Action' has been translated from my Bengali discourse on 'Karma-Yoga' by my nephew, "Babu Surendranath Tagore."

On Tagore's own testimony thus we cannot accept these essays as Tagore's English writings—originals or translations, and hence we are painfully obliged to reprint the Preface only.

Personality, a collection of six lectures delivered in America, was first published by Macmillan, New York, in 1917. The book is dedicated to C.F. Andrews.

Nationalism, a collection of three lectures delivered in Japan, was first published by Macmillan, New York, in 1917. This book is dedicated to C.F. Andrews.

The Centre of Indian Culture, originally a lecture delivered in Madras in February 1919, was published by the society for the Promotion of National Education, Adyar, Madras in 1919. Incidentally, this is supposed to be the first lecture delivered in English in India by Tagore.

Creative Unity was first published by Macmillan, New York, in 1922. It is dedicated to Dr Edwin H. Lewis, of Harvard University.

Talks in China, a collection of seven lectures delivered in China was published in Calcutta in 1925. But Sisir Kumar Das points out that another earlier edition had already been published by Visva-Bharati in 1924, but the edition was possibly withdrawn. Both the editions have the same title—but there is some difference in the contents and the arrangement. Three essays of the 1924 edition do not occur in the 1925 edition. So we publish *Talks in China* in two sections. Section I uses the 1924 edition and Section II, the 1925 edition.

MOHIT K. RAY

PLAYS

Chitra

A PLAY IN ONE ACT

PREFACE

This lyrical drama was written about twenty-five years ago. It is based on the following story from the Mahabharata.

In the course of his wanderings, in fulfilment of a vow of penance, Arjuna came to Manipur. There he saw Chitrāṅgadā, the beautiful daughter of Chitravāhana, the king of the country. Smitten with her charms, he asked the king for the hand of his daughter in marriage. Chitravāhana asked him who he was, and learning that he was Arjuna the Pandava, told him that Prabhanjana, one of his ancestors in the kingly line of Manipur, had long been childless. In order to obtain an heir, he performed severe penances. Pleased with these austerities, the god Shiva gave him this boon, that he and his successors should each have one child. It so happened that the promised child had invariably been a son. He, Chitravāhana, was the first to have only a daughter Chitrāṅgadā to perpetuate the race. He had, therefore, always treated her as a son and had made her his heir. Continuing, the king said:

'The one son that will be born to her must be the perpetuator of my race. That son will be the price that I shall demand for this marriage. You can take her, if you like, on this condition.'

Arjuna promised and took Chitrāṅgadā to wife, and lived in her father's capital for three years. When a son was born to them, he embraced her with affection, and taking leave of her and her father, set out again on his travels.

Characters

Gods
Madana (Eros)
Vasanta (Lycoris)
Mortals
Chitra, *daughter of the King of Manipur*
Arjuna, *a prince of the house of the Kurus. He is of the Kshatriya or 'warrior caste', and during the action is living as a Hermit retired in the forest.*
Villagers *from an outlying district in Manipur*

SCENE I

Chitra. Art thou the god with the five darts, the Lord of Love?

Madana. I am he who was the first born in the heart of the Creator. I bind in bonds of pain and bliss the lives of men and women!

Chitra. I know, I know what that pain is and those bonds.—And who art thou, my lord?

Vasanta. I am his friend—Vasanta—the King of the Seasons. Death and decrepitude would wear the world to the bone but that I follow them and constantly attack them. I am Eternal Youth.

Chitra. I bow to thee, Lord Vasanta.

Madana. But what stern vow is thine, fair stranger? Why dost thou wither thy fresh youth with penance and mortification? Such a sacrifice is not fit for the worship of love. Who art thou and what is thy prayer?

Chitra. I am Chitra, the daughter of the kingly house of Manipur. With god-like grace Lord Shiva promised to my royal grandsire an unbroken line of male descent. Nevertheless, the divine word proved powerless to change the spark of life in my mother's womb—so invincible was my nature, woman though I be.

Madana. I know, that is why thy father brings thee up as his son. He has taught thee the use of the bow and all the duties of a king.

Chitra. Yes, that is why I am dressed in man's attire and have left the seclusion of a woman's chamber. I know no feminine wiles for winning hearts. My hands are strong to bend the bow, but I have never learnt Cupid's archery, the play of eyes.

Madana. That requires no schooling, fair one. The eye does its work untaught, and he knows how well, who is struck in the heart.

Chitra. One day in search of game I roved alone to the forest on the bank of the Purna river. Tying my horse to a tree trunk I entered a dense thicket on the track of a deer. I found a narrow sinuous path meandering through the dusk of the entangled boughs, the foliage vibrated with the chirping of crickets, when of a sudden I came upon a man lying on a bed of dried leaves, across my path. I asked him haughtily to move aside, but he heeded not. Then with the sharp end of my bow I pricked him in contempt. Instantly he leapt up with straight, tall limbs, like a sudden tongue of fire from a heap of ashes. An amused smile flickered round the corners of his mouth, perhaps at the sight of my boyish countenance. Then for the first time in my life I felt myself a woman, and knew that a man was before me.

Madana. At the auspicious hour I teach the man and the woman this supreme lesson to know themselves. What happened after that?

Chitra. With fear and wonder I asked him 'Who are you?' 'I am Arjuna,' he said, 'of the great Kuru clan.' I stood petrified like a statue, and forgot to do him obeisance. Was this indeed Arjuna, the one great idol of my dreams! Yes, I had long ago heard how he had vowed a twelve-years' celibacy. Many a day my young ambition had spurred me on to break my lance with him, to challenge him in disguise to single combat, and prove my skill in arms against him. Ah, foolish heart, whither fled thy presumption? Could I but exchange my youth with all its aspirations for the clod of earth under his feet. I should deem it a most precious grace. I know not in what whirlpool of thought I was lost, when suddenly I saw him vanish through the trees. O foolish woman, neither didst thou greet him, nor speak a word, nor beg forgiveness, but stoodest like a barbarian boor while he contemptuously walked away!... Next morning I laid aside my man's clothing. I donned bracelets, anklets, waist-chain, and a gown of purple red silk. The unaccustomed dress clung about my shrinking shame; but I hastened on my quest, and found Arjuna in the forest temple of Shiva.

Madana. Tell me the story to the end. I am the heart-born god, and I understand the mystery of these impulses.

Chitra. Only vaguely can I remember what things I said, and what answer I got. Do not ask me to tell you all. Shame fell on me like a thunderbolt, yet could not break me to pieces, so utterly hard, so like a man am I. His last words as I walked home pricked my ears like red hot needles. 'I have taken the vow of celibacy. I am not fit to be thy husband!' Oh, the vow of a man! Surely thou knowest, thou god of love, the unnumbered saints and sages have surrendered the merits of their life-long penance at the feet of a woman. I broke my bow in two and burnt my arrows in the fire. I hated my strong, lithe arm, scored by drawing the bowstring. O Love, god Love, thou hast laid low in the dust the vain pride of my manlike strength; and all my man's training lies crushed under thy feet. Now teach me thy lessons; give me the power of the weak and the weapon of the unarmed hand.

Madana. I will be thy friend. I will bring the world-conquering Arjuna a captive before thee, to accept his rebellion's sentence at thy hand.

Chitra. Had I but the time needed, I could win his heart by slow degrees, and ask no help of the gods. I would stand by his side as a comrade, drive the fierce horses of his war-chariot, attend him in the pleasures of the chase, keep guard at night at the entrance of his tent, and help him in all the great duties of a Kshatriya, rescuing the weak, and meting out justice where it is due. Surely at last the day would have come for him to look at me and wonder. 'What boy is this? Has one of my slaves in a former life followed me like my good deeds into this?' I am not the woman who nourishes her despair in lonely silence, feeding it with nightly tears and covering it with the daily patient smile, a widow from her birth. The flower of my desire shall never drop into the dust before it has ripened to fruit. But it is the labour of a lifetime to make one's true self known and honoured. Therefore I have come to thy door, thou world-vanquishing Love, and thou, *Vasanta,* youthful Lord of the Seasons, take from my young body this primal injustice, an unattractive plainness. For a single day make me superbly beautiful, even as beautiful as was the sudden blooming of love in my heart. Give me but one brief day of perfect beauty, and I will answer for the days that follow.

Madana. Lady, I grant thy prayer.

Vasanta. Not for the short span of a day, but for one whole year the charm of spring blossoms shall nestle round thy limbs.

SCENE II

Arjuna. Was I dreaming or was what I saw by the lake truly there? Sitting on the mossy turf, I mused over bygone years in the sloping shadows of the evening, when slowly there came out from the folding darkness of foliage an apparition of beauty in the perfect form of a woman, and stood on a white slab of stone at the water's brink. It seemed that the heart of the earth must heave in joy under her bare white feet. Methought the vague veilings of her body should melt in ecstasy into air as the golden mist of dawn melts from off the snowy peak of the eastern hill. She bowed herself above the shining mirror of the lake and saw the reflection of her face. She started up in awe and stood still; then smiled, and with a careless sweep of her left arm unloosed her hair and let it trail on the earth at her feet. She bared her bosom and looked at her arms, so flawlessly modelled, and instinct with an exquisite caress. Bending her head she saw the sweet blossoming of her youth and the tender bloom and blush of her skin. She beamed with a glad surprise. So, if the white lotus bud on opening her eyes in the morning were to arch her neck and see her shadow in the water, would she wonder at herself the live-long day. But a moment after the smile passed from her face and a shade of sadness crept into her eyes. She bound up her tresses, drew her veil over her arms, and sighing slowly, walked away like a beauteous evening fading into the night. To me the supreme fulfilment of desire seemed to have been revealed in a flash and then to have vanished.... But who is it that pushes the door?

[*Enter* Chitra, *dressed as a woman.*]

Ah! it is she. Quiet, my heart! ... Fear me not, lady! I am a Kshatriya.

Chitra. Honoured sir, you are my guest. I live in this temple. I know not in what way I can show you hospitality.

Arjuna. Fair lady, the very sight of you is indeed the highest hospitality. If you will not take it amiss I would ask you a question.

Chitra. You have permission.

Arjuna. What stern vow keeps you immured in this solitary temple, depriving all mortals of a vision of so much loveliness?

Chitra. I harbour a secret desire in my heart, for the fulfilment of which I offer daily prayers to lord Shiva.

Arjuna. Alas, what can you desire, you who are the desire of the whole world! From the easternmost hill on whose summit the morning sun first prints his fiery foot to the end of the sunset land have I travelled. I have seen whatever is most precious, beautiful and great on the earth. My knowledge shall be yours, only say for what or for whom you seek.

Chitra. He whom I seek is known to all.

Arjuna. Indeed! Who may this favourite of the gods be, whose fame has captured your heart?

Chitra. Sprung from the highest of all royal houses, the greatest of all heroes is he.

Arjuna. Lady, offer not such a wealth of beauty as is yours on the altar of false reputation. Spurious fame spreads from tongue to tongue like the fog of the early dawn before the sun rises. Tell me who in the highest of kingly lines is the supreme hero?

Chitra. Hermit, you are jealous of other men's fame. Do you not know that all over the world the royal house of the Kurus is the most famous?

Arjuna. The house of the Kurus!

Ahitra. And have you never heard of the greatest name of that far-famed house?

Arjuna. From your own lips let me hear it.

Chitra. Arjuna, the conqueror of the world. I have culled from the mouths of the multitude that imperishable name and hidden it with care in my maiden heart. Hermit, why do you look perturbed? Has that name only a deceitful glitter? Say so, and I will not hesitate to break this casket of my heart and throw the false gem to the dust.

Arjuna. Be his name and fame, his bravery and prowess false or true, for mercy's sake do not banish him from your heart—for he kneels at your feet even now.

Chitra. You, Arjuna!

Arjuna. Yes, I am he, the love-hungered guest at your door.

Chitra. Then it is not true that Arjuna has taken a vow of chastity for twelve long years?

Arjuna. But you have dissolved my vow even as the moon dissolves the night's vow of obscurity.

Chitra. Oh, shame upon you! What have you seen in me that makes you false to yourself? Whom do you seek in these dark eyes, in these milk-white arms, if you are ready to pay for her the price of your probity? Not my true self, I know. Surely this cannot be love, this is not man's highest homage to woman! Alas, that this frail disguise, the body, should make one blind to the light of the deathless spirit! Yes, now indeed, I know, Arjuna, the fame of your heroic manhood is false.

Arjuna. Ah, I feel how vain is fame, the pride of prowess! Everything seems to me a dream. You alone are perfect; you are the wealth of the world, the end of all poverty, the goal of all efforts, the one woman! Others there are who can be but slowly known. While to see you for a moment is to see perfect completeness once and for ever.

Chitra. Alas, it is not I, not I, Arjuna! It is the deceit of a god. Go, go, my hero, go. Woo not falsehood, offer not your great heart to an illusion! Go.

SCENE III

Chitra. No, impossible. To face that fervent gaze that almost grasps you like clutching hands of the hungry spirit within; to feel his heart struggling to break its bounds urging its passionate cry through the entire body—and then to send him away like a beggar—no, impossible.

[*Enter* Madana *and* Vasanta.]

Ah, god of love, what fearful flame is this with which thou hast enveloped me! I burn, and I burn whatever I touch.

Madana. I desire to know what happened last night.

Chitra. At evening I lay down on a grassy bed strewn with the petals of spring flowers, and recollected the wonderful praise of my beauty I had heard from Arjuna;—drinking drop by drop the honey that I had stored during the long day. The history of my past life like that of my former existences was forgotten. I felt like a flower, which has but a few fleeting hours to listen to all the humming flatteries and whispered murmurs of the woodlands and then must lower its eyes from the sky, bend its head and at a breath give itself up to the dust without a cry, thus ending the short story of a perfect moment that has neither past nor future.

Vasanta. A limitless life of glory can bloom and spend itself in a morning.

Madana. Like an endless meaning in the narrow span of a song.

Chitra. The southern breeze caressed me to sleep. From the flowering *Malati* bower overhead silent kisses dropped over my body. On my hair, my breast, my feet, each flower chose a bed to die on. I slept. And, suddenly in the depth of my sleep, I felt as if some intense eager look, like tapering fingers of flame, touched my slumbering body. I started up and saw the Hermit standing before me. The moon had moved to the west, peering through the leaves to espy this wonder of divine art wrought in a fragile human frame. The air was heavy with perfume; the silence of the night was vocal with the chirping of crickets; the reflections of the trees hung motionless in the lake; and with his staff in his hand he stood, tall and straight and still, like a forest tree. It seemed to me that I had, on opening my eyes, died to all realities of life and undergone a dream birth into a shadow land. Shame slipped to my feet like loosened clothes. I heard his call—'Beloved, my most beloved!' And all my forgotten lives united as one and responded to it. I said, 'Take me, take all I am!' And I stretched out my arms to him. The moon set behind the trees. One curtain of darkness covered all. Heaven and earth, time and space, pleasure and pain, death and life merged together in an unbearable ecstasy.... With the first gleam of light, the first twitter of birds, I rose up and sat leaning on my left arm. He lay asleep with a vague smile about his lips like the crescent moon in the morning. The rosy red glow of the dawn fell upon his noble forehead. I sighed and stood up. I drew together the leafy lianas to screen the streaming sun from his face. I looked about me and saw the same old earth. I remembered what I used to be, and ran and ran like a deer afraid of her own shadow, through the forest path strewn with *Shephali* flowers. I found a lonely nook, and sitting down covered my face with both hands, and tried to weep and cry. But no tears came to my eyes.

Madana. Alas, thou daughter of mortals! I stole from the divine storehouse the fragrant wine of heaven, filled with it one earthly night to the brim, and placed it in thy hand to drink—yet still I hear this cry of anguish!

Chitra [*bitterly*]. Who drank it? The rarest completion of life's desire, the first union of love was proffered to me, but was wrested from my grasp? This borrowed beauty, this falsehood that enwraps me, will slip from me taking with it the only monument of that sweet union, as the petals fall from an overblown flower; and the woman ashamed of her naked poverty will sit weeping day and night. Lord Love, this cursed appearance companions me like a demon robbing me of all the prizes of love—all the kisses for which my heart is athirst.

Madana. Alas, how vain thy single night had been! The barque of joy came in sight, but the waves would not let it touch the shore.

Chitra. Heaven came so close to my hand that I forgot for a moment that it had not reached me. But when I woke in the morning from my dream I found that my body had become my own rival. It is my hateful task to deck her every day, to send her to my beloved and see her caressed by him. O god, take back thy boon!

Madana. But if I take it from you how can you stand before your lover? To snatch away the cup from his lips when he has scarcely drained his first draught of pleasure, would not that be cruel? With what resentful anger he must regard thee then?

Chitra. That would be better far than this. I will reveal my true self to him, a nobler thing than this disguise. If he rejects it, if he spurns me and breaks my heart, I will bear even that in silence.

Vasanta. Listen to my advice. When with the advent of autumn the flowering season is over then comes the triumph of fruitage. A time will come of itself when the heat-cloyed bloom of the body will droop and Arjuna will gladly accept the abiding fruitful truth in thee. O child, go back to thy mad festival.

SCENE IV

Chitra. Why do you watch me like that, my warrior?

Arjuna. I watch how you weave that garland. Skill and grace, the twin brother and sister, are dancing playfully on your finger tips. I am watching and thinking.

Chitra. What are you thinking, sir?

Arjuna. I am thinking that you, with this same lightness of touch and sweetness, are weaving my days of exile into an immortal wreath, to crown me when I return home.

Chitra. Home! But this love is not for a home!

Arjuna. Not for a home?

Chitra. No. Never talk of that. Take to your home what is abiding and strong. Leave the little wild flower where it was born; leave it beautifully to die at the day's end among all fading blossoms and decaying leaves. Do not take it to your palace hall to fling it on the stony floor which knows no pity for things that fade and are forgotten.

Arjuna. Is ours that kind of love?

Chitra. Yes, no other! Why regret it? That which was meant for idle days should never outlive them. Joy turns into pain when the door by which it should depart is shut against it. Take it and keep it as long as it lasts. Let not the satiety of your evening claim more than the desire of your morning could earn.... The day is done. Put this garland on. I am tired. Take me in your arms, my love. Let all vain bickerings of discontent die away at the sweet meeting of our lips.

Arjuna. Hush! Listen, my beloved, the sound of prayer bells from the distant village temple steals upon the evening air across the silent trees!

SCENE V

Vasanta. I cannot keep pace with thee, my friend! I am tired. It is a hard task to keep alive the fire thou hast kindled. Sleep overtakes me, the fan drops from my hand, and cold ashes cover the glow of the fire. I start up again from my slumber and with all my might rescue the weary flame. But this can go on no longer.

Madana. I know, thou art as fickle as a child. Ever restless is thy play in heaven and on earth. Things that thou for days buildest up with endless detail thou dost shatter in a moment without regret. But this work of ours is nearly finished. Pleasure-winged days fly fast, and the year, almost at its end, swoons in rapturous bliss.

SCENE VI

Arjuna. I woke in the morning and found that my dreams had distilled a gem. I have no casket to inclose it, no king's crown whereon to fix it, no chain from which to hang it, and yet have not the heart to throw it away. My Kshatriya's right arm, idly occupied in holding it, forgets its duties.

[*Enter* Chitra.]

Chitra. Tell me your thoughts, sir!

Arjuna. My mind is busy with thoughts of hunting to-day. See, how the rain pours in torrents and fiercely beats upon the hillside. The dark shadow of the clouds hangs heavily over the forest, and the swollen stream, like reckless youth, overleaps all barriers with mocking laughter. On such rainy days we five brothers would go to the Chitraka forest to chase wild beasts. Those were glad times. Our hearts danced to the drumbeat of rumbling clouds. The woods resounded with the screams of peacocks. Timid deer could not hear our approaching steps for the patter of rain and the noise of waterfalls; the leopards would leave their tracks on the wet earth, betraying their lairs. Our sport over, we dared each other to swim across turbulent streams on our way back home. The restless spirit is on me. I long to go hunting.

Chitra. First run down the quarry you are now following. Are you quite certain that the enchanted deer you pursue must needs be caught? No, not yet. Like a dream the wild creature eludes you when it seems most nearly yours. Look how the wind is chased by the mad rain that discharges a thousand arrows after it. Yet it goes free and unconquered. Our sport is like that, my love! You give chase to the fleet-footed spirit of beauty, aiming at her every dart you have in your hands. Yet this magic deer runs ever free and untouched.

Arjuna. My love, have you no home where kind hearts are waiting for your return? A home which you once made sweet with your gentle service and whose light went out when you left it for this wilderness?

Chitra. Why these questions? Are the hours of unthinking pleasure over? Do you not know that I am no more than what you see before you? For me there is no vista beyond. The dew that hangs on the tip of a *Kinsuka* petal has neither name nor destination. It offers no answer to any question. She whom you love is like that perfect bead of dew.

Arjuna. Has she no tie with the world? Can she be merely like a fragment of heaven dropped on the earth through the carelessness of a wanton god?

Chitra. Yes.

Arjuna. Ah, that is why I always seem about to lose you. My heart is unsatisfied, my mind knows no peace. Come closer to me, unattainable one! Surrender yourself to the bonds of name and home and parentage. Let my heart feel you on all sides and live with you in the peaceful security of love.

Chitra. Why this vain effort to catch and keep the tints of the clouds, the dance of the waves, the smell of the flowers?

Arjuna. Mistress mine, do not hope to pacify love with airy nothings. Give me something to clasp, something that can last longer than pleasure, that can endure even through suffering.

Chitra. Hero mine, the year is not yet full, and you are tired already! Now I know that it is Heaven's blessing that has made the flower's term of life short. Could this body of mine have drooped and died with the flowers of last spring it surely would have died with honour. Yet, its days are numbered, my love. Spare it not, press it dry of honey, for fear your beggar's heart come back to it again and again with unsated desire, like a thirsty bee when summer blossoms lie dead in the dust.

SCENE VII

Madana. To-night is thy last night.

Vasanta. The loveliness of your body will return tomorrow to the inexhaustible stores of the spring. The ruddy tint of thy lips freed from the memory of Arjuna's kisses, will bud anew as a pair of fresh *Asoka* leaves, and the soft, white glow of thy skin will be born again in a hundred fragrant jasmine flowers.

Chitra. O gods, grant me this my prayer! To-night, in its last hour let my beauty flash its brightest, like the final flicker of a dying flame.

Madana. Thou shalt have thy wish.

SCENE VIII

Villagers. Who will protect us now?

Arjuna. Why, by what danger are you threatened?

Villagers. The robbers are pouring from the northern hills like a mountain flood to devastate our village.

Arjuna. Have you in this kingdom no warden?

Villagers. Princess Chitra was the terror of all evil doers. While she was in this happy land we feared natural deaths, but had no other fears. Now she has gone on a pilgrimage, and none knows where to find her.

Arjuna. Is the warden of this country a woman?

Villagers. Yes, she is our father and mother in one. [*Exeunt.*]

[*Enter* Chitra.]

Chitra. Why are you sitting all alone?

Arjuna. I am trying to imagine what kind of woman Princess Chitra may be. I hear so many stories of her from all sorts of men.

Chitra. Ah, but she is not beautiful. She has no such lovely eyes as mine, dark as death. She can pierce any target she will, but not our hero's heart.

Arjuna. They say that in valour she is a man, and a woman in tenderness.

Chitra. That, indeed, is her greatest misfortune. When a woman is merely a woman; when she winds herself round and round men's hearts with her smiles and sobs and services and caressing endearments; then she is happy. Of what use to her are learning and great achievements? Could you have seen her only yesterday in the court of the Lord Shiva's temple by the forest path, you would have passed by without deigning to look at her. But have you grown so weary of woman's beauty that you seek in her for a man's strength?

With green leaves wet from the spray of the foaming waterfall, I have made our noonday bed in a cavern dark as night. There the cool of the soft green mosses thick on the black and dripping stone, kisses your eyes to sleep. Let me guide you thither.

Arjuna. Not to-day, beloved.

Chitra. Why not to-day?

Arjuna. I have heard that a horde of robbers has neared the plains. Needs must I go and prepare my weapons to protect the frightened villagers.

Chitra. You need have no fear for them. Before she started on her pilgrimage, Princess Chitra had set strong guards at all the frontier passes.

Arjuna. Yet permit me for a short while to set about a Kshatriya's work. With new glory will I ennoble this idle arm, and make of it a pillow more worthy of your head.

Chitra. What if I refuse to let you go, if I keep you entwined in my arms? Would you rudely snatch yourself free and leave me? Go then! But you must know that the liana, once broken in two, never joins again. Go, if your thirst is quenched. But, if not, then remember that the goddess of pleasure is fickle, and waits for no man. Sit for a while, my lord! Tell me what uneasy thoughts tease you. Who occupied your mind to-day? Is it Chitra?

Arjuna. Yes, it is Chitra. I wonder in fulfilment of what vow she has gone on her pilgrimage. Of what could she stand in need?

Chitra. Her needs? Why, what has she ever had, the unfortunate creature? Her very qualities are as prison walls, shutting her woman's heart in a bare cell. She is obscured, she is unfulfilled. Her womanly love must content itself dressed in rags; beauty is denied her. She is like the spirit of a cheerless morning, sitting upon the stony mountain peak, all her light blotted out by dark clouds. Do not ask me of her life. It will never sound sweet to man's ear.

Arjuna. I am eager to learn all about her. I am like a traveller come to a strange city at midnight. Domes and towers and garden-trees look vague and shadowy, and the dull moan of the sea comes fitfully through the silence of sleep. Wistfully he waits for the morning to reveal to him all the strange wonders. Oh, tell me her story.

Chitra. What more is there to tell?

Arjuna. I seem to see her, in my mind's eye, riding on a white horse, proudly holding the reins in her left hand, and in her right a bow, and like the Goddess of Victory dispensing glad hope all round her. Like a watchful lioness she protects the litter at her dugs with a fierce love. Woman's arms, though adorned with naught but unfettered strength, are beautiful! My heart is restless, fair one, like a serpent reviving from his long winter's sleep. Come, let us both race on swift horses side by side, like twin orbs of light sweeping through space. Out from this slumbrous prison of green gloom, this dank, dense cover of perfumed intoxication, choking breath.

Chitra. Arjuna, tell me true, if, now at once, by some magic I could shake myself free from this voluptuous softness, this timid bloom of beauty shrinking from the rude and healthy touch of the world, and fling it from my body like borrowed clothes, would you be able to bear it? If I stand up straight and strong with the strength of a daring heart spurning the wiles and arts of twining weakness, if I hold my head high like a tall young mountain fir, no longer trailing in the dust like a liana, shall I then appeal to man's eye? No, no, you could not endure it. It is better that I should keep spread about me all the dainty playthings of fugitive youth, and wait for you in patience. When it pleases you to return, I will smilingly pour out for you the wine of pleasure in the cup of this beauteous body. When you are tired and satiated with this wine, you can go to work or play; and when I grow old I will accept humbly and gratefully whatever corner is left for me. Would it please your heroic soul if the playmate of the night aspired to be the helpmate of the day, if the left aim learnt to share the burden of the proud right arm.

Arjuna. I never seem to know you aright. You seem to me like a goddess hidden within a golden image. I cannot touch you, I cannot pay you my dues in return for your priceless gifts. Thus my love is incomplete. Sometimes in the enigmatic depth of your sad look, in your playful words mocking at their own meaning. I gain glimpses of being trying to rend asunder the languorous grace of her body, to emerge in a chaste fire of pain through a vaporous veil of smiles. Illusion is the first appearance of Truth. She advances towards her lover in disguise. But a time comes when she throws off her ornaments and veils and stands clothed in naked dignity. I grope for that ultimate *you,* that bare simplicity of truth.

Why these tears, my love? Why cover your face with your hands? Have I pained you, my darling? Forget what I said. I will be content with the present. Let each separate moment of beauty come to me like a bird of mystery from its unseen nest in the dark bearing a message of music. Let me for ever sit with my hope on the brink of its realization, and thus end my days.

SCENE IX

Chitra [*cloaked*]. My lord, has the cup been drained to the last drop? Is this, indeed, the end? No, when all is done something still remains, and that is my last sacrifice at your feet.

I brought from the garden of heaven flowers of incomparable beauty with which to worship you, god of my heart. If the rites are over, if the flowers have faded, let me throw them out of the temple. [*Unveiling in her original male attire*] Now, look at your worshipper with gracious eyes.

I am not beautifully perfect as the flowers with which I worshipped. I have many flaws and blemishes. I am a traveller in the great world-path, my garments are dirty, and my feet are bleeding with thorns. Where should I achieve flower-beauty, the unsullied loveliness of a moment's life? The gift that I proudly bring you is the heart of a woman. Here have all pains and joys gathered, the hopes and fears and shames of a daughter of the dust; here love springs up struggling toward immortal life. Herein lies an imperfection which yet is noble and grand. If the flower-service is finished, my master, accept *this* as your servant for the days to come!

I am Chitra, the king's daughter. Perhaps you will remember the day when a woman came to you in the temple of Shiva, her body loaded with ornaments and finery. That shameless woman came to court you as though she were a man. You rejected her; you did well. My lord, I am that woman. She was my disguise. Then by the boon of gods I obtained for a year the most radiant form that a mortal ever wore, and wearied my hero's heart with the burden of that deceit. Most surely I am not that woman.

I am Chitra. No goddess to be worshipped, nor yet the object of common pity to be brushed aside like a moth with indifference. If you deign to keep me by your side in the path of danger and daring, if you allow me to share the great duties of your life, then you will know my true self. If your babe, whom I am nourishing in my womb be born a son, I shall myself teach him to be a second Arjuna, and send him to you when the time comes, and then at last you will truly know me. To-day I can only offer you Chitra, the daughter of a king.

Arjuna. Beloved, my life is full.

Sacrifice and Other Plays

Sanyasi

OR

The Ascetic

'LEAD US FROM THE UNREAL
TO THE REAL'

A scene from *Sanyasi* staged in China in 1924

SCENE I

Sanyasi [*outside the cave*]. The division of days and nights is not for me, nor that of months and years. For me, the stream of time has stopped, on whose waves dances the world, like straws and twigs. In this dark cave I am alone, merged in myself,—and the eternal night is still, like a mountain lake afraid of its own depth. Water oozes and drips from the cracks, and in the pools float the ancient frogs. I sit chanting the incantation of nothingness. The world's limits recede, line after line.—The stars, like sparks of fire, flown from the anvil of time, are extinct; and that joy is mine which comes to the God Shiva, when, after aeons of dream, he wakes up to find himself alone in the heart of the infinite annihilation. I am free, I am the great solitary One. When I was thy slave, O Nature, thou didst set my heart against itself, and madest it carry the fierce war of suicide through its world. Desires, that have no other ends, but to feed upon themselves and all that comes to their mouths, lashed me into fury. I ran about, madly chasing my shadow. Thou drovest me with thy lightning lashes of pleasure into the void of satiety. And the hungers, who are thy decoys, ever led me into the endless famine, where food turned into dust, and drink into vapour.

Till, when my world was spotted with tears and ashes, I took my oath, that I would have revenge upon thee, interminable Appearance, mistress of endless disguises. I took shelter in the darkness,—the castle of the Infinite,—and fought the deceitful light, day after day, till it lost all its weapons and lay powerless at my feet. Now. when I am free of fear and desires, when the mist has vanished, and my reason shines pure and bright, let me go out into the kingdom of lies, and sit upon its heart, untouched and unmoved.

SCENE II

Sanyasi [*by the roadside*]. How small is this earth and confined, watched and followed by the persistent horizons. The trees, houses, and crowd of things are pressing upon my eyes. The light, like a cage, has shut out the dark eternity; and the hours hop and cry within its barriers, like prisoned birds. But why are these noisy men rushing on, and for what purpose? They seem always afraid of missing something,—the something that never comes to their hands.

[*The crowd passes.*]

[*Enter a* village elder *and two* women.]

First Woman. O my, O my! You *do* make me laugh.

Second Woman. But who says you are old?

Village Elder. There are fools who judge men by their outside.

First Woman. How sad! We have been watching your outside from our infancy. It is just the same all through these years.

Village Elder. Like the morning sun.

First Woman. Yes, like the morning sun in its shining baldness.

Village Elder. Ladies, you are overcritical in your taste. You notice things that are unessential.

Second Woman. Leave off your chatter, Ananga. Let us hasten home, or my man will be angry.

First Woman. Good bye, sir. Please judge us from our outside, we won't mind that.

Village Elder. Because you have no inside to speak of.

[*They go.*]

[*Enter three* villagers.]

First Villager. Insult me? the scoundrel! He shall regret it.

Second Villager. He must be taught a thorough lesson.

First Villager. A lesson that will follow him to his grave.

Third Villager. Yes, brother, set your heart upon it. Never give him quarter.

Second Villager. He has grown too big.

First Villager. Big enough to burst at last.

Third Villager. The ants, when they begin to grow wings, perish.

Second Villager. But have you got a plan?

First Villager. Not one, but hundreds. I will drive my ploughshare over his household.—I will give him a donkey-ride through the town, with his cheeks painted white and black. I will make the world too hot for him, and— [*They go.*]

[*Enter two* students.]

First Student. I am sure Professor Madhab won in the debate.

Second Student. No, it was Professor Janardan.

First Student. Professor Madhab maintained his point to the last. He said that the subtle is the outcome of the gross.

Second Student. But Professor Janardan conclusively proved that the subtle is the origin of the gross.

First Student. Impossible.

Second Student. It is clear as the day-light.

First Student. Seeds come from the tree.

Second Student. The tree comes from the seed.

First Student. Sanyasi, which of these is true? Which is the original, the subtle or the gross?

Sanyasi. Neither.

Second Student. Neither. Well, that sounds satisfactory.

Sanyasi. The origin is the end, and the end is the origin. It is a circle.—The distinction between the subtle and gross is in your ignorance.

First Student. Well, it sounds very simple—and I think this was what my master meant.

Second Student. Certainly this agrees more with what *my* master teaches. [*They go out.*]

Sanyasi. These birds are word-peckers. When they pick up some wriggling nonsense, which can fill their mouth, they are happy.

[*Enter two* flower-girls, *singing.*]

The weary hours pass by.
The flowers that blossom in the light

Fade and drop in the shadow.
I thought I would weave a garland
In the cool of the morning for my love.
But the morning wears on,
The flowers are not gathered.
And my love is lost.

A Wayfarer. Why such regret, my darlings? When the garlands are ready, the necks will not be wanting.

First Flower-girl. Nor the halter.

Second Flower-girl. You are bold. Why do you come so close?

Wayfarer. You quarrel for nothing, my girl. I am far enough from you to allow an elephant to pass between us.

Second Flower-girl. Indeed. Am I such a fright? I wouldn't have eaten you, if you had come. [*They go out laughing.*]

[*Comes an old* beggar.]

Beggar. Kind sirs, have pity on me. May God prosper you. Give me one handful from your plenty.

[*Enters a* soldier.]

Soldier. Move away. Don't you see the Minister's son is coming?

[*They go out.*]

Sanyasi. It is midday. The sun is growing strong. The sky looks like an overturned burning copper bowl. The earth breathes hot sighs, and the whirling sands dance by. What sights of man have I seen! Can 1 ever again shrink back into the smallness of these creatures, and become one of them? No, I am free. I have not this obstacle, this world round me. I live in a pure desolation.

[*Enter the girl* Vasanti *and a* woman.]

Woman. Girl, you are Raghu's daughter, aren't you? You should keep away from this road. Don't you know it goes to the temple?

Vasanti. I am on the farthest side. Lady.

Woman. But I thought my cloth-end touched you. I am taking my offerings to the goddess,—I hope they are not polluted.

Vasanti. I assure you, your cloth did not touch me.

[*The* woman *goes*.]

I am Vasanti, Raghu's daughter. May I come to you, father?

Sanyasi. Why not, child?

Vasanti. I am a pollution, as they call me.

Sanyasi. But they are all that,—a pollution. They roll in the dust of existence. Only he is pure who has washed away the world from his mind. But what have you done, daughter?

Vasanti. My father, who is dead, had defied their laws and their gods. He would not perform their rites.

Sanyasi. Why do you stand away from me?

Vasanti. Will you touch me?

Sanyasi. Yes, because nothing can touch me truly. I am ever away in the endless. You can sit here, if you wish.

Vasanti [*breaking into a sob*]. Never tell me to leave you, when once you have taken me near you.

Sanyasi. Wipe away your tears, child. I am a Sanyasi. I have neither hatred, nor attachment in my heart,—I never claim you as mine; therefore I can never discard you. You are to me as this blue sky is,—you are,—yet you are not.

Vasanti. Father, I am deserted by gods and men alike.

Sanyasi. So am I. I have deserted both gods and men.

Vasanti. You have no mother?

Sanyasi. No.

Vasanti. Nor father?

Sanyasi. No.

Vasanti. Nor any friend?

Sanyasi. No.

Vasanti. Then I shall be with you.—You won't leave me?

Sanyasi. I have done with leaving. You can stay near me, yet never coming near me.

Vasanti. I do not understand you, father. Tell me, is there no shelter for me in the whole world?

Sanyasi. Shelter? Don't you know this world is a bottomless chasm? The swarm of creatures, coming out from the hole of nothingness, seeks for shelter, and enters into the gaping mouth of this emptiness, and is lost. These are the ghosts of lies around you, who hold their market of illusions,—and the foods which they sell are shadows. They only deceive your hunger, but do not satisfy. Come away from here, child, come away.

Vasanti. But, father, they seem so happy in this world. Can we not watch them from the roadside?

Sanyasi. Alas, they do not understand. They cannot see that this world is death spread out to eternity.—It dies every moment, yet never comes to the end.—And we, the creatures of this world, live by feeding upon death.

Vasanti. Father, you frighten me.

[*Enters a* traveller.]

Traveller. Can I get a shelter near this place?

Sanyasi. Shelter there is nowhere, my son, but in the depth of one's self.—Seek that; hold to it fast, if you would be saved.

Traveller. But I am tired, and want shelter.

Vasanti. My hut is not far from here. Will you come?

Traveller. But who are you?

Vasanti. Must you know me? I am Raghu's daughter.

Traveller. God bless you, child, but I cannot stay. [*Goes.*]

[*Men come bearing somebody on a bed.*]

First Bearer. He is still asleep.

Second Bearer. How heavy the rascal is!

A Traveller [*outside their group.*]. Whom do you carry?

Third Bearer. Bindé, the weaver, was sleeping as one dead, and we have taken him away.

Second Bearer. But I am tired, brothers. Let us give him a shake, and waken him up.

Bindé [*wakes up.*]. Ee, a, u—

Third Bearer. What's that noise?

Bindé. I say. Who are you? Where am I being carried?

[*They put down the bed from their shoulders.*]

Third Bearer. Can't you keep quiet, like all decent dead people?

Second Bearer. The cheek of him! He must talk, even though he is dead.

Third Bearer. It would be more proper of you, if you kept still.

Bindé. I am sorry to disappoint you, gentlemen, you have made a mistake.—I was not dead, but fast asleep.

Second Bearer. I admire this fellow's impudence. Not only must he die, but argue.

Third Bearer. He won't confess the truth. Let us go, and finish the rites of the dead.

Bindé. I swear by your beard, my brother, I am as alive as any of you. [*They take him away, laughing.*]

Sanyasi. The girl has fallen asleep, with her arm beneath her little head; I think I must leave her now, and go. But, coward, must you run away,—run away from this tiny thing? These are nature's spiders' webs, they have danger merely for moths, and not for a Sanyasi like me.

Vasanti [*awaking with a start*]. Have you left me, Master?—Have you gone away?

Sanyasi. Why should I go away from you? What fear have I? Afraid of a shadow?

Vasanti. Do you hear the noise in the road?

Sanyasi. But stillness is in my soul.

[*Enters a young* woman, *followed by* men.]

Woman. Go now. Leave me. Don't talk to me of love.

First Man. Why, what has been my crime?

Woman. You men have hearts of stone.

First Man. Incredible. If our hearts were of stone, how could Cupid's darts make damage there?

Other Man. Bravo. Well said.

Second Man. Now, what is your answer to that, my dear?

Woman. Answer! You think you have said something very fine, —don't you? It is perfect rubbish.

First Man. I leave it to your judgment, gentlemen. What I said was this, that if our hearts be of stone, how can—

Third Man. Yes, yes, it has no answer at all.

First Man. Let me explain it to you. She said we men have hearts of stone, didn't she? Well, I said, in answer, if our hearts were truly of stone, how could Cupid's darts damage them? You understand?

Second Man. Brother, I have been selling molasses in the town for the last twenty-four years,—do you think I cannot understand what you say? [*They go out.*]

Sanyasi. What are you doing, my child?

Vasanti. I am looking at your broad palm, father. My hand is a little bird that finds its nest here. Your palm is great, like the great earth which holds all. These lines are the rivers, and these are hills. [*Puts her cheek upon it.*]

Sanyasi. Your touch is soft, my daughter, like the touch of sleep. It seems to me this touch has something of the great darkness, which touches one's soul with the wand of the eternal.—But, child, you are the moth of the daylight. You have your birds and flowers and fields—what can you find in me, who have my centre in the One and my circumference nowhere?

Vasanti. I do not want anything else. Your love is enough for me.

Sanyasi. The girl imagines I love her,—foolish heart. She is happy in that thought. Let her nourish it. For they have been brought up in illusions, and they must have illusions to console them.

Vasanti. Father, this creeper trailing on the grass, seeking some tree to twine itself round, is my creeper. I have tended it and watered it from the time when it had pushed up only two little leaves into the air, like an infant's cry. This creeper is me,—it has grown by the road-side, it can be so easily crushed. Do you see these beautiful little flowers, pale blue with white spots in their hearts,—these white spots are their dreams. Let me gently brush your forehead with these flowers. To me, things that are beautiful are the keys to all that I have not seen and not known.

Sanyasi. No, no, the beautiful is mere phantasy. To him who knows, the dust and the flower are the same.—But what languor is this that is creeping into my blood and drawing before my eyes a thin mist veil of all the rainbow colours? Is it nature herself weaving her dreams round me, clouding my senses? (*Suddenly he tears the creeper, and rises up*.) No more of this; for this is death. What game of yours is this with me, little girl? I am a sanyasi, I have cut all my knots, I am free.—No, no, not those tears. I cannot bear them. —But where was hidden in my heart this snake, this anger, that hissed out of its dark with its fang? No, they are not dead,—they outlive starvation. These hell-creatures clatter their skeletons and dance in my heart, when their mistress, the great witch, plays upon her magic flute.—Weep not, child, come to me. You seem to me like a cry of a lost world, like the song of a wandering star. You bring to my mind something, which is infinitely more than this Nature,—more than the sun and stars. It is as great as the darkness. I understand it not. I have never known it, therefore I fear it. I must leave you.—Go back whence you came,—the messenger of the unknown.

Vasanti. Leave me not, father,—I have none else but you.

Sanyasi. I must go, I thought that I had known,—but I do not know. Yet I must know. I leave you, to know who you are.

Vasanti. Father, if you leave me, I shall die.

Sanyasi. Let go my hand. Do not touch me. I must be free.—

[*He runs away*.]

SCENE III

[*The SANYASI is seen, sitting upon a boulder in a mountain path.*]

[*A shepherd boy passes by, singing.*]

Do not turn away your face, my love,
The spring has bared open its breast.
The flowers breathe their secrets in the dark.
The rustle of the forest leaves comes across the sky,
Like the sobs of the night.
Come, love, show me your face.

Sanyasi. The gold of the evening is melting in the heart of the blue sea. The forest, on the hillside, is drinking the last cup of the daylight. On the left, the village huts are seen through the trees with their evening lamps lighted, like a veiled mother watching by her sleeping children. Nature, thou art my slave. Thou hast spread thy many-coloured carpet in the great hall where I sit alone, like a king, and watch thee dance with thy starry necklace twinkling on thy breast.

[*Shepherd girls pass by, singing.*]

The music comes from across the dark river and calls me.
I was in the house and happy,
But the flute sounded in the still air of night,
And a pain pierced my heart.
Oh, tell me the way who know it,—
Tell me the way to him.
I will go to him with my one little flower,
And leave it at his feet,
And tell him that his music is one with my love.

[*They go.*]

Sanyasi. I think such an evening had come to me only once before in all my births. Then its cup overbrimmed with love and music, and I sat with someone, the memory of whose face is in that setting star of the evening.—But where is my little girl, with her dark sad eyes, big with tears? Is she there, sitting outside her hut, watching that same star through the immense loneliness of the evening? But the star must set, the evening close her eyes in the night, and tears must cease and sobs be stilled in sleep. No, I will not go back. Let the world-dreams take their own shape. Let me not trouble its course and create new phantasies. I will see, and think, and know.

[*Enters a ragged* girl.]

Girl. Are you there, father?

Sanyasi. Come, child, sit by me. I wish I could own that call of yours. Someone did call me father, once, and the voice was somewhat like yours. The father answers now,—but where is that call?

Girl. Who are you?

Sanyasi. I am a sanyasi. Tell, me child, what is your father?

Girl. He gathers sticks from the forest.

Sanyasi. And you have a mother?

Girl. No. She died when I was young.

Sanyasi. Do you love your father?

Girl. I love him more than anything else in the world. I have no one else but him.

Sanyasi. I understand you. Give me your little hand,—let me hold it in my palm,—in this big palm of mine.

Girl. Sanyasi, do you read palms? Can you read in my palm all that I am and shall be?

Sanyasi. I think I can read, but dimly know its meaning. One day, I shall know it.

Girl. Now I must go to meet my father.

Sanyasi. Where?

Girl. Where the road goes into the forest. He will miss me, if he does not find me there.

Sanyasi. Bring your head near to me, child. Let me give you my kiss of blessing, before you go. [girl *goes.*]

[*A* mother *enters, with two children.*]

Mother. How stout and chubby Misri's children are. They are something to look at. But the more I feed you, the more you seem to grow thin every day.

First Girl. But why do you always blame us for that, mother? Can we help it?

Mother. Don't I tell you to take plenty of rest? But you must always be running about.

Second Girl. But mother, we run about on your errands.

Mother. How dare you answer me like that?

Sanyasi. Where are you going, daughter?

Mother. My salutation, father. We are going home.

Sanyasi. How many are you?

Mother. My mother-in-law, and my husband and two other children, beside these.

Sanyasi. How do you spend your days?

Mother. I hardly know how my days pass. My man goes to the field, and I have my house to look after. Then, in the evening, I sit to spin with my elder girls. [*To the girls*] Go and salute the sanyasi. Bless them, father. [*They go.*]

[*Enter two* men.]

First Man. Friend, go back from here. Do not come any further.

Second Man. Yes, I know. Friends meet in this earth by chance, and the chance carries us on together some portion of the way, and then comes the moment when we must part.

Second Friend. Let us carry away with us the hope that we part to meet again.

First Friend. Our meetings and partings belong to all the movements of the world. Stars do not take special notice of us.

Second Friend. Let us salute those stars which *did* throw us together. If for a moment, still it has been much.

First Friend. Look back for a minute before you go. Can you see that faint glimmer of the water in the dark, and those *casuarina* trees on the sandy bank? Our village is all one heap of dark shadows. You can only see the lights. Can you guess which of those lights are ours?

Second Friend. Yes, I think I can.

First Friend. That light is the last farewell look of our past days upon their parting guest. A little further on, and there will remain one blot of darkness. [*They go away.*]

Sanyasi. The night grows dark and desolate. It sits like a woman forsaken,—those stars are her tears, turned into fire. O my child, the sorrow of your little heart has filled, for ever, all the nights of my life with its sadness. Your dear caressing hand has left its touch in this night air,—I feel it on my forehead,—it is damp with your tears. My darling, your sobs that pursued me, when I fled away, have clung to my heart. I shall carry them to my death.

SCENE IV

[*In the village path.*]

Sanyasi. Let my vows of sanyasi go, I break my staff and my alms-bowl. This stately ship, this world which is crossing the sea of time,—let it take me up again, let me join once more the pilgrims. O the fool, who wanted to get safety in swimming alone and gave up the light of the sun and stars, to pick his way with his glow-worm's lamp! The bird flies in the sky, not to fly away into the emptiness, but to come back again to this great earth.—I am free. I am free from the bodiless chain of the Nay. I am free among things, and forms and purpose. The finite is the true infinite, and love knows its truth. My girl, you are the spirit of all that is,—I can never leave you.

[*Enters a* village elder.]

Sanyasi. Do you know, brother, where Raghu's daughter is?

Elder. She has left her village, and we are glad.

Sanyasi. Where has she gone?

Elder. Do you ask where? It is all one to her where she goes. [*Goes out.*]

Sanyasi. My darling has gone to seek a somewhere in the emptiness of nowhere. She must find me.

[*A crowd of* villagers *enter.*]

First Man. So our King's son is going to be married to-night.

Second Man. Can you tell me, when is the wedding hour?

Third Man. The wedding hour is only for the bride-groom and the bride. What have we got to do with it?

A Woman. But won't they give us cakes for the happy day?

First Man. Cakes? You *are* silly. My uncle lives in the town—I have heard from him that we shall have curds and parched rice.

Second Man. Grand.

Fourth Man. But we shall have a great deal more water than curds. You may be sure of that.

First Man. Moti, you are a dull fellow. Water in the curds at a prince's wedding!

Fourth Man. But we are not princes ourselves, Panchu. For us, poor people, the curds have the trick of turning into water most parts.

First Man. Look there. That son of the charcoal-burner is still busy with his work. We mustn't allow that.

Second Man. We shall burn him into charcoal, if he does not come out.

Sanyasi. Do you know, any of you, where is Raghu's daughter?

The Woman. She has gone away.

Sanyasi. Where?

Woman. That we don't know.

First Man. But we are sure that she is not the bride for our prince. [*They laugh and go out.*]

[*Enters* a woman, *with a child.*]

Woman. My obeisance to you, father. Let my child touch your feet with his head. He is sick. Bless him, father.

Sanyasi. But, daughter, I am no longer a sanyasi. Do not mock me with your salutation.

Woman. Then who are you? What are you doing?

Sanyasi. I am seeking.

Woman. Seeking whom?

Sanyasi. Seeking my lost world back.—Do you know Raghu's daughter? Where is she?

Woman. Raghu's daughter? She is dead.

Sanyasi. No, she cannot be dead. No. No.

Woman. But what is her death to you. Sanyasi?

Sanyasi. Not only to me; it would be death to all.

Woman. I do not understand you.

Sanyasi. She can never be dead.

Malini

ACT I

The Balcony of the Palace facing the street.

Malini. The moment has come for me, and my life, like the dew drop upon a lotus leaf, is trembling upon the heart of this great time. I shut my eyes and seem to hear the tumult of the sky, and there is an anguish in my heart, I know not for what.

[*Enters* Queen.]

Queen. My child, what is this? Why do you forget to put on dresses that befit your beauty and youth? Where are your ornaments? My beautiful dawn, how can you absent the touch of gold from your limbs?

Malini. Mother, there are some who are born poor, even in a king's house. Wealth does not cling to those whose destiny it is to find riches in poverty.

Queen. That the child whose only language was the baby cry should talk to me in such riddles!—My heart quakes in fear when I listen to you. Where did you pick up your new creed, which goes against all our holy books? My child, they say that the Buddhist monks, from whom you take your lessons, practice black arts; that they cast their spells upon men's minds, confounding them with lies. But I ask you, is religion a thing that one has to find by seeking? Is it not like sunlight, given to you for all days? I am a simple woman. I do not understand men's creeds and dogmas. I only know that women's true objects of worship come to their own arms, without asking, in the shape of their husbands and their children.

[*Enters* King.]

King. My daughter, storm clouds are gathering over the King's house. Go no farther along your perilous path. Pause, if only for a short time.

Queen. What dark words are these?

King. My foolish child, if you must bring your new creed into this land of the old, let it not come like a sudden flood threatening those who dwell on the bank. Keep your faith to your own self. Rake not up public hatred and mockery against it.

Queen. Do not chide my girl, and teach her the crookedness of your diplomacy. If my child should choose her own teachers and pursue her own path, I do not know who can blame her.

King. Queen, my people are agitated, they clamour for my daughter's banishment.

Queen. Banishment? Of your own daughter?

King. The Brahmins, frightened at her heresy, have combined, and—

Queen. Heresy indeed. Are all truths confined only in their musty, old books? Let them fling away their worm-eaten creeds, and come and take their lessons from this child. I tell you, King, she is not a common girl,—she is a pure flame of fire. Some divine spirit has taken birth in her. Do not despise her, lest some day you strike your forehead, and weep, and find her no more.

Malini. Father, grant to your people their request. The great moment has come. Banish me.

King. Why, child? What want do you feel in your father's house?

Malini. Listen to me, father. Those, who cry for my banishment, cry for me. Mother, I have no words in which to tell you what I have in my mind. Leave me without regret, like the tree that sheds its flowers unheeding. Let me go out to all men,—for the world has claimed me from the King's hands.

King. Child, I do not understand you.

Malini. Father, you are a King. Be strong and fulfil your mission.

Queen. Child, is there no place for you here, where you were born? Is the burden of the world waiting for your little shoulders?

Malini. I dream, while I am awake, that the wind is wild, and the water is troubled; the night is dark, and the boat is moored in the haven. Where is the captain, who shall take the wanderers home? I feel I know the path, and the boat will thrill with life at my touch, and speed on.

Queen. Do you hear, King? Whose words are these? Do they come from this little girl? Is she your daughter, and have I borne her?

King. Yes, even as the night bears the dawn,—the dawn that is not of the night, but of all the world.

Queen. King, have you nothing to keep her bound to your house,—this image of light?—My darling, your hair has come loose on your shoulders. Let me bind it up.—Do they talk of banishment, King? If this be a part of their creed, then let come the new religion, and let those Brahmins be taught afresh what is truth.

King. Queen, let us take away our child from this balcony. Do you see the crowd gathering in the street?

[*They all go out.*]

[*Enter a crowd of* Brahmins, *in the street, before the palace balcony. They shout.*]

Brahmins. Banishment of the King's daughter!

Kemankar. Friends, keep your resolution firm. The woman, as an enemy, is to be dreaded more than all others. For reason is futile against her and forces are ashamed; man's power gladly surrenders itself to her powerlessness, and she takes her shelter in the strongholds of our own hearts.

First Brahmin. We must have audience with our King, to tell him that a snake has raised its poisonous hood from his own nest, and is aiming at the heart of our sacred religion.

Supriya. Religion? I *am* stupid. I do not understand you. Tell me, sir, is it your religion that claims the banishment of an innocent girl?

First Brahmin. You are a marplot, Supriya, you are ever a hindrance to all our enterprises.

Second Brahmin. We have united in defence of our faith, and you come like a subtle rift in the wall, like a thin smile on the compressed lips of contempt.

Supriya. You think that, by the force of numbers, you will determine truth, and drown reason by your united shouts?

First Brahmin. This is rank insolence, Supriya.

Supriya. The insolence is not mine but theirs who shape their scripture to fit their own narrow hearts.

Second Brahmin. Drive him out. He is none of us.

First Brahmin. We have all agreed upon the banishment of the Princess.—He who thinks differently, let him leave this assembly.

Supriya. Brahmins, it was a mistake on your part to elect me as one of your league. I am neither your shadow, nor an echo of your texts. I never admit that truth sides with the shrillest voice and I am ashamed to own as mine a creed that depends on force for its existence. [*To* Kemankar] Dear friend, let me go.

Kemankar. No, I will not. I know you are firm in your action, only doubting when you debate. Keep silence, my friend; for the time is evil.

Supriya. Of all things the blind certitude of stupidity is the hardest to bear. To think of saving your religion by banishing a girl from her home! But let me know what is her offence. Does she not maintain that truth and love are the body and soul of religion? If so, is that not the essence of all creeds?

Kemankar. Religion is one in its essence, but different in its forms. The water is one, yet by its different banks it is bounded and preserved for different peoples. What if you have a well-spring of your own in your heart, spurn not your neighbours who must go for their draught of water to their ancestral pond with the green of its gradual slopes mellowed by ages and its ancient trees bearing eternal fruit.

Supriya. I shall follow you, my friend, as I have ever done in my life, and not argue.

[*Enters* third Brahmin.]

Third Brahmin. I have good news. Our words have prevailed, and the King's army is about to take our side openly.

Second Brahmin. The army?—I do not quite like it.

First Brahmin. Nor do I. It smells of rebellion.

Second Brahmin. Kemankar, I am not for such extreme measures.

First Brahmin. Our faith will give us victory, not our arms. Let us make penance, and recite sacred verses. Let us call on the names of our guardian gods.

Second Brahmin. Come, Goddess, whose wrath is the sole weapon of thy worshippers, deign to take form and crush even to dust the blind pride of unbelievers. Prove to us the strength of our faith, and lead us to victory.

All. We invoke thee, Mother, descend from thy heavenly heights and do thy work among mortals.

[*Enters* Malini.]

Malini. I have come.

[*They all bow to her, except* Kemankar *and* Supriya, *who stand aloof and watch.*]

Second Brahmin. Goddess.—Thou hast come at last, as a daughter of man, withdrawing all thy terrible power into the tender beauty of a girl. Whence hast thou come, Mother? What is thy wish?

Malini. I have come down to my exile at your call.

Second Brahmin. To exile from heaven, because thy children of earth have called thee?

First Brahmin. Forgive us, Mother. Utter ruin threatens this world and it cries aloud for thy help.

Malini. I will never desert you. I always knew that your doors were open for me. The cry went from you for my banishment and I woke up, amidst the wealth and pleasure of the King's house.

Kemankar. The Princess.

All. The King's daughter.

Malini. I am exiled from my home, so that I may make your home my own. Yet tell me truly, have you need of me? When I lived in seclusion, a lonely girl, did you call to me from the outer world? Was it no dream of mine?

First Brahmin. Mother, you have come, and taken your seat in the heart of our hearts.

Malini. I was born in a King's house, never once looking out from my window. I had heard that it was a sorrowing world,—the world out of my reach. But I did not know where it felt its pain. Teach me to find this out.

First Brahmin. Your sweet voice brings tears to our eyes.

Malini. The moon has just come out of those clouds. Great peace is in the sky. It seems to gather all the world in its arms, under the fold of one vast moonlight. There goes the road, losing itself among the solemn trees with their still shadows. There are the houses, and there the temple; the river bank in the distance looks dim and desolate. I seem to have come down, like a sudden shower from a cloud of dreams, into this world of men, by the roadside.

First Brahmin. You are the divine soul of this world.

Second Brahmin. Why did not our tongues burst in pain, when they shouted for your banishment?

First Brahmin. Come, Brahmins, let us restore our Mother to her home.

[*They shout.*]

Victory to the Mother of the world! Victory to the Mother in the heart of the Man's daughter!

[Malini *goes, surrounded by them.*]

Kemankar. Let the illusion vanish. Where are you going, Supriya, like one walking in his sleep?

Supriya. Leave hold of me, let me go.

Kemankar. Control yourself. Will you, too, fly into the fire with the rest of the blinded swarm?

Supriya. Was it a dream, Kemankar?

Kemankar. It was nothing but a dream. Open your eyes, and wake up.

Supriya. Your hope of heaven is false, Kemankar. Vainly have I wandered in the wilderness of doctrines,—I never found peace. The God, who belongs to the multitude, and the God of the books are not my own God. These never answered my questions and never consoled me. But, at last, I have found the divine breathing and alive in the living world of men.

Kemankar. Alas, my friend, it is a fearful moment when a man's heart deceives him. Then blind desire becomes his gospel and fancy usurps the dread throne of his gods. Is yonder moon, lying asleep among soft fleecy clouds, the true emblem of everlasting reality? The naked day will come to-morrow, and the hungry crowd begin again to drag the sea of existence with their thousand nets. And then this moon-light night will hardly be remembered, but as a thin film of unreality made of sleep and shadows and delusions. The magic web, woven of the elusive charms of a woman, is like that,—and can it take the place of highest truth? Can any creed, born of your fancy, satisfy the gaping thirst of the midday, when it is wide awake in its burning heat?

Supriya. Alas, I know not.

Kemankar. Then shake yourself up from your dreams, and look before you. The ancient house is on fire, whose nurslings are the ages. The spirits of our forefathers are hovering over the impending ruins, like crying birds over their perishing nests. Is this the time for vacillation, when the night is dark, the enemies knocking at the gate, the citizens asleep, and men drunken with delusions laying their hands upon their brothers' throats?

Supriya. I will stand by you.

Kemankar. I must go away from here.

Supriya. Where? And for what?

Kemankar. To foreign lands. I shall bring soldiers from outside. For this conflagration cries for blood, to be quenched.

Supriya. But our own soldiers are ready.

Kemankar. Vain is all hope of help from them. They, like moths, are already leaping into the fire. Do you not hear how they are shouting like fools? The whole town has gone mad, and is lighting her festival lamps at the funeral pyre of her own sacred faith.

Supriya. If you must go, take me with you.

Kemankar. No. You remain here, to watch and keep me informed. But, friend, let your heart be not drawn away from me by the novelty of the falsehood.

Supriya. Falsehood is new, but our friendship is old. We have ever been together from our childhood. This is our first separation.

Kemankar. May it prove our last! In evil times the strongest bonds give way. Brothers strike brothers and friends turn against friends. I go out into the dark, and in the darkness of night I shall come back to the gate. Shall I find my friend watching for me, with the lamp lighted? I take away that hope with me. [*They go.*]

[*Enter* King, *with the* Prince, *in the balcony.*]

King. I fear I must decide to banish my daughter.

Prince. Yes, Sire, delay will be dangerous.

King. Gently, my son, gently. Never doubt that I will do my duty. Be sure I will banish her. [Prince *goes.*]

[*Enters* Queen.]

Queen. Tell me, King, where is she? Have you hidden her, even from me?

King. Whom?

Queen. My Malini.

King. What? Is she not in her room?

Queen. No, I cannot find her. Go with your soldiers and search for her through all the town, from house to house. The citizens have stolen her. Banish them all. Empty the whole town, till they return her.

King. I will bring her back,—even if my Kingdom goes to ruin.

[*The* Brahmins *and soldiers bring* Malini, *with torches lighted.*]

Queen. My darling, my cruel child. I never keep my eyes off you,— how could you evade me, and go out?

Second Brahmin. Do not be angry with her, Queen. She came to our home to give us her blessings.

First Brahmin. Is she only yours? And does she not belong to us as well?

Second Brahmin. Our little mother, do not forget us. You are our star, to lead us across the pathless sea of life.

Malini. My door has been opened for you. These walls will nevermore separate us.

Brahmins. Blessed are we, and the land where we were born.

[*They go.*]

Malini. Mother, I have brought the outer world into your house. I seem to have lost the bounds of my body. I am one with the life of this world.

Queen. Yes, child. Now you shall never need to go out. Bring in the world to you, and to your mother.—It is close upon the second watch of the night. Sit here. Calm yourself. This flaming life in you is burning out all sleep from your eyes.

Malini [*embracing her mother*]. Mother, I am tired. My body is trembling. So vast is this world.—Mother dear, sing me to sleep. Tears come to my eyes, and a sadness descends upon my heart.

ACT II

The Palace Garden

Malini. What can I say to you? I do not know how to argue. I have not read your books.

Supriya. I am learned only among the fools of learning. I have left all arguments and books behind me. Lead me, princess, and I shall follow you, as the shadow follows the lamp.

Malini. But, Brahmin, when you question me, I lose all my power and do not know how to answer you. It is a wonder to me to see that even you, who know everything, come to me with your questions.

Supriya. Not for knowledge I come to you. Let me forget all that I have ever known. Roads there are, without number, but the light is missing.

Malini. Alas, sir, the more you ask me, the more I feel my poverty. Where is that voice in me, which came down from heaven, like an unseen flash of lightning, into my heart? Why did you not come that day, but keep away in doubt? Now that I have met the world face to face my heart has grown timid, and I do not know how to hold the helm of the great ship that I must guide. I feel I am alone, and the world is large, and ways are many, and the light from the sky comes of a sudden to vanish the next moment. You who are wise and learned, will you help me?

Supriya. I shall deem myself fortunate, if you ask my help.

Malini. There are times when despair comes to choke all the life-currents; when suddenly, amidst crowds of men, my eyes turn upon myself and I am frightened. Will you befriend me in those moments of blankness, and utter me one word of hope that will bring me back to life.

Supriya. I shall keep myself ready. I shall make my heart simple and pure, and my mind peaceful, to be able truly to serve you.

[*Enters* Attendant.]

Attendant. The citizens have come, asking to see you.

Malini. Not to-day. Ask their pardon for me. I must have time to fill my exhausted mind, and have rest to get rid of weariness.

[Attendant *goes.*]

Tell me again about Kemankar, your friend. I long to know what your life has been and its trials.

Supriya. Kemankar is my friend, my brother, my master. His mind has been firm and strong, from early days, while my thoughts are always flickering with doubts. Yet he has ever kept me close to his heart, as the moon does its dark spots. But, however strong a ship may be, if it harbours a small hole in its bottom, it must sink.—That I would make you sink, Kemankar, was in the law of nature.

Malini. You made him sink?

Supriya. Yes, I did. The day when the rebellion slunk away in shame before the light in your face and the music in the air that touched you, Kemankar alone was unmoved. He left me behind him, and said that he must go to the foreign land to bring soldiers, and uproot the new creed from the sacred soil of Kashi.—You know what followed. You made me live again in a new land of birth. 'Love for all life' was a mere word, waiting from the old time to be made real,—and I saw that truth in you in flesh. My heart cried for my friend, but he was away, out of my reach; then came his letter, in which he wrote that he was coming with a foreign army at his back, to wash away the new faith in blood, and to punish you with death.—I could wait no longer. I showed the letter to the King.

Malini. Why did you forget yourself, Supriya? Why did fear overcome you? Have I not room enough in my house for him and his soldiers?

[*Enters* King.]

King. Come to my arms, Supriya, I went at a fit time to surprise Kemankar and to capture him. An hour later, and a thunderbolt would have burst upon my house in my sleep. You are my friend, Supriya, come—

Supriya. God forgive me.

King. Do you not know, that a King's love is not unsubstantial? I give you leave to ask for any reward that comes to your mind. Tell me, what do you want?

Supriya. Nothing, Sire, nothing. I shall live, begging from door to door.

King. Only ask me, and you shall have provinces worthy to tempt a king.

Supriya. They do not tempt me.

King. I understand you. I know towards what moon you raise your hands. Mad youth, be brave to ask even that which seems so impossible. Why are you silent? Do you remember the day when you prayed for my Malini's banishment? Will you repeat that prayer to me, to lead my daughter to exile from her father's house?—My daughter, do you know that you owe your life to this noble youth? And is it hard for you to pay off that debt with your—?

Supriya. For pity's sake, Sire, no more of this. Worshippers there are many who by life-long devotion have gained the highest fulfilment of their desire. Could I be counted one of them I should be happy. But to accept it from the King's hands as the reward of treachery? Lady mine, you have the plenitude and peace of your greatness; you know not the secret cravings of a poverty-stricken soul. I dare not ask from you an atom more than that pity of love which you have for every creature in the world.

Malini. Father, what is your punishment for the captive?

King. He shall die.

Malini. On my knees I beg from you his pardon.

King. But he is a rebel, my child.

Supriya. Do you judge him, King? He also judged you, when he came to punish you, not to rob your kingdom.

Malini. Spare him his life, father. Then only will you have the right to bestow on him your friendship, who has saved you from a great peril.

King. What do you say, Supriya? Shall I restore a friend to his friend's arms?

Supriya. That will be king-like in its grace.

King. It will come in its time, and you will find back your friend. But a King's generosity must not stop there. I must give you something which exceeds your hope,—yet not as a mere reward. You have won my heart, and my heart is ready to offer you its best treasure.—My child, where was this shyness in you before now? Your dawn had no tint of rose,—its light was white and dazzling. But to-day a tearful mist of tenderness sweetly tempers it for mortal eyes. [*To* Supriya] Leave my feet, rise up and come to my heart. Happiness is pressing it like pain. Leave me now for a while. I want to be alone with my Malini. [Supriya *goes.*] I feel I have found back my child once again,—not the bright star of the sky, but the sweet flower that blossoms on earthly soil. She is my daughter, the darling of my heart.

[*Enters* Attendant.]

Attendant. The captive, Kemankar, is at the door.

King. Bring him in. Here comes he, with his eyes fixed, his proud head held high, a brooding shadow on his forehead, like a thunder cloud motionless in a suspended storm.

Malini. The iron chain is shamed of itself upon those limbs. The insult to greatness is its own insult. He looks like a god defying his captivity.

[*Enters* Kemankar *in chains.*]

King. What punishment do you expect from my hands?

Kemankar. Death.

King. But if I pardon you?

Kemankar. Then I shall have time again to complete the work I began.

King. You seem out of love with your life. Tell me your last wish, if you have any.

Kemankar. I want to see my friend, Supriya, before I die.

King [*to the* attendant]. Ask Supriya to come.

Malini. There is a power in that face that frightens me. Father, do not let Supriya come.

King. Your fear is baseless, child.

[Supriya *enters, and walks towards* Kemankar, *with arms extended.*]

Kemankar. No, no, not yet. First let us have our say, and then the greeting of love.—Come closer to me. You know I am poor in words,—and my time is short. My trial is over, but not yours. Tell me, why have you done this?

Supriya. Friend, you will not understand me. I had to keep my faith, even at the cost of my love.

Kemankar. I understand you, Supriya. I have seen that girl's face, glowing with an inner light, looking like a voice becoming visible. You offered, to the fire of those eyes, the faith in your fathers' creed, the faith in your country's good, and built up a new one on the foundation of a treason.

Supriya. Friend, you are right. My faith has come to me perfected in the form of that woman. Your sacred books were dumb to me. I have read, by the help of the light of those eyes, the ancient book of creation, and I have known that true faith is there, where there is man, where there is love. It comes from the mother in her devotion, and it goes back to her from her child. It descends in the gift of a giver and it appears in the heart of him who takes it. I accepted the bond of this faith which reveals the infinite in man, when I set my eyes upon that face full of light and love and peace of hidden wisdom.

Kemankar. I also once set my eyes on that face, and for a moment dreamt that religion had come at last, in the form of a woman, to lead man's heart to heaven. For a moment, music broke out from the very ribs of my breast and all my life's hopes blossomed in their fulness. Yet did not I break through these meshes of illusion to wander in foreign lands? Did not I suffer humiliation from unworthy hands in patience, and bear the pain of separation from you, who have been my friend from my infancy? And what have you been doing meanwhile? You sat in the shade of the King's garden, and spent your sweet leisure in idly weaving a lie to condone your infatuation and calling it a religion.

Supriya. My friend, is not this world wide enough to hold men whose natures are widely different? Those countless stars of the sky, do they fight for the mastery of the One? Cannot faiths hold their separate lights in peace for the separate worlds of minds that need them?

Kemankar. Words, mere words. To let falsehood and truth live side by side in amity, the infinite world is not wide enough. That the corn ripening for the food of man should make room for thorny weeds, love is not so hatefully all-loving. That one should be allowed to sap the sure ground of friendship with betrayal of trust, could tolerance be so traitorously wide as that? That one should die like a thief to defend his faith and the other live in honour and wealth who betrayed it—no, no, the world is not so stony-hard as to bear without pain such hideous contradictions in its bosom.

Supriya [*to* Malini]. All these hurts and insults I accept in your name, my lady, Kemankar, you are paying your life for your faith,—I am paying more. It is your love, dearer than my life.

Kemankar. No more of this prating. All truths must be tested in death's court. My friend, do you remember our student days when we used to wrangle the whole night through, to come at last to our teacher, in the morning, to know in a moment which of us was right? Let that morning break now. Let us go there to that land of the final, and stand before death with all our questions, where the changing mist of doubts will vanish at a breath, and the mountain peaks of eternal truth will appear, and we two fools will look at each other and laugh.—Dear friend, bring before death that which you deem your best and immortal.

Supriya. Friend, let it be as you wish.

Kemankar. Then come to my heart. You had wandered far from your comrade, in the infinite distance,—now, dear friend, come eternally close to me, and accept from one, who loves you, the gift of death. [*Strikes* Supriya *with his chains, and* Supriya *falls*.]

Kemankar [*embracing the dead body of* Supriya]. Now call your executioner.

King [*rising up*]. Where is my sword?

Malini. Father, forgive Kemankar!

Sacrifice

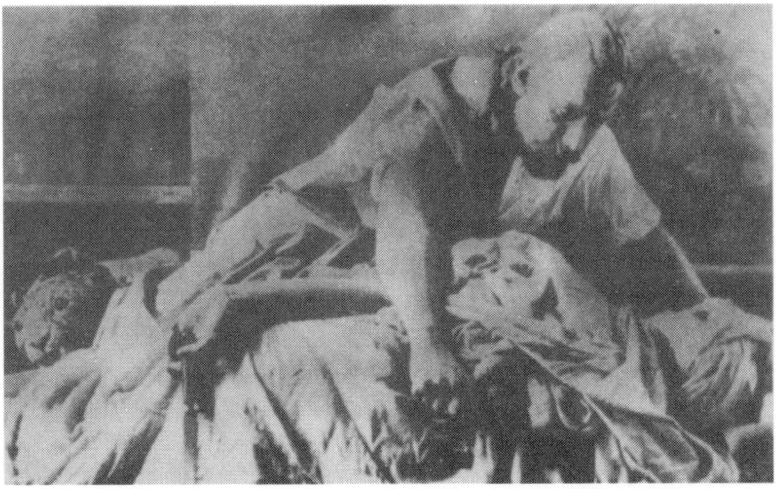

Tagore as Raghupati in his play *Bisarjan* (Sacrifice)

A temple of the Goddess Kali in Tripura.

[*Enters* Gunavati, *the Queen.*]

Gunavati. Have I offended thee, dread Mother? Thou grantest children to the beggar woman, who sells them to live, and to the adulteress, who kills them to save herself from infamy, and here I am, the Queen, with all the world lying at my feet, hankering in vain for the baby-touch at my bosom, to feel the stir of a dearer life within my life. What sin have I committed, Mother, to merit this, to be banished from the mothers' heaven?

[*Enters* Raghupati, *the priest.*]

O Master, have I ever been remiss in my worship? and my husband, is he not godlike in his purity? Then why has the Goddess, who weaves the web of this world-illusion, assigned my place in the barren waste of childlessness?

Raghupati. Our Mother is all caprice, she knows no law, our sorrows and joys are mere freaks of her mind. Have patience, daughter, to-day we shall offer special sacrifice in your name to please her.

Gunavati. Accept my grateful obeisance, father. My offerings are already on their way to the temple,—red bunches of hybiscus and beasts of sacrifice. [*They go out.*]

[*Enter* Govinda, *the King;* Jaising, *the servant of temple; and* Aparna, *the beggar girl.*]

Jaising. What is your wish, Sire?

Govinda. Is it true that this poor girl's pet goat has been brought by force to the temple to be killed? Will Mother accept such a gift with grace?

Jaising. King, how are we to know whence the servants collect our daily offerings of worship? But, my child, why is this weeping? Is it worthy of you to shed tears for that which Mother herself has taken?

Aparna. Mother! I am his mother. If I return late to my hut, he refuses his grass, and bleats, with his eyes on the road. I take him up in my arms, when I come, and share my food with him. He knows no mother but me.

Jaising. Sire, could I make the goat live again, by giving up a portion of my life, gladly would I do it. But how can I restore that which Mother herself has taken?

Aparna. Mother has taken? It is a lie. Not mother, but demon.

Jaising. O, the blasphemy!

Aparna. Mother, art thou there to rob a poor girl of her love? Then where is the throne, before which to condemn thee? Tell me, King.

Govinda. I am silent, my child. I have no answer.

Aparna. This blood-streak running down the steps, is it his? O my darling, when you trembled and cried for dear life, why did your call not reach my heart through the whole deaf world?

Jaising [*To the image*]. I have served thee from my infancy, Mother Kali, yet I understand thee not. Does pity only belong to weak mortals, and not to gods? Come with me, my child, let me do for you what I can. Help must come from man, when it is denied from gods.

[*All go out but the King.*]

[*Enter* Raghupati; Nakshatra, *who is the King's brother; and the courtiers.*]

All. Victory be to the King!

Govinda. Know you all, that I forbid shedding of blood in the temple from to-day for ever.

Minister. You forbid sacrifice to the Goddess?

General Nayan Rai. Forbid sacrifice?

Nakshatra. How terrible! Forbid sacrifice?

Raghupati. Is it a dream?

Govinda. No dream, father. It is awakening. Mother came to me, in a girl's disguise, and told me that blood she cannot suffer.

Raghupati. She has been drinking blood for ages. Whence comes this loathing all of a sudden?

Govinda. No, she never drank blood, she kept her face averted.

Raghupati. I warn you, think and consider. You have no power to alter laws laid down in scriptures.

Govinda. God's words are above all laws.

Raghupati. Do not add pride to your folly. Do you have the effrontery to say that *you* alone have heard God's words, and not I?

Nakshatra. It is strange, that the King should have heard from gods and not the priest.

Govinda. God's words are ever ringing in the world, and he who is wilfully deaf cannot hear them.

Raghupati. Atheist! Apostate!

Govinda. Father, go to your morning service, and declare to all worshippers that hence-forward they will be punished with banishment who shed creatures' blood in their worship of the Mother of all creatures.

Raghupati. Is this your last word?

Govinda. Yes.

Raghupati. Then curse upon you! Do you, in your enormous pride, imagine that the Goddess, dwelling in your land, is your subject? Do you presume to bind her with your laws and rob her of her dues? You shall never do it. I declare it,—I who am her servant. [*Goes.*]

Nayan Rai. Pardon me, Sire, but have you the right?

Minister. King, is it too late to revoke your order?

Govinda. We dare not delay to uproot sin from our realm.

Minister. Sin can never have such a long lease of life. Could they be sinful,—the rites that have grown old at the feet of the Goddess? [*The King is silent.*]

Nakshatra. Indeed they could not be.

Minister. Our ancestors have performed these rites with reverence; can you have the heart to insult them?

[*The King remains silent.*]

Nayan Rai. That which has the sanction of ages, do you have the right to remove it?

Govinda. No more doubts and disputes. Go and spread my order in all my lands.

Minister. But, Sire, the Queen has offered her sacrifice for this morning's worship; it is come near the temple gate.

Govinda. Send it back. [*He goes.*]

Minister. What is this?

Nakshatra. Are we, then, to come down to the level of Buddhists, and treat animals as if they have their right to live? Preposterous! [*They all go out.*]

[*Enters* Raghupati—Jaising *following him with a jar of water to wash his feet.*]

Jaising. Father.

Raghupati. Go!

Jaising. Here is some water.

Raghupati. No need of it!

Jaising. Your clothes.

Raghupati. Take them away!

Jaising. Have I done anything to offend you?

Raghupati. Leave me alone. The shadows of evil have thickened. The King's throne is raising its insolent head above the temple altar. Ye Gods of these degenerate days, are ye ready to obey the King's laws with bowed heads, fawning upon him like his courtiers?

Jaising. Whatever has happened, father?

Raghupati. I cannot find words to say. Ask the Mother Goddess who has been defied.

Jaising. Defied? By whom?

Raghupati. By King Govinda.

Jaising. King Govinda defied Mother Kali?

Raghupati. Defied you and me, all scriptures, all countries, all time, defied Mahakali, the Goddess of the endless stream of time,—sitting upon that puny little throne of his.

Jaising. King Govinda?

Raghupati. Yes, yes, your King Govinda, the darling of your heart. Ungrateful! I have given all my love to bring you up, and yet King Govinda is dearer to you than I am.

Jaising. The child raises its arms to the full moon, sitting upon his father's lap. You are my father and my full moon is King Govinda. Then is it true, what I hear from people, that our King forbids all sacrifice in the temple? But in this we cannot obey him.

Raghupati. Banishment is for him who does not obey.

Jaising. It is no calamity to be banished from a land where Mother's worship remains incomplete. No, so long as I live, the service of the temple shall be fully performed.

[*They go out.*]

[*Enter* Gunavati *and her* Attendant.]

Gunavati. What is it you say? The Queen's sacrifice turned away from the temple gate? Is there a man in this land who carries more than one head on his shoulders, that he could dare think of it? Who is that doomed creature?

Attendant. I am afraid to name him.

Gunavati. Afraid to name him, when I ask you? Whom do you fear more than me?

Attendant. Pardon me.

Gunavati. Give my salutation to the priest, and ask him to come.

[Attendant *goes out.*]

[*Enter* Govinda.]

Gunavati. Have you heard, King? My offerings have been sent back from Mother's temple.

Govinda. I know it.

Gunavati. You know it, and yet bear the insult?

Govinda. I beg to ask your pardon for the culprit.

Gunavati. I know, King, your heart is merciful, but this is no mercy. It is feebleness. If your kindness hampers you, leave the punishment in my hand. Only, tell me, who is he?

Govinda. It is I, my Queen. My crime is in nothing else but having given you pain.

Gunavati. I do not understand you.

Govinda. From to day shedding of blood in gods' temples is forbidden in my land.

Gunavati. Who forbids it?

Govinda. Mother herself.

Gunavati. Who heard it?

Govinda. I.

Gunavati. You! That makes me laugh. The Queen of all the world comes to the gate of Tripura's King with her petition.

Govinda. Not with her petition, but with her sorrow.

Gunavati. Your dominion is outside the temple limit. Do not send your commands there, where they are impertinent.

Govinda. The command is not mine, it is Mother's.

Gunavati. If you have no doubt in your decision, do not cross my faith. Let me perform my worship according to my light.

Govinda. I promised my Goddess to prevent sacrifice of life in her temple, and I must carry it out.

Gunavati. I also promised my Goddess the blood of three hundred kids and one hundred buffaloes, and I will carry it out. You may leave me now.

Govinda. As you wish. [*He goes out.*]

[*Enters* Raghupati.]

Gunavati. My offerings have been turned back from the temple, father.

Raghupati. The worship offered by the most ragged of all beggars is not less precious than yours, Queen. But the misfortune is that Mother has been deprived.

Gunavati. What will come of all this, father?

Raghupati. That is only known to her who fashions this world with her dreams. But this is certain, that the throne which casts its shadow upon Mother's shrine will burst like a bubble, vanishing in the void.

Gunavati. Have mercy and save us, father.

Raghupati. Ha, ha! I am to save you,—you, the consort of a King who boasts of his kingdom on the earth and in heaven as well, before whom the gods and the Brahmins must—Oh, shame! Oh, the evil age, when the Brahmin's futile curse recoils upon himself, to sting him into madness.

[*About to tear his sacrificial thread.*]

Gunavati [*preventing him*]. Have mercy upon me.

Raghupati. Then give back to Brahmins what is theirs by right.

Gunavati. Yes, I will. Go, master, to your worship, and nothing will hinder you.

Raghupati. Indeed your favour overwhelms me. At the merest glance of your eyes gods are saved from ignominy and the Brahmin is restored to his sacred offices. Thrive and grow fat and sleek till the dire day of judgment comes.

[*Goes out.*]

[*Re-enters King* Govinda.]

Govinda. My Queen, the shadow of your angry brows hides all light from my heart.

Gunavati. Go! Do not bring a curse upon this house.

Govinda. Woman's smile removes all curse from the house, her love is God's grace.

Gunavati. Go, and never show your face to me again.

Govinda. I shall come back, my Queen, when you remember me.

Gunavati [*clinging to the King's feet*]. Pardon me, King. Have you become so hard, that you forget to respect woman's pride? Do you not know, beloved, that thwarted love takes the disguise of anger?

Govinda. I would die, if I lost my trust in you. I know, my love, that clouds are for moments only, and the sun is for all days.

Gunavati. Yes, the clouds will pass by, God's thunder will return to his armoury, and the sun of all days will shine upon the traditions of all time. Yes, my King, order it so, that Brahmins be restored to their rights, the Goddess to her offerings, and the King's authority to its earthly limits.

Govinda. It is not the Brahmin's right to violate the eternal good. Creature's blood is not the offering for gods. And it is within the rights of the King and the peasant alike to maintain truth and righteousness.

Gunavati. I prostrate myself on the ground before you; I beg at your feet. The custom that comes through all ages is not the King's own. Like the heaven's air, it belongs to all men. Yet your Queen begs it of you, with clasped hands, in the name of your people. Can you still remain silent, proud man, refusing entreaties of love in favour of duty which is doubtful? Then go, go, go from me. [*They go.*]

[*Enter* Raghupati, Jaising *and* Nayan Rai.]

Raghupati. General, your devotion to Mother is well-known.

Nayan Rai. It runs through generations of my ancestors.

Raghupati. Let this sacred love give you indomitable courage. Let it make your sword-blade mighty as God's thunder, and win its place above all powers and positions of this world.

Nayan Rai. The Brahmin's blessings will never be in vain.

Raghupati. Then I bid you collect your soldiers and strike Mother's enemy down to the dust.

Nayan Rai. Tell me, father, who is the enemy?

Raghupati. Govinda.

Nayan Rai. Our King?

Raghupati. Yes, attack him with all your force.

Nayan Rai. It is evil advice. Father, is this to try me?

Raghupati. Yes, it is to try you, to know for certain whose servant you are. Give up all hesitation. Know that the Goddess calls, and all earthly bonds must be severed.

Nayan Rai. I have no hesitation in my mind. I stand firm in my post, where my Goddess has placed me.

Raghupati. You are brave.

Nayan Rai. Am I the basest of Mother's servants, that the order should come for me to turn traitor? She herself stands upon the faith of man's heart. Can she ask me to break it? Then to-day comes to dust the King, and to-morrow the Goddess herself.

Jaising. Noble words.

Raghupati. The King, who has turned traitor to Mother, has lost all claims to your allegiance.

Nayan Rai. Drive me not, father, into a wilderness of debates. I know only one path,—the straight path of faith and truth. This stupid servant of Mother shall never swerve from that highway of honour. [*Goes out.*]

Jaising. Let us be strong in our faith as he is, master. Why ask the aid of soldiers? We have the strength within ourselves for the task given to us from above. Open the temple gate wide, father. Sound the drum. Come, come, O citizens, to worship her, who takes all fear away from our hearts. Come, Mother's children.

[Citizens *come.*]

First Citizen. Come, come, we are called.

All. Victory to Mother! [*They sing and dance.*]

The dread Mother dances naked in the battlefield,
Her lolling tongue burns like a red flame of fire,
Her dark tresses fly in the sky, sweeping away the sun and stars,
Red streams of blood run from her cloud-black limbs,
And the world trembles and cracks under her tread.

Jaising. Do you see the beasts of sacrifice coming towards the temple, driven by the Queen's attendants?

[*They cry.*]

Victory to Mother! Victory to our Queen!

Raghupati. Jaising, make haste and get ready for the worship.

Jaising. Everything is ready, father.

Raghupati. Send a man to call Prince Nakshatra in my name.

[Jaising *goes.*]

[Citizens *sing and dance, enters King* Govinda.]

Govinda. Silence, Raghupati! Do you dare to disregard my order?

Raghupati. Yes, I do.

Govinda. Then you are not for my land.

Raghupati. No, my land is there, where the King's crown kisses the dust. Ho! Citizens! Let Mother's offerings be brought in here. [*They beat drums.*]

Govinda. Silence! [*To his attendants*] Ask my General to come. Raghupati, you drive me to call soldiers to defend God's right. I feel the shame of it; for the force of arms only reveals man's weakness.

[*Enter General* Nayan Rai *and* Chandpal, *who is the second in command of the army.*]

Govinda. Stand here with your soldiers to prevent sacrifice of life in the temple.

Nayan. Pardon me, Sire. The King's servant is powerless in the temple of God.

Govinda. General, it is not for you to question my order. You are to carry out my words. Their merits and demerits belong only to me.

Nayan. I am your servant, my King, but I am a man above all. I have reason and my religion. I have my King,—and also my God.

Govinda. Then surrender your sword to Chandpal. He will protect the temple from pollution of blood.

Nayan Rai. Why to Chandpal? This sword was given to my forefathers by your royal ancestors. If you want it back, I will give it up to you. Be witness, my fathers, who are in the heroes' paradise, the sword that you made sacred with your loyal faith and bravery, I surrender to my King.

[*Goes out.*]

Raghupati. The Brahmin's curse has begun its work already.

[*Enters* Jaising.]

Jaising. The beasts have been made ready for the sacrifice.

Govinda. Sacrifice?

Jaising [*on his knees*]. King, listen to my earnest entreaties. Do not stand in the way, hiding the Goddess, man as you are.

Raghupati. Shame, Jaising. Rise up and ask my pardon. I am your Master. Your place is at my feet, not the King's. Fool! Do you ask King's sanction to do God's service? Leave alone the worship and the sacrifice. Let us wait and see how his pride prevails in the end. Come away. [*They go out.*]

[*Enters* Aparna, *the beggar girl.*]

Aparna. Where is Jaising? He is not here, but only you,—the image whom nothing can move. You rob us of all our best without uttering a word. We pine for love, and die beggars for want of it. Yet it comes to you unasked, though you need it not. Like a grave, you hoard it under your miserly stone, keeping it from the use of the yearning world. Jaising, what happiness do you find from her? What can she speak to you? O my heart, my famished heart!

[*Enters* Raghupati.]

Raghupati. Who are you?

Aparna. I am a beggar girl. Where is Jaising?

Raghupati. Leave this place at once. I know you are haunting this temple, to steal Jaising's heart from the Goddess.

Aparna. Has the Goddess anything to fear from me? I fear her. [*She goes out.*]

[*Enter* Jaising *and Prince* Nakshatra.]

Nakshatra. Why have you called me?

Raghupati. Last night the Goddess told me in a dream, that you shall become king within a week.

Nakshatra. Ha, ha, this is news indeed.

Raghupati. Yes, you shall be King.

Nakshatra. I cannot believe it.

Raghupati. You doubt my words?

Nakshatra. I do not want to doubt them. But suppose, by chance, it never comes to pass.

Raghupati. No, it shall be true.

Nakshatra. But, tell me, how can it ever become true?

Raghupati. The Goddess thirsts for King's blood.

Nakshatra. King's blood?

Raghupati. You must offer it to her before you can be king.

Nakshatra. I know not where to get it.

Raghupati. There is King Govinda.—Jaising, keep still.—Do you understand? Kill him in secret. Bring his blood, while warm, to the altar.—Jaising, leave this place, if you cannot remain still,—

Nakshatra. But he is my brother, and I love him.

Raghupati. Your sacrifice will be all the more precious.

Nakshatra. But, father, I am content to remain as I am. I do not want the kingdom.

Raghupati. There is no escape for you, because the Goddess commands it. She is thirsting for blood from the King's house. If your brother is to live, then you must die.

Nakshatra. Have pity on me, father.

Raghupati. You shall never be free in life, or in death, until her bidding is done.

Nakshatra. Advise me, then, how to do it.

Raghupati. Wait in silence. I will tell you what to do, when the time comes. And now, go. [Nakshatra *goes*.]

Jaising. What is it that I heard? Merciful Mother, is it your bidding? To ask brother to kill brother? Master, how could you say that it was Mother's own wish?

Raghupati. There was no other means but this to serve my Goddess.

Jaising. Means? Why means? Mother, have you not your own sword to wield with your own hand? Must your wish burrow underground, like a thief, to steal in secret? Oh, the sin!

Raghupati. What do you know about sin?

Jaising. What I have learnt from you.

Raghupati. Then come and learn your lesson once again from me. Sin has no meaning in reality. To kill is but to kill, it is neither sin nor anything else. Do you not know that the dust of this earth is made of countless killings? Old Time is ever writing the chronicle of the transient life of creatures in letters of blood. Killing is in the wilderness, in the habitations of man, in birds' nests, in insects' holes, in the sea, in the sky; there is killing for life, for sport, for nothing whatever. The world is ceaselessly killing; and the great Goddess Kali, the spirit of ever changing time, is standing with her thirsty tongue hanging down from her mouth, with her cup in hand, into which is running the red life-blood of the world, like juice from the crushed cluster of grapes.

Jaising. Stop, master. Is then love a falsehood and mercy a mockery, and the one thing true, from the beginning of time, the lust for destruction? Would it not have destroyed itself long ago? You are playing with my heart, my master. Look there, she is gazing at me. My blood-thirsty Mother, wilt thou accept my blood? Is it so delicious to thee? Master, did you call me? The Mother, who is thirsting for our love, you accuse of blood-thirstiness!

Raghupati. Then let the sacrifice be stopped in the temple.

Jaising. Yes, let it be stopped.—No, no, master, you know what is right and what is wrong. The heart's laws are not the laws of scripture. Eyes cannot see with their own light,—the light must come from the outside. Tell me, father, is it true that the Goddess seeks King's blood?

Raghupati. Alas, child, have you lost your faith in me?

Jaising. My world stands upon my faith in you. If the Goddess must have King's blood, let me bring it to her. I will never allow a brother to kill his brother.

Raghupati. But there can be no evil in carrying out God's wishes.

Jaising. No, it must be good, and I will earn the merit of it.

Raghupati. But, my boy, I have reared you from your childhood, and you have grown close to my heart. I can never bear to lose you, by any chance.

Jaising. I will not let your love for me be soiled with sin. Release Prince Nakshatra from his promise.

Raghupati. I will think, and decide to-morrow. [*He goes.*]

Jaising. Deeds are better, however cruel they may be, than the hell of thinking and doubting. You are true, my master, to kill is no sin, to kill a brother is no sin, to kill a king is no sin.—Where do you go, my brothers? To the fair at Nishipur? There the women are to dance? Oh, this world is pleasant! And the dancing limbs of the girls are beautiful. In what careless merriment the crowds flow through the roads, making the sky ring with their laughter and song. I will follow them.

[*Enters* Raghupati.]

Raghupati. Jaising.

Jaising. I do not know you. I drift with the crowd. Why ask me to stop? Go your own way.

Raghupati. Jaising.

Jaising. The road is straight before me. With an alms bowl in hand and the beggar girl as my sweetheart I shall walk on. Who says that the world's ways are devious? Anyhow we reach the end,—the end where all laws and rules are no more, where the errors and hurts of life are forgotten. What is the use of all these scriptures, and the teacher and his instructions?—My master, my father, what wild words are these of mine? I was living in a dream. There stands the temple, cruel and immovable as truth. What was your order, my teacher? I have not forgotten it. (*Bringing out the knife*) I am sharpening your words in my mind, till they become one with this knife in keenness. Have you any other order to give me?

Raghupati. My boy, my darling, how can I tell you how deep is my love for you?

Jaising. No, master, do not tell me of love. Let me think only of duty. Love, like the green grass and the trees and life's music, is only for the surface of the world. It comes and vanishes like a dream. But underneath is duty, like the rude layers of stone, like a huge load that nothing can move.

[*They go out.*]

[*Enter King* Govinda *and* Chandpal.]

Chandpal. Sire, I warn you to be careful.

Govinda. Why? What do you mean?

Chandpal. I have overheard a conspiracy to take away your life.

Govinda. Who wants my life?

Chandpal. I am afraid to tell you, lest the news become to you more deadly than the knife itself. It was Prince Nakshatra, who—

Govinda. Nakshatra?

Chandpal. He has promised to Raghupati to bring your blood to the Goddess.

Govinda. To the Goddess? Then I cannot blame him. For a man loses his humanity when it concerns his gods. You go to your work and leave me alone. [Chandpal *goes out.*]

(*Addressing the image*) Accept these flowers, Goddess, and let your creatures live in peace. Mother, those who are weak in this world are so helpless, and those who are strong are so cruel. Greed is pitiless, ignorance blind, and pride takes no heed when it crushes the small under its foot. Mother, do not raise your sword and lick your lips for blood; do not set brother against brother, and woman against man. If it is your desire to strike me by the hand of one I love, then let it be fulfilled. For the sin has to ripen to its ugliest limits, before it can burst and die a hideous death.

[Jaising *rushes in.*]

Jaising. Tell me, Goddess, dost thou truly want King's blood? Ask it in thine own voice, and thou shalt have it.

A Voice. I want King's blood.

Jaising. King, say your last prayer, for your time has come.

Govinda. What makes you say it, Jaising?

Jaising. Did you not hear what the Goddess said?

Govinda. It was not the Goddess. I heard the familiar voice of Raghupati.

Jaising. Drive me not from doubt to doubt. It is all the same, whether the voice comes from the Goddess, or from my master.—

[*He unsheathes his knife, and then throws it away.*]

Listen to the cry of thy children, Mother. Let there be only flowers for thy offerings,—no more blood. They are red even as blood,—these bunches of hybiscus. They have come out of the heart-burst of the earth, pained at the slaughter of her children. Accept this. Thou must accept this. I defy thy anger. Blood thou shalt never have. Redden thine eyes. Raise thy sword. Bring thy furies of destruction. I do not fear thee. King, leave this temple to its Goddess, and go to your men. [Govinda *goes.*]

Alas, alas, in a moment I gave up all that I had, my master, my Goddess. [Raghupati *comes.*]

Raghupati. I have heard all. Traitor, you have betrayed your master.

Jaising. Punish me, father.

Raghupati. What punishment will you have?

Jaising. Punish me with my life.

Raghupati. No, that is nothing. Take your oath touching the feet of the Goddess.

Jaising. I touch her feet.

Raghupati. Say, I will bring kingly blood to the altar of the Goddess, before it is midnight.

Jaising. I will bring kingly blood to the altar of the Goddess, before it is midnight. [*They go out.*]

[*Enters* Gunavati.]

Gunavati. I failed. I have hoped that, if I remained hard and cold for some days, he would surrender. Such faith I had in my power, vain woman that I am. I showed my sullen anger, and remained away from him; but it was fruitless. Woman's anger is like a diamond's glitter; it only shines, but cannot burn. I would it were like thunder, bursting upon the King's house, startling him up from his sleep, and dashing his pride to the ground.

[*Enters the boy* Druva.]

Gunavati. Where are you going?

Druva. I am called by the King. [*Goes out.*]

Gunavati. There goes the darling of the King's heart. He has robbed my unborn children of their father's love, usurped their right to the first place in the King's breast. O Mother Kali, your creation is infinite and full of wonders, only send a child to my arms in merest whim, a tiny little warm living flesh to fill my lap, and I shall offer you whatever you wish. [*Enters* Nakshatra.] Prince Nakshatra, why are you so excited.

Nakshatra. Tell me what you want of me.

Gunavati. The thief that steals the crown awaiting you,—remove him. Do you understand?

Nakshatra. Yes, except who the thief is.

Gunavati. That boy, Druva. Do you not see how he is growing in the King's lap, till one day he reaches the crown?

Nakshatra. Yes, I have often thought of it. I have seen my brother putting his crown on the boy's head in play.

Gunavati. Playing with the crown is a dangerous game. If you do not remove the player, he will make a game of you.

Nakshatra. Yes, I like it not.

Gunavati. Offer him to Kali. Have you not heard that Mother is thirsting for blood?

Nakshatra. But, sister, this is not my business.

Gunavati. Fool, can you feel yourself safe, so long as Mother is not appeased? Blood she must have; save your own, if you can.

Nakshatra. But she wants King's blood.

Gunavati. Who told you that.

Nakshatra. I know it from one to whom the Goddess herself sends her dreams.

Gunavati. Then that boy must die for the King. His blood is more precious to your brother than his own, and the King can only be saved by paying the price, which is more than his life.

Nakshatra. I understand.

Gunavati. Then lose no time. Run after him. He is not gone far. But remember. Offer him in my name.

Nakshatra. Yes, I will.

Gunavati. The Queen's offerings have been turned back from Mother's gate. Pray to her that she may forgive me.

[*They go out.*]

[*Enters* Jaising.]

Jaising. Goddess, is there any little thing, that yet remains, out of the wreck of thee? If there be but a faintest spark of thy light in the remotest of the stars of evening, answer my cry, though thy voice be the feeblest. Say to me, 'Child, here I am.'—No, she is nowhere. She is naught. But take pity upon Jaising, O Illusion! Art thou so irredeemably false, that not even my love can send the slightest tremor of life through thy nothingness? O fool, for whom have you upturned your cup of life, emptying it to the last drop? for this unanswering void,—truthless, merciless, and motherless?

[*Enters* Aparna.]

Aparna, they drive you away from the temple; yet you come back over and over again. For you are true, and truth cannot be banished. We enshrine falsehood in our temple, with all devotion; yet she is never there. Leave me not, Aparna. Sit here by my side. Why are you so sad, my darling? Do you miss some god, who is god no longer? But is there any need of God in this little world of ours? Let us be fearlessly godless and come closer to each other. They want our blood. And for this, they have come down to the dust of our earth, leaving their magnificence of heaven. For in their heaven there are no men, no creatures, who can suffer. No, my girl, there is no Goddess.

Aparna. Then leave this temple, and come away with me.

Jaising. Leave this temple? Yes, I will leave, Alas, Aparna, I must leave. Yet I cannot leave it, before I have paid my last dues to the.— But let that be. Come closer to me, my love. Whisper something to my ears, which will overflow this life with sweetness, flooding death itself.

Aparna. Words do not flow when the heart is full.

Jaising. Then lean your head on my breast. Let the silence of two eternities, life and death, touch each other.—But no more of this. I must go.

Aparna. Jaising, do not be cruel. Can you not feel what I have suffered?

Jaising. Am I cruel? Is this your last word to me? Cruel, as that block of stone, whom I called Goddess? Aparna, my beloved, if you were the Goddess, you would know what fire is this that burns my heart. But you *are* my Goddess. Do you know how I know it?

Aparna. Tell me.

Jaising. You bring to me your sacrifice every moment, as a mother does to her child. God must be all sacrifice, pouring out his life in all creation.

Aparna. Jaising, come, let us leave this temple and go away together.

Jaising. Save me, Aparna, have mercy upon me and leave me. I have only one object in my life. Do not usurp its place.

[*Rushes out.*]

Aparna. Again and again I have suffered. But my strength is gone. My heart breaks. [*She goes out.*]

[*Enter* Raghupati *and Prince* Nakshatra.]

Raghupati. Prince, where have you kept the boy?

Nakshatra. He is in the room where the vessels for worship are kept. He has cried himself to sleep. I think I shall never be able to bear it, when he wakes up again.

Raghupati. Jaising was of the same age when he came to me. And I remember how he cried till he slept at the feet of the Goddess,—the temple lamp dimly shining on his tear-stained child-face. It was a stormy evening like this.

Nakshatra. Father, delay not. I wish to finish it all, while he is sleeping. His cry pierces my heart like a knife.

Raghupati. I will drug him to sleep, if he wakes up.

Nakshatra. The King will soon find it out, if you are not quick. For, in the evening, he leaves the care of his kingdom to come to this boy.

Raghupati. Have more faith in the Goddess. The victim is now in her own hands and it shall never escape.

Nakshatra. But Chandpal is so watchful.

Raghupati. Not more so than our Mother.

Nakshatra. I thought I saw a shadow pass by.

Raghupati. The shadow of your own fear.

Nakshatra. Do we not hear the sound of a cry?

Raghupati. The sound of your own heart. Shake off your despondency, Prince. Let us drink this wine duly consecrated. So long as the purpose remains in the mind, it looms large and fearful. In action it becomes small. The vapour is dark and diffused. It dissolves into water drops that are small and sparkling. Prince, it is nothing. It takes only a moment,—not more than it does to snuff a candle.

Nakshatra. I think we should not be too rash. Leave this work till tomorrow night.

Raghupati. To-night is as good as tomorrow night, perhaps better.

Nakshatra. Listen to the sound of footsteps.

Raghupati. I do not hear it.

Nakshatra. See there,—the light.

Raghupati. The King comes. I fear we have delayed too long.

[*King* Govinda *comes with attendants.*]

Govinda. Make them prisoners. [*To* Raghupati] Have you anything to say?

Raghupati. Nothing.

Govinda. Do you admit your crime?

Raghupati. Crime? Yes, my crime was that, in my weakness, I delayed in carrying out Mother's service. The punishment comes from the Goddess. You are merely her instrument.

Govinda. According to my law, my soldiers shall escort you to exile, Raghupati, where you shall spend eight years of your life.

Raghupati. King, I never bent my knees to any mortal in my life. I am a Brahmin. Your caste is lower than mine. Yet, in all humility, I pray to you, give me only one day's time.

Govinda. I grant it.

Raghupati [*mockingly*]. You are the King of all kings. Your majesty and mercy are alike immeasurable. Whereas I am a mere worm, hiding in the dust. [*He goes out.*]

Govinda. Nakshatra, admit your guilt.

Nakshatra. I am guilty, Sire, and I dare not ask for your pardon.

Govinda. Prince, I know you are tender of heart. Tell me, who beguiled you with evil counsel?

Nakshatra. I will not take other names, King. My guilt is my own. You have pardoned your foolish brother more than once, and once more he begs to be pardoned.

Govinda. Nakshatra, leave my feet. The judge is still more bound by his laws than his prisoner.

Attendants. Sire, remember that he is your brother, and pardon him.

Govinda. Let me remember that I am a king. Nakshatra shall remain in exile for eight years, in the house we have built, by the sacred river, outside the limits of Tripura. [*Taking* Nakshatra's *hands*] The punishment is not yours only, brother, but also mine,— the more so because I cannot share it bodily.

[*They all go out.*]

[*Enter* Raghupati *and* Jaising.]

Raghupati. My pride wallows in the mire. I have shamed my Brahminhood. I am no longer your master, my child. Yesterday I had the authority to command you. To-day I can only beg your favour. Life's days are mere tinsel, most trifling of God's gifts, and I had to beg for one of those days from the King with bent knees. Let that one day be not in vain. Let its infamous black brows be red with King's blood before it dies. Why do you not speak, my boy? Though I forsake my place as your master, yet have I not the right to claim your obedience as your father,—I who am more than a father to you, because father to an orphan? You are still silent, my child? Then let my knees bend to you, who were smaller than my knees when you first came to my arms.

Jaising. Father, do not torture the heart that is already broken. If the Goddess thirsts for kingly blood, I will bring it to her before tonight. I will pay all my debts, yes, every farthing. Keep ready for my return. I will delay not. [*Goes out.*]

[*Storm outside.*]

Raghupati. She is awake at last, the Terrible. Her curses go shrieking through the town. The hungry furies are shaking the cracking branches of the world tree with all their might, for the stars to break and drop. My Mother, why didst thou keep thine own people in doubt and dishonour so long? Leave it not for thy servant to raise thy sword. Let thy mighty arm do its own work!—I hear steps.

[*Enters* Aparna.]

Aparna. Where is Jaising?

Raghupati. Away evil omen. [Aparna *goes out.*] But if Jaising never comes back? No, he will not break his promise.

Victory to thee, Great Kali, the giver of all success!—But if he meet with obstruction? If he be caught and lose his life at the guards' hands?—Victory to thee, watchful Goddess, Mother invincible! Do not allow thy repute to be lost, and thine enemies to laugh at thee. If thy children must lose their pride and faith in their Mother, and bow down their heads in shame before the rebels, who then shall remain in this orphaned world to carry thy banner?—I hear his steps. But so soon? Is he coming back foiled in his purpose? No, that cannot be. Thy miracle needs not time, O Mistress of all time, terrible with thy necklace of human skulls.

[*Rushes in* Jaising.]

Jaising, where is the blood?

Jaising. It is with me. Let go my hands. Let me offer it myself [*Entering the temple*] Must thou have kingly blood, Great Mother, who nourishest the world at thy breast with life?—I am of the royal caste, a Kshatriya. My ancestors have sat upon thrones, and there are rulers of men in my mother's line. I have kingly blood in my veins. Take it, and quench thy thirst for ever.

[*Stabs himself and falls.*]

Raghupati. Jaising! O cruel, ungrateful! You have done the blackest crime. You kill your father! Jaising, forgive me, my darling. Come back to my heart, my heart's one treasure! Let me die in your place.

[*Enters* Aparna.]

Aparna. It will madden me. Where is Jaising? Where is he?

Raghupati. Come, Aparna, come, my child, call him with all your love. Call him back to life. Take him to you, away from me, only let him live.

[Aparna *enters the temple and swoons.*]

Raghupati [*beating his forehead on the temple floor*]. Give him, give him, give him.—Give him back to me! [*Stands up addressing the image.*] Look how she stands there, the silly stone,—deaf, dumb, blind,—the whole sorrowing world weeping at her door,—the noblest hearts wrecking themselves at her stony feet. Give me back my Jaising. Oh, it is all in vain. Our bitterest cries wander in emptiness,—the emptiness that we vainly try to fill with these stony images of delusion. Away with them! Away with these our impotent dreams, that harden into stones, burdening our world.

[*He throws away the image, and comes out into the courtyard.*]

[*Enters* Gunavati.]

Gunavati. Victory to thee, great Goddess!—But, where is the Goddess?

Raghupati. Goddess there is none.

Gunavati. Bring her back, father. I have brought her my offerings. I have come at last, to appease her anger with my own heart's blood. Let her know that the Queen is true to her promise. Have pity on me, and bring back the Goddess only for this night. Tell me,—where is she?

Raghupati. She is nowhere,—neither above, nor below.

Gunavati. Master, was not the Goddess here in the temple?

Raghupati. Goddess?—If there were any true Goddess anywhere in the world, could she bear this thing to usurp her name?

Gunavati. Do not torture me. Tell me truly. Is there no Goddess?

Raghupati. No, there is none.

Gunavati. Then who was here?

Raghupati. Nothing, nothing.

[Aparna *comes out from the temple.*]

Aparna. Father.

Raghupati. My sweet child! 'Father,'—did you say? Do you rebuke me with that name? My son, whom I have killed, has left that one dear call behind him in your sweet voice.

Aparna. Father, leave this temple. Let us go away from here.

[*Enters the King.*]

Govinda. Where is the Goddess?

Raghupati. The Goddess is nowhere.

Govinda. But what blood-stream is this?

Raghupati. King, Jaising, who loved you so dearly, has killed himself.

Govinda. Killed himself? Why?

Raghupati. To kill the falsehood, that sucks the life-blood of man.

Govinda. Jaising is great. He has conquered death. My flowers are for him.

Gunavati. My King.

Govinda. Yes, my love.

Gunavati. The Goddess is no more.

Govinda. She has burst her cruel prison of stone, and come back to woman's heart.

Aparna. Father, come away.

Raghupati. Come, child. Come, Mother. I have found thee. Thou art the last gift of Jaising.

The King and the Queen

ACT I

The Palace Garden. King Vikram *and Queen* Sumitra.

Vikram. Why have you delayed in coming to me for so long, my love?

Sumitra. Do you not know, my King, that I am utterly yours, wherever I am? It was your house, and its service, that kept me away from your presence, but not from you.

Vikram. Leave the house, and its service, alone. My heart cannot spare you for my world, I am jealous of its claims.

Sumitra. No, King, I have my place in your heart, as your beloved, and in your world, as your Queen.

Vikram. Alas, my darling, where have vanished those days of unalloyed joy, when we first met in love; when our world awoke not,—only the flush of the early dawn of our union broke through our hearts in over-flowing silence? You had sweet shyness in your eyelids, like a dew drop on the tip of a flower-petal, and the smile flickered on your lips like a timid evening lamp in the breeze. I remember the eager embrace of your love, when the morning broke and we had to part, and your unwilling steps, heavy with languor, that took you away from me. Where were the house, and its service, and the cares of your world?

Sumitra. But then we were scarcely more than a boy and a girl; and to-day we are the King and the Queen.

Vikram. The King and the Queen? Mere names. We are more than that; we are lovers.

Sumitra. You are my King, my husband, and I am content to follow your steps. Do not shame me by putting me before your kingship.

Vikram. Do you not want my love?

Sumitra. Love me truly by not making your love extravagant; for truth can afford to be simple.

Vikram. I do not understand woman's heart.

Sumitra. King, if you thriftlessly squander your all upon me, then I shall be deprived.

Vikram. No more vain words, Queen. The birds' nests are silent with love. Let lips keep guard upon lips, and allow not words to clamour.

[*Enters* Attendant.]

Attendant. The minister begs audience, to discuss a grave matter of state.

Vikram. No, not now. [Attendant *goes.*]

Sumitra. Sire, ask him to come.

Vikram. The state and its matter can wait. But sweet leisure comes rarely. It is frail, like a flower. Respite from duty is a part of duty.

Sumitra. Sire, I beg of you, attend to your work.

Vikram. Again, cruel woman. Do you imagine that I always follow you to win your unwilling favour, drop by drop? I leave you and go. [*He goes.*]

[*Enters* Devadatta, *the King's Brahmin friend.*]

Sumitra. Tell me, sir, what is that noise outside the gate?

Devadatta. That noise? Command me, and with the help of soldiers I shall drive away that noise, ragged and hungry.

Sumitra. Do not mock me. Tell me what has happened.

Devadatta. Nothing. It is merely hunger,—the vulgar hunger of poverty. The famished horde of barbarians is rudely clamouring, making the drowsy cuckoos in your royal garden start up in fear.

Sumitra. Tell me, father, who are hungry?

Devadatta. It is their ill-fate. The King's poor subjects have been practising long to live upon half a meal a day, but they have not yet become experts in complete starvation. It is amazing.

Sumitra. But, father, the land is smiling with ripe corn. Why should the King's subjects die of hunger?

Devadatta. The corn is his, whose is the land,—it is not for the poor. They, like intruding dogs at the King's feast, crouch in the corner for their crumbs, or kicks.

Sumitra. Does it mean, that there is no King in this land?

Devadatta. Not one, but hundreds.

Sumitra. Are not the King's officers watchful?

Devadatta. Who can blame your officers? They came penniless from the alien land. Is it to bless the King's subjects with their empty hands?

Sumitra. From the alien land? Are they my relatives?

Devadatta. Yes, Queen.

Sumitra. What about Jaisen?

Devadatta. He rules the province of Singarh with such scrupulous care, that all the rubbish, in the shape of food and raiment, has been cleared away; only the skin and bones remain.

Sumitra. And Shila?

Devadatta. He keeps his eyes upon the trade; he relieves all merchants of their excessive profits, taking the burden upon his own broad shoulders.

Sumitra. And Ajit?

Devadatta. He lives in Vijaykote. He smiles sweetly, strokes the land on its back with his caressing hand, and whatever comes to his touch gathers with care.

Sumitra. What shame is this. I must remove this refuse from my father's land and save my people. Leave me now, the King comes. [*Enters the King.*] I am the mother of my people. I cannot bear their cry. Save them, King.

Vikram. What do you want me to do?

Sumitra. Turn those out from your kingdom, who are oppressing the land.

Vikram. Do you know who they are?

Sumitra. Yes, I know.

Vikram. They are your own cousins.

Sumitra. They are not a whit more my own than my people. They are robbers, who, under the cover of your throne, seek for their victims.

Vikram. They are Jaisen, Shila, Ajit.

Sumitra. My country must be rid of them.

Vikram. They will not move without fight.

Sumitra. Then fight them, Sire.

Vikram. Fight? But let me conquer *you* first, and then I shall have time to conquer my enemies.

Sumitra. Allow me, King, as your Queen. I will save your subjects myself. [*Goes.*]

Vikram. This is how you make my heart distraught. You sit alone upon your peak of greatness, where I do not reach you. You go to attend your own God, and I go seeking you in vain.

[*Enters* Devadatta.]

Devadatta. Where is the Queen, Sire? Why are you alone?

Vikram. Brahmin, this is all your conspiracy. You come here to talk of the state news to the Queen?

Devadatta. The state is shouting its own news loud enough to reach the Queen's ears. It has come to that pass, when it takes no heed lest your rest be broken. Do not be afraid of me, King. I have come to ask my Brahmin's dues from the Queen. For my wife is out of humour, her larder is empty, and in the house there are a number of empty stomachs. [*He goes.*]

Vikram. I wish all happiness to my people. Why should there be suffering, and injustice? Why should the strong cast his vulture's eyes upon the poor man's comforts, pitifully small? (*Enters* Minister.) Banish all the foreign robbers from my kingdom, this moment. I must not hear the cry of the oppressed for a day longer.

Minister. But, King, the evil that has been slowly growing for long, you cannot uproot in a day.

Vikram. Strike at its root with vigour, and fell it with your axe in a day,—the tree that has taken a hundred years to grow.

Minister. But we want arms and soldiers.

Vikram. Where is my general?

Minister. He himself is a foreigner.

Vikram. Then invite the hungry people. Open my treasure; stop this cry with food; send them away with money,—And if they want to have my kingdom, let them do so in peace, and be happy. [*He goes.*]

[*Enter* Sumitra *and* Devadatta.]

Minister. Queen, my humble salutation to you.

Sumitra. We cannot allow misery to go unchecked in our land.

Minister. What are your commands, Queen?

Sumitra. Call immediately, in my name, all our chiefs who are foreigners.

Minister. I have done so already. I have taken upon myself to invite them into the capital, in the King's name, without asking for his sanction, for fear of refusal.

Sumitra. When did you send your messengers?

Minister. It will soon be a month hence. I am expecting their answers every moment. But I am afraid they will not respond.

Sumitra. Not respond to the King's call?

Devadatta. The King has become a piece of wild rumour, which they can believe, or not, as they like.

Sumitra. Keep your soldiers ready, Minister, for these people. They shall have to answer to me, as my relatives.

[*The* Minister *goes.*]

Devadatta. Queen, they will not come.

Sumitra. Then the King shall fight them.

Devadatta. The King will not fight.

Sumitra. Then I will.

Devadatta. You!

Sumitra. I will go to my brother Kumarsen, Kashmir's King, and with his help fight these rebels, who are a disgrace to Kashmir. Father, help me to escape from this kingdom, and do your duty, if things come to the worst.

Devadatta. I salute thee, Mother of the people. [*He goes.*]

[*Enters* Vikram.]

Vikram. Why do you go away, Queen? My hungry desire is revealed to you in its naked poverty. Do you therefore go away from me in derision?

Sumitra. I feel shamed to share alone your heart, which is for all men.

Vikram. Is it absolutely true, Queen, that you stand on your giddy height, and I grovel in the dust? No. I know my power. There is an unconquerable force in my nature, which I have turned into love for you.

Sumitra. Hate me, King, hate me. Forget me. I shall bear it bravely,—but do not wreck your manhood against a woman's charms.

Vikram. So much love, yet such neglect? Your very indifference, like a cruel knife, cuts into my bosom, laying bare the warm bleeding love,—and then, to fling it into the dust!

Sumitra. I throw myself at your feet, my beloved. Have you not forgiven your Queen, again and again, for wrongs done? Then why is this wrath, Sire, when I am blameless?

Vikram. Rise up, my love. Come to my heart. Shut my life from all else for a moment, with your encircling arms, rounding it into a world completely your own.

A Voice from Outside. Queen.

Sumitra. It is Devadatta.—Yes, father, what is the message?

[*Enters* Devadatta.]

Devadatta. They have defied the King's call,—the foreign governors of the provinces,—and they are preparing for rebellion.

Sumitra. Do you hear, King?

Vikram. Brahmin, the palace garden is not the council-house.

Devadatta. Sire, we rarely meet our King in the council-house, because it is not the palace garden.

Sumitra. The miserable dogs, grown fat upon the King's table sweepings, dare dream of barking against their master? King, is it time for debating in the council chamber? Is not the course clear before you? Go with your soldiers and crush these miscreants.

Vikram. But our general himself is a foreigner.

Sumitra. Go yourself.

Vikram. Am I your misfortune, Queen,—a bad dream, a thorn in your flesh? No, I will never move a step from here. I will offer them terms of peace. Who is it that has caused this mischief? The Brahmin and the woman conspired to wake up the sleeping snake from its hole. Those who are too feeble to protect themselves are the most thoughtless in causing disasters to others.

Sumitra. O the unfortunate land, and the unfortunate woman who is the Queen of this land.

Vikram. Where are you going?

Sumitra. I am going to leave you.

Vikram. Leave me?

Sumitra. Yes. I am going to fight the rebels.

Vikram. Woman, you mock me.

Sumitra. I take my farewell.

Vikram. You dare not leave me.

Sumitra. I dare not stay by your side, when I weaken you.

Vikram. Go, proud woman. I will never ask you to turn back,—but claim no help from me. [Sumitra *goes.*]

Devadatta. King, you allow her to go alone?

Vikram. She is not going. I do not believe her words.

Devadatta. I think she is in earnest.

Vikram. It is her woman's wiles. She threatens me, while she wants to spur me into action; and I despise her methods. She must not think that she can play with my love. She shall regret it. O my friend, must I learn my lesson at last, that love is not for the King,—and learn it from that woman, whom I love like my doom? Devadatta, you have grown with me from infancy,—can you not forget, for a moment, that I am a king, and feel that I have a man's heart that knows pain?

Devadatta. My heart is yours, my friend, which is not only ready to receive your love, but your anger.

Vikram. But why do you invite the snake into my nest?

Devadatta. Your house was on fire,—I merely brought the news, and wakened you up. Am I to blame for that?

Vikram. What is the use of waking? When all are mere dreams, let me choose my own little dream, if I can, and then die. Fifty years hence, who will remember the joys and sorrows of this moment? Go, Devadatta, leave me to my kingly loneliness of pain.

[*Enters a* Courtier *who is a foreigner.*]

Courtier. We ask justice from your hands, King,—we, who came to this land with the Queen.

Vikram. Justice for what?

Courtier. It has come to our ears, that false accusations against us are brought before you, for no other cause than that we are foreigners.

Vikram. Who knows, if they are not true? But so long as I trust you, can you not remain silent? Have I ever insulted you with the least suspicion—the suspicions that are bred like maggots in the rotten hearts of cowards? Treason I do not fear. I can crush it under my feet. But I fear to nourish littleness in my own mind.—You can leave me now.

[*The* courtier *goes.*]

[*Enter* Minister *and* Devadatta.]

Minister. Sire, the Queen has left the palace, riding on her horse.

Vikram. What do you say? Left my palace?

Minister. Yes, King.

Vikram. Why did you not stop her?

Minister. She left in secret.

Vikram. Who brought you the news?

Minister. The priest. He saw her riding before the palace temple.

Vikram. Send for him.

Minister. But Sire, she cannot be far. She has only just left. You can yet bring her back.

Vikram. Bringing her back is not important. The great fact is, that she left me.—Left me! And all the King's soldiers and forts, and prisons and iron chains, could not keep fast this little heart of a woman.

Minister. Alas, King. Calumny, like a flood-burst, when the dyke is broken, will rush in from all sides.

Vikram. Calumny! Let the people's tongues rot with their own poison.

Devadatta. In the days of eclipse, men dare look at the midday sun through their broken pieces of glass, blackened with soot. Great Queen, your name will be soiled, tossed from mouth to mouth, but your light will ever shine far above all soiling.

Vikram. Bring the priest to me. [Minister *goes*.] I can yet go to seek her, and bring her back. But is this my eternal task? That she should always avoid me, and I should ever run after the fugitive heart? Take your flight, woman, day and night, homeless, loveless, without rest and peace. [*Enters* priest.] Go, go, I have heard enough, I do not want to know more. [*The* priest *is about to go*.] Come back.—Tell me, did she come down to the temple to pray, with tears in her eyes?

Priest. No, Sire. Only, for a moment, she checked her horse and turned her face to the temple, bowing her head low,—then rode away fast as lightning. I cannot say, if she had tears in her eyes. The light from the temple was dim.

Vikram. Tears in her eyes? You could not even imagine such enormity? Enough. You may go. [*The* Priest *goes*.] My God, you know that all the wrong that I have done to her, was that I loved her. I was willing to lose my heaven and my kingdom for her love. But they have not betrayed me, only she has.

[*Enters* Minister.]

Minister. Sire, I have sent messengers on horse-back in pursuit of her.

Vikram. Call them back. The dream has fled away. Where can your messengers find it? Get ready my army. I will go to war myself, and crush the rebellion.

Minister. As you command. [*Goes away*.]

Vikram. Devadatta, why do you sit silent and sad? The thief has fled, leaving the booty behind, and now I pick up my freedom. This is a moment of rejoicing to me. False, false friend, false are my words. Cruel pain pierces my heart.

Devadatta. You shall have no time for pain, or for love, now,—your life will become one stream of purpose, and carry your kingly heart to its great conquest.

Vikram. But I am not yet completely freed in my heart. I still believe she will soon come back to me, when she finds that the world is not her lover, and that man's heart is the only world for a woman. She will know what she has spurned, when she misses it; and my time will come when, her pride gone, she comes back, and jealously begins to woo me.

[*Enters* Attendant.]

Attendant. A letter from the Queen.

[*Gives the letter, and goes*.]

Vikram. She relents already. [*Reads the letter*.] Only this. Just two lines, to say that she is going to her brother in Kashmir, to ask him to help her to quell the rebellion in my kingdom. This is insult! Help from Kashmir!

Devadatta. Lose no time to forestall her,—and let that be your revenge.

Vikram. My revenge? You shall know it.

ACT II

Tent in Kashmir. Vikram *and the* General.

General. Pardon me, King, if I dare offer you advice in the interest of your kingdom.

Vikram. Speak to me.

General. The rebellion in our land has been quelled. The rebels themselves are fighting on your side. Why waste our strength and time in Kashmir, when your presence in your own capital is so urgently needed?

Vikram. The fight here is not over yet.

General. But Kumarsen, the Queen's brother, is already punished for his sister's temerity. His army is routed, he is hiding for his life. His uncle, Chandrasen, is only too eager to be seated upon the vacant throne. Make him the king, and leave this unfortunate country to peace.

Vikram. It is not for punishment, that I stay here; it is for fight. The fight has become like a picture to a painter. I must add bold lines, blend strong colours, and perfect it every day. My mind grows more and more immersed in it, as it blossoms into forms; and I leave it with a sigh, when it is finished. The destruction is merely its materials, out of which it takes its shape. It is a creation. It is beautiful, as red bunches of *palash,* that break out like a drunken fury, yet every one of its flowers delicately perfect.

General. But, Sire, this cannot go on for ever. You have other duties. The minister has been sending me message after message, entreating me to help you to see how this war is ruining your country.

Vikram. I cannot see anything else in the world but what is growing under my masterly hands. Oh, the music of swords. Oh, the great battles, that clasp your breast tight like hard embraces of love. Go, General, you have other works to do,—your advices flash out best on the points of your swords. [General *goes.*] This is deliverance. The bondage has fled of itself, leaving the prisoner free. Revenge is stronger than the thin wine of love. Revenge is freedom,—freedom from the coils of cloying sweetness.

[*Enters* General.]

General. I can espy a carriage coming towards our tent, perhaps bringing an envoy of peace. It has no escort of armed soldiers.

Vikram. Peace must follow the war. The time for it has not yet come.

General. Let us hear the messenger first, and then,—

Vikram. And then continue the war.

[*Enters a* Soldier.]

Soldier. The Queen has come asking for your audience.

Vikram. What do you say?

Soldier. The Queen has come.

Vikram. Which Queen?

Soldier. Our Queen, Sumitra.

Vikram. Go, General, see who has come. [*The* general *and the* Soldier *go.*] This is the third time that she has come, vainly attempting to coax me away, since I have carried war into Kashmir. But these are no dreams—these battles. To wake up suddenly, and then find again the same palace gardens, the flowers, the Queen, the long days made of sighs and small favours. No, a thousand times, no. She has come to make me captive, to take me as her trophy from the war-field into her palace hall. She may as well try to capture the thunderstorms.

[*Enters* General.]

General. Yes, Sire, it is our own Queen, who wants to see you. It breaks my heart when I cannot allow her to come freely into your presence.

Vikram. This is neither the time, nor the place, to see a woman.

General. But, Sire.

Vikram. No, no. Tell my guards to keep a strict watch at my tent door,—not for enemies, but for women.

[General goes.]

[*Enters* Shankar.]

Shankar. I am Shankar,—King Kumarsen's servant. You have kept me captive in your tent.

Vikram. Yes, I know you.

Shankar. Your Queen waits outside your tent.

Vikram. She will have to wait for me farther away.

Shankar. It makes me blush to say, that she has come humbly to ask your pardon; or, if that is impossible, to accept her punishment from your hand. For she owns that she alone was to blame,—and she asks you, in the name of all that is sacred, to spare her brother's country and her brother.

Vikram. But you must know, old man, it is war,—and this war is with her brother, and not herself. I have no time to discuss the rights and wrongs of the question with a woman. But, being a man, you ought to know that when once a war is started, rightly or wrongly, it is our man's pride that must carry it on to the end.

Shankar. But do you know, Sire, you are carrying on this war with a woman, and she is your Queen. Our King is merely espousing her cause, being her brother. I ask you, is it king-like, or manlike, to magnify a domestic quarrel into a war, carrying it from country to country?

Vikram. I warn you, old man, your tongue is becoming dangerous. You may tell the Queen, in my name, that when her brother, Kumarsen, owns his defeat and surrenders himself into our hands, the question of pardoning will then be discussed.

Shankar. That is as impossible as for the morning sun to kiss the dust of the western horizon. My King will never surrender himself alive into your hands, and his sister will never suffer it.

Vikram. Then the war must continue. But do you not think that bravery ceases to be bravery at a certain point, and becomes mere fool-hardiness? Your King can never escape me. I have surrounded him on all sides, and he knows it.

Shankar. Yes, he knows it and also knows that there is a great gap.

Vikram. What do you mean?

Shankar. I mean death,—the triumphal gate through which he will escape you, if I know him right. And there waits his revenge. [*He goes*.]

[*Enters* Attendant.]

Attendant. Sire, Chandrasen, and his wife Revati, Kumarsen's uncle and aunt, have come to see you.

Vikram. Ask them in.

[*Enter* Chandrasen *and* Revati.]

Vikram. My obeisance to you both.

Chandrasen. May you live long.

Revati. May you be victorious.

Chandrasen. What punishment have you decided for him?

Vikram. If he surrenders, I shall pardon him.

Revati. Only this, and nothing more? If tame pardon comes at the end, then why is there such preparation? Kings are not overgrown children, and war is no mere child's play.

Vikram. To rob was not my purpose, but to restore my honour. The head that bears the crown cannot bear insult.

Chandrasen. My son, forgive him. For he is neither mature in age, nor in wisdom. You may deprive him of his right to the throne, or banish him, but spare him his life.

Vikram. I never wished to take his life.

Revati. Then why such an army and arms? You kill the soldiers, who have done you no harm, and spare him who is guilty?

Vikram. I do not understand you.

Chandrasen. It is nothing. She is angry with Kumarsen for having brought our country into trouble, and for giving you just cause for anger, who are so nearly related to us.

Vikram. Justice will be meted out to him, when he is captured.

Revati. I have come to ask you never to suspect that we are hiding him. It is the people. Burn their crops and their villages,—drive them with hunger, and then they will bring him out.

Chandrasen. Gently, wife, gently. Come to the palace, son, the reception of Kashmir awaits you there.

Vikram. You go there now, and I shall follow you. [*They go out.*] Oh, the red flame of hell-fire. The greed and hatred in a woman's heart. Did I catch a glimpse of my own face in her face, I wonder? Are there lines like those on my forehead, the burnt tracks made by a hidden fire? Have my lips grown as thin and curved at both ends as hers, like some murderer's knife? No, my passion is for war,—it is neither for greed, nor for cruelty; its fire is like love's fire, that knows no restraint, that counts no cost, that burns itself, and all that it touches, either into a flame, or to ashes.

[*Enters* Attendant.]

Attendant. The Brahmin, Devadatta, has come, awaiting your pleasure.

Vikram. Devadatta has come? Bring him in,—No, no, stop. Let me think,—I know him. He has come to turn me back from the battle-field. Brahmin, you undermined the river banks, and now, when the water overflows, you piously pray that it may irrigate your fields, and then tamely go back. Will it not wash away your houses, and ruin the country? The joy of the terrible is blind,—its term of life is short, and it must gather its plunder in fearful haste, like a mad elephant uprooting the lotus from the pond. Wise councils will come, in their turn, when the great force is spent,—No, I must not see the Brahmin.

[*Enters* Amaru, *the chieftain of Trichür hills.*]

Amaru. Sire, I have come at your bidding, and I own you as my King.

Vikram. You are the chief of this place?

Amaru. Yes. I am the chief of Trichur. You are the King of many kings, and I am your servant. I have a daughter, whose name is Ila. She is young and comely. Do not think me vain, when I say that she is worthy to be your spouse. She is waiting outside. Permit me, King, and I shall send her to you as the best greeting of this land of flowers.

[*He goes out.*]

[*Enters* Ila *with her* Attendant.]

Vikram. Ah! She comes, as a surprise of dawn, when the moment before it seemed like a dark night. Come, maiden, you have made the battle-field forget itself. Kashmir has shot her best arrow, at last, to pierce the heart of the war-god. You make me feel that my eyes had been wandering among the wilderness of things, to find at last their fulfilment. But why do you stand so silent, with your eyes on the ground? I can almost see a trembling of pain in your limbs, whose intensity makes it invisible.

Ila [*kneeling*]. I have heard that you are a great King. Be pleased to grant me my prayer.

Vikram. Rise up, fair maiden. This earth is not worthy to be touched by your feet. Why do you kneel in the dust? There is nothing that I cannot grant you.

Ila. My father has given me to you. I beg myself back from your hands. You have wealth untold, and territories unlimited,—go and leave me behind in the dust; there is nothing that you can want.

Vikram. Is there, indeed, nothing that I can want? How shall I show you my heart? Where is its wealth? Where are its territories? It is empty. Had I no kingdom, but only you—

Ila. Then first take my life,—as you take that of the wild deer of the forest, piercing her heart with your arrows,—

Vikram. But why, child,—why such contempt for me? Am I so utterly unworthy of you? I have won kingdoms with the might of my arms. Can I not hope to beg your heart for me?

Ila. But my heart is not mine. I have given it to one who left me months ago, promising to come back and meet me in the shade of our ancient forest. Days pass, and I wait, and the silence of the forest grows wistful. If he find me not, when he comes back! If he go away for ever, and the forest shadows keep their ancient watch for the love-meeting that remains eternally unfulfilled! King, do not take me away,—leave me for him, who has left me, to find me again.

Vikram. What a fortunate man is he. But I warn you, girl, gods are jealous of our love. Listen to my secret. There was a time when I despised the whole world, and only loved. I woke up from my dream, and found that the world was there,—only my love burst as a bubble. What is his name, for whom you wait?

Ila. He is Kashmir's King. His name is Kumarsen.

Vikram. Kumarsen!

Ila. Do you know him? He is known to all. Kashmir has given its heart to him.

Vikram. Kumarsen? Kashmir's King?

Ila. Yes. He must be your friend.

Vikram. But do you not know, that the sun of his fortune has set? Give up all hope of him. He is like a hunted animal, running and hiding from one hole to another. The poorest beggar in these hills is happier than he.

Ila. I hardly understand you, King.

Vikram. You, women, sit in the seclusion of your hearts, and only love. You do not know how the roaring torrent of the world passes by, and we, men, are carried away in its waves in all directions. With your sad, big eyes, filled with tears, you sit and watch, clinging to flimsy hope. But learn to despair, my child.

Ila. Tell me the truth, King. Do not deceive me. I am so very little and so trivial. But I am all his own. Where,—in what homeless wilds,—is my lover roaming? I will go to seek him,—I, who never have been out of my house. Show me the way,—

Vikram. His enemy's soldiers are after him,—he is doomed.

Ila. But are you not his friend? Will you not save him? A king is in danger, and will you suffer it as a King? Are you not honour-bound to succour him? I know that all the world loved him. But where are they, in his time of misfortune? Sire, you are great in power, but what is your power for, if you do not help the great? Can you keep yourself aloof? Then show me the way,— I will offer my life for him,—the one, weak woman.

Vikram. Love him, love him with all you have—Love him, who is the King of your precious heart. I have lost my love's heaven myself,—but let me have the happiness to make you happy. I will not covet your love.—The withered branch cannot hope to blossom with borrowed flowers. Trust me. I am your friend. I will bring him to you.

Ila. Noble King. I owe you my life and my heaven of happiness.

Vikram. Go, and be ready with your bridal dress. I will change the tune of my music. (Ila *goes.*) This war is growing tiresome. But peace is insipid. Homeless fugitive, you are more fortunate than I am. Woman's love, like heaven's watchful eyes, follows you wherever you go in this world, making your defeat a triumph and misfortune splendid, like sunset clouds.

[*Enters* Devadatta.]

Devadatta. Save me from my pursuers.

King. Who are they?

Devadatta. They are your guards, King. They kept me under strict watch for this ever-lasting half-hour. I talked to them of art and letters; they were amused. They thought I was playing the fool to please them. Then I began to recite to them the best lyrics of Kalidas,—and it soothed this pair of yokels to sleep. In perfect disgust, I left their tent to come to you.

King. These guards should be punished for their want of taste in going off to sleep when the prisoner recited Kalidas.

Devadatta. We shall think of the punishment later on. In the meanwhile, we must leave this miserable war and go back home. Once I used to think that only they died of love's separation, who were the favoured of fortune, delicately nurtured. But since I left home to come here, I have discovered that even a poor Brahmin is not too small to fall a victim to angered love.

Vikram. Love and death are not too careful in their choice of victims. They are impartial. Yes, friend, let us go back home. Only I have one thing to do, before I leave this place. Try to find out, from the chief of Trichur, Kumarsen's hiding-place. Tell him, when you find him, that I am no longer his enemy. And, friend, if somebody else is there with him,—if you meet her,—

Devadatta. Yes, yes, I know. She is ever in our thoughts, yet she is beyond our words. She, who is noble, her sorrow has to be great.

Vikram. Friend, you have come to me, like the first sudden breeze of spring. Now my flowers will follow, with all the memories of the past happy years. [Devadatta *goes*.]

[*Enters* Chandrasen.]

Vikram. I have glad tidings for you. I have pardoned Kumarsen.

Chandrasen. You may have pardoned him,—but now that I represent Kashmir, he must await his country's judgment at my hands. He shall have his punishment from me.

Vikram. What punishment?

Chandrasen. He shall be deprived of his throne.

Vikram. Impossible. His throne I will restore to him.

Chandrasen. What right have you in Kashmir's throne?

Vikram. The right of the victorious. This throne is now mine, and I will give it to him.

Chandrasen. *You* give it to him! Do I not know proud Kumarsen, from his infancy? Do you think he will accept his father's throne as a gift from you? He can bear your vengeance, but not your generosity.

[*Enters a* Messenger.]

Messenger. The news has reached us that Kumarsen is coming in a closed carriage to surrender himself. [*Goes out.*]

Chandrasen. Incredible! The lion comes to beg his chains! Is life so precious?

Vikram. But why does he come in a closed carriage?

Chandrasen. How can he show himself? The eyes of the crowd in the streets will pierce him, like arrows, to the quick. King, put out the lamp, when he comes, receive him in darkness. Do not let him suffer the insult of the light.

[*Enters* Devadatta.]

Devadatta. I hear that the King, Kumarsen, is coming to see you of his own will.

Vikram. I will receive him with solemn rituals,—with you as our priest. Ask my general to employ his soldiers to make preparation for a wedding festival.

[*Enter the* Brahmin elders.]

All. Victory be to you.

First Elder. We hear that you have invited our King, to restore him to his throne,—. Therefore we have come to bless you for the joy that you have given to Kashmir.

[*They bless him, and* Vikram *bows to them.*
The Brahmins *go out. Enters* Shankar.]

Shankar [*to* Chandrasen]. Sire, is it true that Kumarsen is coming to surrender himself to his enemies?

Chandrasen. Yes, it is true.

Shankar. Worse than a thousand lies. O my beloved King, I am your old servant, I have suffered pain that only God knows, yet never complained. But how can I bear this? That you should travel through all the roads of Kashmir, to enter your cage of prison? Why did not your servant die before this day?

[*Enters* a Soldier.]

Soldier. The carriage is at the door.

Vikram. Have they no instruments at hand,—flutes and drums? Let them strike a glad tune. [*Coming near the door*] I welcome you, my kingly friend, with all my heart.

[*Enters* Sumitra, *with a covered tray in her hands*.]

Vikram. Sumitra. My Queen!

Sumitra. King Vikram, day and night you sought him in hills and forests, spreading devastation, neglecting your people and your honour, and to-day he sends through me to you his coveted head,—the head upon which death sits even more majestic than his crown.

Vikram. My Queen.

Sumitra. Sire, no longer your Queen; for merciful death has claimed me. [*Falls and dies*.]

Shankar. My King, my Master, my darling boy, you have done well. You have come to your eternal throne. God has allowed me to live for so long to witness this glory. And now, my days are done, and your servant will follow you.

[*Enters* Ila, *dressed in a bridal dress*.]

Ila. King, I hear the bridal music. Where is my lover? I am ready.

Autumn-Festival

CHARACTERS

Sanyasi, *Emperor Vijayaditya in disguise*
Thakurdada
Luckeswar
Upananda
Rajah
Boys
Minister, Courtiers, etc.

Scene. The forest near the river Vetasini.
Luckeswar *and* Upananda.

Luckeswar. Have you brought me the money which is long overdue?

Upananda. My master died last night.

Luckeswar. Died! Absurd! That trick won't do. What about the money?

Upananda. He hasn't left anything except the *vina* which was his only means of paying off your debt.

Luckeswar. Only the *vina!* That's a consoling piece of news to bring to me.

Upananda. I haven't come to give you news. There was a time when I was a beggar in the street; he sheltered me and allowed me to share his food, which was scanty enough. I have come to offer my service till his debt is fully paid.

Luckeswar. Indeed! Now that he is no more you have come to share *my* food, which is not overabundant. I am not such an ass as to be taken in by you. However let me first know what you can do.

Upananda. I can copy manuscripts and illuminate them. Food I won't take in your house. I shall earn it and also pay off the debt.

Luckeswar [*aside*]. The *vina* player was a big fool and he has moulded this boy in his own pattern. This vagabond is pining to take up some voluntary burden to be crushed to death. For some creatures this is the only natural death.—

Good, I agree. But you must pay me the money on the third day of each month, otherwise—

Upananda. Otherwise what! Your threats are of no use. In memory of my dear master I take this up. But no threats for me, I warn you.

Luckeswar. Don't take offence, my child. You are made of gold, every inch of you; you are a jewel. You know I have my god in the temple, his worship depends upon my charity. If, owing to any irregularity in your payment, I have to curtail the temple expenses, the sin will be on your head. [Upananda *moves away to another side of the forest.*] Who's that! It must be my own boy prowling about this place. I am sure the rogue is seeking for the place where I keep my treasure hidden. Simply out of fear of these prying noses I have to remove it from place to place.— Dhanapati, why on earth are you here?

Dhanapati. If you give me leave, I can have my game here this morning with the other boys.

Luckeswar [*aside*]. I know their game. They have got scent of that big pearl which I hid near this spot. [*To* Dhanapati] No, that won't do! Come at once to your multiplication table.

Dhanapati. But, Sir, it is a beautiful day—

Luckeswar. What do you mean by the day being beautiful! Come at once! [*Drags him away.*]

[*Enter* boys *with* Thakurdada.]

First boy. You belong to our party, Thakurdada!

Second boy. No, to ours.

Thakurdada. Children, I don't sell myself in shares. I must remain undivided. Now for the song. [*They sing.*]

Over the green and yellow ricefields sweeps the shadows of the autumn clouds followed by the swift-chasing sun.
The bees forget to sip their honey; drunken with light they foolishly hover and hum.
The ducks in the islands of the river clamour in joy for nothing.

[*Enter another group of* boys.]

Third boy. Was it fair? Why didn't you call us when you came out?

Thakurdada. It is your part to call me out. Don't quarrel, finish the song. [*They sing*.]

Let none go back home, brothers, this morning, let none go to work.
Let us take the blue sky by storm and plunder space as we run.
Laughter floats in the air like foam on the flood.
Brothers, let us squander our morning in futile songs.

First boy. Look there Thakurdada, a sanyasi is coming.

Second boy. It's grand! We shall have a game with the sanyasi. We shall be his followers.

Third boy. We shall follow him to the end of the earth and nobody will be able to find us out.

Thakurdada. Hush, he has come.

The boys [*shouting*]. Sanyasi Thakur! Sanyasi Thakur!

Thakurdada. Stop that noise! The father will be angry.

First boy. Sanyasi Thakur, will you be angry with us?

Second boy. We shall become your followers for this morning.

Sanyasi. Excellent! When you have had your turn, I shall be your followers. That will be splendid fun!

Thakurdada. My salutation. Who are you, father?

Sanyasi. I am a student.

Thakurdada. Student!

Sanyasi. I have come out to fling to the four winds my books.

Thakurdada. I understand. You want to be lightened of your learning, to follow the path of wisdom unburdened.

First boy. Thakurdada is wasting time with talk, and our holiday will come to its close.

Sanyasi. You are right, my boys. My holidays are also near their end.

The boys. Have you long holidays?

Sanyasi. Oh! no, extremely short. My school-master is already after me.

First boy. You frighten us! Even *you* have school-masters?

Sanyasi. What boy is that under the shade of that tree, merged in his manuscripts?

Boys. He is Upananda.

First boy. Upananda, we are Sanyasi Thakur's followers, come and become our chief.

Upananda. Not to-day. I have my work.

Second boy. No work. You *must* come!

Upananda. I must finish copying manuscripts.

Third boy. Father, you ask him to come. He won't listen to us.

Sanyasi [*to* Upananda]. What work have you, my son? To-day is not meant for work.

Upananda. I know it is our holiday. But I have my debt to pay and I must work.

Thakurdada. Upananda, your debt! To whom?

Upananda. My master has died, he is in debt to Luckeswar. I must pay it off.

Thakurdada. Alas! that such a boy as you must pay your debts, and on such a day! The first breath of the autumn has sent a shiver through the white crest of flowering grass and the *shiuli* blossoms have offered their fragrance to the air, as if in the joy of reckless sacrifice, and it pains me to see that boy sitting in the midst of all this, toiling to pay his debts.

Sanyasi. Why, this is as beautiful as all these flowers,—his paying his debts. He has made this morning glorious, sitting in its centre. Baba, you go on writing, let me watch you. Every line you finish brings you freedom, and thus you fill your holiday with truth. Give me one of your manuscripts and let me help you.

Thakurdada. I have my spectacles with me, let me also sit down to this work.

First boy. We shall also write. This is great fun!

Second boy. Yes, yes, let us try.

Upananda. But it will be such a great trouble to you, father.

Sanyasi. That is why I join you. We shall take trouble for fun. What do you say to that, boys?

The boys [*clapping hands*]. Yes, yes.

First boy. Give me one of the books.

Second boy. And me also.

Upananda. But are you sure you can do it.

The boys. O! Yes!

Upananda. You won't be tired?

Second boy. Never.

Upananda. You will have to be very careful.

First boy. Try us.

Upananda. There must be no mistakes.

Second boy. Not a bit.

Sanyasi. Baba Upananda, what was your master's name?

Upananda. Surasen.

Sanyasi. Surasen, the *vina* player?

Upananda. Yes, father. Was he known to you?

Sanyasi. I came to this place with the one hope of hearing him.

Upananda. Had he such fame?

Thakurdada. Was he such a master, that a sanyasi like yourself should have come all this way to hear him? Then we must have missed knowing him truly.

Sanyasi. But the Rajah of this place?

Thakurdada. The Rajah never even saw him. But where could you have heard him play?

Sanyasi. I suppose you know that there is a Rajah whose name is Vijayaditya.

Thakurdada. We may be very provincial, but surely you don't expect us not to know him.

Sanyasi. Very likely. Surasen played the *vina* in his court, where I was present. The Rajah tried hard to keep him permanently in his capital, but he failed.

Thakurdada. What a pity that we did not honour him.

Sanyasi. But that neglect has only made him all the greater. God has called him to His own court. Upananda, how did you come to know him?

Upananda. At my father's death I came to this town seeking shelter. It was at the end of July and the rain was pouring down in torrents. I was trying to find a corner in Lokanath temple, when the priest came and drove me out, expecting me to be of a low caste. My master was playing the *vina* in the temple. At once he came up and putting his arms round my neck asked me to come to his house. From that day he brought me up suffering calumny for my sake.

Sanyasi. How did you learn illuminating manuscripts?

Upananda. At first I asked him to teach me to play the *vina,* so that I could earn something and be useful to him. He said, 'Baba, this art is not for filling one's stomach.' And so he taught me how to use paints for copying books.

Sanyasi. Though Surasen's *vina* is silent, I hear the undying music of his life through you. My boy go on with your writing.

The boys [*starting up*]. There he comes, Lucki's owl! We must run away. [*They go.*]

[*Enters* Luckeswar.]

Luckeswar. Horror! Upananda is sitting exactly on the spot where the pearl is hidden. I *was* simple to think he was a fool seeking to pay off other people's debts. He is cleverer than he looked. He is after my pearl. I see he has captured a sanyasi to help him. Upananda!

Upananda. What's the matter!

Luckeswar. Get up from that spot at once! What business have you to be sitting there!

Upananda. And what business have *you* to be shouting at me like that! Does this place belong to you?

Luckeswar. It is no concern of yours, if it does or does not.—You *are* cunning! The other day this fellow came to me, looking innocent as a babe whose mother's milk had hardly dried on his lips. And I believed him when he said that he came to pay his master's debts. Of course, it is in the King's statute also,—

Upananda. I sat down to my work here for that very purpose.

Luckeswar. That very purpose! How old am I do you think? Only born overnight?

Sanyasi. But why do you suspect him and of what?

Luckeswar. As if you know nothing! False Sanyasi!

Upananda [*getting excited*]. Won't I just smash his teeth with this pestle of mine!

[Luckeswar *hides himself behind the* Sanyasi.]

Sanyasi. Don't be excited. Luckeswar knows human nature better than any of you here. Directly he sets his eyes upon me, I am caught,—a sanyasi false from his matted hair to his bare foot. I have passed through many countries and everywhere they believed in me, but Luckeswar is hard to deceive.

Luckeswar [*aside*]. I am afraid I am mistaken. It was rash on my part. He may curse me. I still have three boats on the sea. [*Taking the dust off* sanyasi's *feet.*] My salutation to you, father! I did make a blunder. Thakurdada, you had better take our Sanyasi to our house. I'll give him some alms. But you go first; don't delay, I shall be there in a minute.

Thakurdada. You are excessively kind. Do you think that father has come crossing hills and seas to accept a handful of rice from you?

Sanyasi. Why not Thakurdada! Where that handful of rice is so very dear, I must claim it. Come Luckeswar!

Luckeswar. I shall follow you. Upananda, you get up first! Get up, I say, with your books and other nonsense.

Upananda. Very well, I get up. Than I cut off all connection with you for good.

Luckeswar. That will be a great relief to me. I was getting on splendidly before I had any connection with you.

Upananda. My debt is paid with this insult that I suffer from your hands. [*Goes*.]

Luckeswar. My God! Sepoys riding on horses are coming this way! I wonder if our Rajah also—I prefer Upananda to him. [*To* Sanyasi] Father, by your holy feet I entreat you, sit on this spot, just on this spot; no, slightly to the left, slightly more. Yes, now it is all right. Sit firmly on this plot of grass. Let the Rajah come or the Emperor, don't you budge an inch. If you keep my words, I'll satisfy you later on.

Thakurdada. What is the matter with Luckeswar? Has he gone mad?

Luckeswar. Father, the very sight of me suggests money to my Rajah. My enemies have falsely informed him that I keep my treasure hidden underground. Since this report, our Rajah has been digging an enormous number of wells in this kingdom. When asked for reasons, he said it was to remove the scarcity of water from this land. And now I can't sleep at nights because of the fear that a sudden fit of his generosity might lead him to remove the water scarcity from the floor of my own dwelling.

[*Enters the King's* Messenger.]

Messenger. Father, my salutation! You are Apurva-Ananda?

Sanyasi. Some people know me by that name.

Messenger. The rumour is abroad of your extraordinary powers. Our Rajah is desirous of seeing you.

Sanyasi. He will see me whenever he sets his eyes on me.

Messenger. If you would kindly—

Sanyasi. I have given my word to somebody that I shall remain immovable in this place.

Messenger. The King's garden is close by.

Sanyasi. All the less trouble for him to come.

Messenger. I shall make known to him your wishes. [*Goes*.]

Thakurdada. Since an irruption of Rajahs is apprehended, I take my leave.

Sanyasi. Do you gather my scattered friends together and keep them ready for me.

Thakurdada. Let disasters come in the shape of Kings or of anarchy, I firmly hold by you. [*Goes*.]

[*Enters* Luckeswar.]

Luckeswar. I have overheard all. You are the famous Apurva-Ananda! I ask your pardon for the liberties I have taken.

Sanyasi. I readily pardon you for your calling me a sham sanyasi.

Luckeswar. But father, mere pardon does not cost much. You cannot dismiss Luckeswar with that. I must have a boon,—quite a substantial one.

Sanyasi. What boon do you ask?

Luckeswar. I must confess to you, father, that I have piled up a little money for myself, though not quite to the measure of what people imagine. But the amount does not satisfy me. Tell me the secret of some treasure, which may lead me to the end of my wanderings.

Sanyasi. I am also seeking for this.

Luckeswar. I can't believe it.

Sanyasi. Yes, it is true.

Luckeswar. Then you are wider awake than we are.

Sanyasi. Certainly.

Luckeswar [*whispering*]. Have got on the track?

Sanyasi. Otherwise I shouldn't be roving about like this.

Luckeswar [*touching his feet*]. Do make it a little plain to me. I swear I shall keep it secret from everybody else.

Sanyasi. Then listen. I am on the quest of the golden lotus on which Lakshmi keeps her feet.

Luckeswar. How bold! This takes my breath away. But, do you think you can find it unaided? It means expense. Do one thing, let us go shares in it.

Sanyasi. In that case you will have to be a sanyasi, never touching gold for a long time.

Luckeswar. That is hard.

Sanyasi. You can only prosper in this business if you give up all others.

Luckeswar. That sounds very much like bankruptcy. But all the same I *do* believe in you—which astounds even myself. There comes our Rajah! Let me hide behind this tree.

[*Hides himself*.]

[*Enters the* Rajah.]

Rajah. My salutation!

Sanyasi. Victory to you! What is your desire?

Rajah. Surely you can divine it already. My desire is to rule over a kingdom which is supreme.

Sanyasi. Then begin by giving up what is small.

Rajah. The overlordship of Vijayaditya has become intolerable to me.

Sanyasi. To tell you the truth he is growing too much even for me.

Rajah. Is that so?

Sanyasi. Yes. All my practices are to bring him under control.

Rajah. Is that why you have become a sanyasi?

Sanyasi. Yes.

Rajah. Do you think your charms will be potent enough to bring you success?

Sanyasi. It is not impossible.

Rajah. In that case do not forget me.

Sanyasi. I shall bring him to your court.

Rajah. Yes, his pride must be brought low.

Sanyasi. That will do him good.

Rajah. With your leave I take my departure. [*Goes.*]

[*Returning*] Father, I am sure you know Vijayaditya personally—is he as great as the people make him out to be?

Sanyasi. He is like an ordinary person,—it is his dress which gives him a false distinction.

Rajah. Just what I thought. Quite an ordinary person!

Sanyasi. I want to convince him that he is very much so. I must free his mind from the notion that he is a different creature from others.

Rajah. Yes, yes, let him feel it. Fools puff him up and he believes them, being the greatest of their kind. Pull down his conceit to the dust.

Sanyasi. I am engaged in that difficult task. [*The* Rajah *goes.*]

[*Enters* Upananda.]

Upananda. Father, the burden is not yet off my mind.

Sanyasi. What is it that troubles you, my son?

Upananda. In my anger, at the insult offered to me, I thought I was right in disowning my debt to him. Therefore I went back home. But just as I was dusting my master's *vina* its strings struck up a chord and it sent a thrill through my heart. I felt that I must do something super-human for my master. If I can lay down my life to pay his debts for him, this beautiful day of October will then have its full due from me.

Sanyasi. Baba, what you say is true.

Upananda. Father, you have seen many countries, do you know of any great man who is likely to buy a boy like me for a thousand *kahan*? That is all that I need for the debt.

Sanyasi. What do you say to trying Vijayaditya, who used to be so fond of your master?

Upananda. Vijayaditya? But he is our emperor.

Sanyasi. Is that so?

Upananda. Don't you know that?

Sanyasi. But what if he *is* your emperor?

Upananda. Do you think he will care to pay any price for a boy like myself?

Sanyasi. I can assure you, that he will be ashamed of his full treasury, if he does not pay your debt.

Upananda. Is that possible, father?

Sanyasi. Do you think in God's world Luckeswar is the only possibility?

Upananda. But I must not idly wait for chances. In the meanwhile, let me go on with my work and pay off in small parts what I owe.

Sanyasi. Yes, my boy, take up your burden.

Upananda. I feel ever so much stronger, for having known you. Now I take my leave. [*Goes.*]

[*Enters* Luckeswar.]

Luckeswar. I give it up. It is not in my power to be your follower. With an infinite struggle I have earned what I have done. To leave all that, at your bidding, and then to repent of my rashness till the end of my days, would be worse than madness; it would be so awfully unlike myself. Now then, father, you must move from your seat.

Sanyasi [*rising*]. Then I have got my release from you?

Luckeswar [*taking out a jewel case from under some turf and dry leaves*]. For this tiny little thing I have been haunting this place, like a ghost from the morning. You are the first human being to whom I have shown this. [*Holding it up to him and then hastily withdrawing it.*] No, impossible! I fully trust you, yet I have not the power to put it into your hands even for a moment. Merely holding it in the light makes my heart palpitate. Can you tell me, father, what kind of man is Vijayaditya? If I try to sell it to him, are you sure he won't take it away by force? Can you trust him?

Sanyasi. Not always.

Luckeswar. Well, that does not sound promising. I suspect, after all, this will lie underground, and after my death nobody will be able to find it.

Sanyasi. Neither Kings nor Emperors, but the dust will claim it as its final tribute.

Luckeswar. Let it; that does not trouble me. But my anxiety is lest some one should discover it, when I am no more.... However, father, I shall never forget about that golden lotus. I feel sure you will get it some day; but all the same I cannot be your follower. [*Goes.*]

[*Enters* Thakurdada.]

Sanyasi. After long days I have learnt one thing at last, and that I must tell you.

Thakurdada. Father, you are very kind to me.

Sanyasi. I know why this world is so beautiful,—simply because it is ever paying back its debt. The ricefield has done its utmost to earn its fulfilment and the Betasini River is what it is because it keeps nothing back.

Thakurdada. I understand, father. There is One Who has given Himself in creation in his abundance of joy. And Creation is every moment working to repay the gift, and this perpetual sacrifice is blossoming everywhere in beauty and life.

Sanyasi. Wherever there is sluggishness, there accumulates debt, and there it is ugly.

Thakurdada. Because where there is a lacking in the gift, the harmony is broken in the eternal rhythm of the payment and repayment.

[*Enters* Luckeswar.]

Luckeswar. What are you two people conspiring about?

Sanyasi. About that golden lotus.

Luckeswar. Have you already given away your secret to Thakurdada? You hope to be successful when you do your business in such a manner? But is Thakurdada the proper man to help you? How much capital has he, do you think?

Sanyasi. You don't know the secret. He has quite a big amount, though he does not show it.

Luckeswar [*slapping* Thakurdada *on the shoulder*]. You are deep. I never thought of that. And yet people only suspect *me* and not you, not even the Rajah himself.... Father, I can't bear Thakurdada to steal a march on me. Let all three of us join in this business. Look there, a crowd of people is coming this way. They must have got news that a Swami is here. Father, they will wear out your feet upto the knees taking the dust of them. But I warn you, father, you are too simple. Don't take anybody else into your confidence.... But, Thakurdada, you must know business is not mere child's play. The chances of loss are eleven to one—keep that in mind. I give it up. But no, I must take time to decide.

[*Goes.*]

[*Enter* Villagers.]

First Villager. Where is the sanyasi they talked about?

Second Villager. Is this the man?

Third Villager. He looks like a fraud. Where is the real one?

Sanyasi. A real one is difficult to find. I am playing at Sanyasi to amuse boys.

First Villager. But we are not boys.

Sanyasi. I know the distinction.

Second Villager. Then why did someone say, that some swami is somewhere about?

First Villager. But your appearance is good. Have you learnt some charms?

Sanyasi. I am willing to learn. But who is to teach me?

Second Villager. There is a proper man. He lives in Bhairabpur. He has control over some spirits, and there is no doubt of that. Only the other day a boy was about to die. And what do you think this man did? He simply let the boy's life-spark fly into the inside of a panther. You won't believe it, but I can assure you, that panther is still alive, though the boy died. You may laugh, but my own brother-in-law has seen the panther with his own eyes. If anybody tries to injure it, the father rushes at him with his big stick. The man is quite

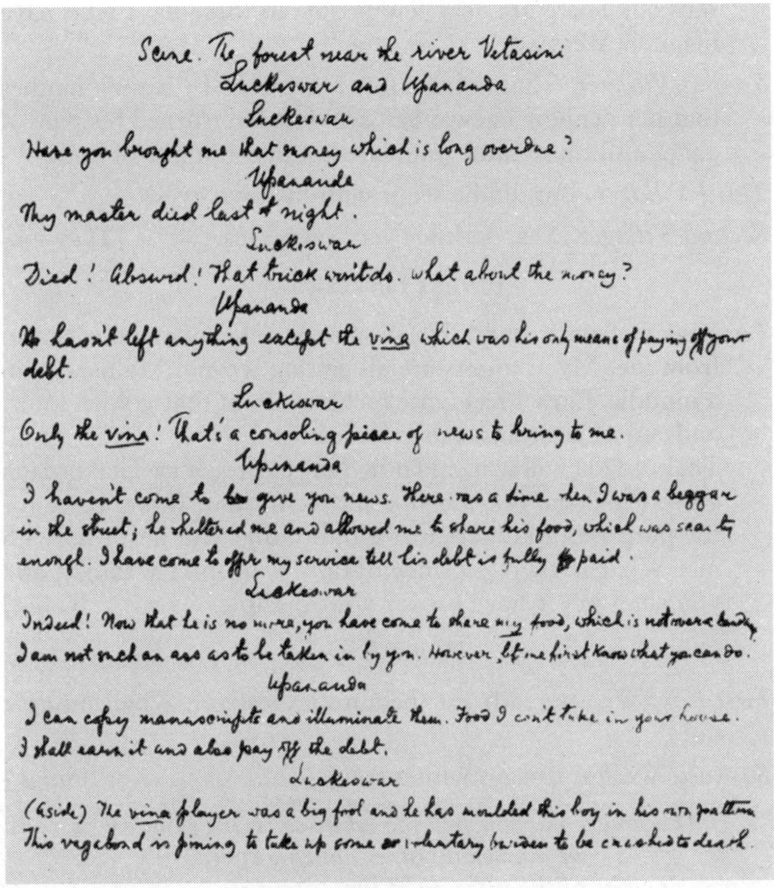

Scene. The forest near the river Vetasini
Luckeswar and Upananda

Luckeswar

Have you brought me that money which is long overdue?

Upananda

My master died last night.

Luckeswar

Died! Absurd! That trick won't do. What about the money?

Upananda

He hasn't left anything except the *vina* which was his only means of paying off your debt.

Luckeswar

Only the *vina*! That's a consoling piece of news to bring to me.

Upananda

I haven't come to give you news. There was a time when I was a beggar in the street; he sheltered me and allowed me to share his food, which was scanty enough. I have come to offer my service till his debt is fully paid.

Luckeswar

Indeed! Now that he is no more, you have come to share my food, which is not over abundant. I am not such an ass as to be taken in by you. However, let me first know what you can do.

Upananda

I can copy manuscripts and illuminate them. Food I can't take in your house. I shall earn it and also pay off the debt.

Luckeswar

(Aside) The *vina* player was a big fool and he has moulded this boy in his own pattern. This vagabond is pining to take up some voluntary burden to be crushed to death.

Facsimile of a page from *Autumn-Festival*

ruining himself by offering kids twice a day to this beast. If you must learn charms, this is the man for you.

Third Villager. What is the use of wasting time? Didn't I tell you in the beginning, that I didn't believe a word about this sanyasi. There are very few people in these days who have magic powers.

Second Villager. That is true. But I was told by Kalu's mother that her nephew knew a Sanyasi who overturned his pipe of ganja and there came out a skull and a full pot of liquor.

Third Villager. But did he see it with his own eyes?

Second Villager. Yes, with his very own eyes. [*They go.*]

[*Enters* Luckeswar.]

Luckeswar. I can't stand this. You must take away your charm from me. My accounts are all getting wrong. My head is in a muddle. Now I feel quite reckless about that golden lotus, and now it seems pure foolishness. Now I am afraid Thakurdada will win, and now I say to myself let Thakurdada go to the dogs. But this doesn't seem right. It is sorcery for the purpose of kidnapping. No, no, that will never do with me. What is there to smile about? I am pretty tough, and you shall never have *me* for your disciple. [*Goes.*]

[*Enter* Boys.]

First Boy. We are ready for the autumn festival. What must we do?

Sanyasi. We must begin with a song. [*Sings.*]

The breeze has touched the white sails, the boat revels
in the beauty of its dancing speed.
It sings of the treasure of the distant shore, it lures
my heart to the voyage of the perilous quest.
The captain stands at his helm with the sun shining
on his face and the rain-clouds looming behind.
My heart aches to know how to sing to him of tears
and smiles made one in joy.

Sanyasi. Now you have seen the face of the autumn.

First Boy. But where is it, father?

Sanyasi. Don't you see those white clouds sailing on?

Second Boy. Yes, yes.

Third Boy. Yes, I can see them.

Sanyasi. The sky fills up.

First Boy. With what?

Sanyasi. With light. And don't you feel the touch of the dew in the air?

Second Boy. Yes.

Sanyasi. Only look at that Betasini River—what headlong rush to spend herself. And see the shiver in the young shoots of rice. Thakurdada, let the boys sing the welcome song of the autumn and go round the forests and hills yonder.

[Thakurdada *sings and the* Boys *join him*.]

I have spread my heart in the sky and found your touch in my dreams.
Take away that veil from your face, let me see your eyes.
There rings your welcome at the doors of the forest fairies;
your anklet bells sound
in all my thoughts
filling my work with music.

[*The* Boys *go out singing*.]

[*Enters* Luckeswar.]

Thakurdada. Hallo! Our Luckeswar in a sanyasi's garb!

Luckeswar. I have become your disciple at last father. Here is my pearl-case, and here are the jewel caskets. Take care of them.

Sanyasi. Why has this sudden change come over you?

Luckeswar. The Emperor Vijayaditya's army is marching towards this town. Nobody will dare touch you, so you are the safest man to whom I can entrust my treasure.—I am your devoted follower,—protect me!

[*Enters the* Rajah.]

Rajah. Father!

Sanyasi. Sit down. You seem to be out of breath. Rest awhile.

Rajah. No time for rest. I am informed that Vijayaditya is almost upon us. His flag has been seen.

Sanyasi. Very likely. He must be feeling eager to acquire new dominions.

Rajah. What do you say? New dominions?

Sanyasi. Why do you take offence at it, my son? You also had a similar idea.

Rajah. Oh! no, that was quite different. But whatever that might be, I ask for your protection. Some mischief-makers must have carried tales to him. Please tell him, they are all lies. Am I mad, that I should want to be the Emperor? Have I got the power.

Sanyasi. Thakurdada!

Thakurdada. Yes, my master!

Sanyasi. Simply with this rag upon my back and a few boys as my followers, I was fully successful in making this day glorious. But look at this wretched man,—this emperor,—he has power only to ruin it.

Rajah. Hush! Somebody may overhear you!

Sanyasi. I must fight it out with that—

Rajah. I won't allow it. You are becoming dangerous. Can't you keep your sentiments to yourself?

Sanyasi. But I already had a discussion about this with you, haven't I?

Rajah. What an awful man you are! Luckeswar, why are you here? Leave this place at once.

Luckeswar. Sire, I can tell you, it is not for the pure pleasure of your presence that I am here. I should be only too glad to get away, but I am fixed to this spot. I have not the power to move.

[*Enter* Vijayaditya's Minister *and courtiers.*]

Minister. Victory to the Emperor Vijayaditya! [*They all bow.*]

Rajah. Stop that stupid jest! I am not Vijayaditya. I am his most unworthy servant—Somapal.

Minister [*to the* Sanyasi]. Sire, the time has come for you to come back to your capital.

Thakurdada. My master, is this a dream?

Sanyasi. Whether your dream or theirs is true who can tell.

Thakurdada. Then—

Sanyasi. Yes, these people happen to know me as Vijayaditya.

Thakurdada. But this new situation has made things critical for me.

Luckeswar. And for me also. I surrendered myself to the Sanyasi in order to be saved from the Emperor. But I do not know in whose hands I am now.

Rajah. Sire, did you come to try me?

Sanyasi. And also myself.

Rajah. What is to be my punishment?

Sanyasi. To leave you to your memory.

[*Enters* Upananda.]

Upananda. Who are these people? Oh! here is the Rajah. [*About to leave.*]

Sanyasi. Upananda, do not go! Tell me what you had come to say.

Upananda. I came to tell you that I had earned this three *Kahans* by my day's work.

Sanyasi. Give them to me. They are too valuable to go for clearing Luckeswar's debt. I take these for myself.

Upananda. Must you take these, father?

Sanyasi. Yes, I must. Do you think I have mastered my greed, because I have become a sanyasi? These tempt me beyond anything else.

Luckeswar. This sounds ominous! I am undone!

Sanyasi. Where is my treasurer?

Treasurer. Here I am.

Sanyasi. Let this man have a thousand *Kahan* from my treasury.

Upananda. Then does he buy me?

Sanyasi. You are mine. [*To the* Minister] You were troubled, because no son had been born to my house. But I have earned my son, by my merit, and here he is.

Luckeswar. How unlucky for me that I am too old for such adoption!

Sanyasi. Luckeswar!

Luckeswar. Command me!

Sanyasi. I have protected your jewels from the grasp of Vijayaditya. Now they are given back to you.

Luckeswar. If the Maharajah had given them back in secret, I could feel secure. Who is to save them now?

Sanyasi. That is my business. But Luckeswar, something is due to me from you.

Luckeswar [*aside*]. Curse me! I knew it would come at last.

Sanyasi. Thakurdada is witness to my claim.

Luckeswar [*aside*]. There will be no lack of false witnesses for him now.

Sanyasi. You wanted to give me alms. You owe me a handful of rice. Do you think you will be able to fill an Emperor's hand?

Luckeswar. But, Sire, it was a sanyasi's hand which gave me courage to propose what I did.

Sanyasi. Then I free you from your promise.

Luckeswar. With the Maharajah's leave I take my departure. Everybody's eyes seem to be turned upon these caskets.

[*He goes.*]

[*Enter the* Boys.]

Boys [*shouting*]. Sanyasi Thakur! [*They suddenly stop and are about to run away.*]

Thakurdada. Boys, do not go.

Sanyasi. Rajah, leave me. [Rajah *goes*.]

[*To his courtiers*] And you also. [*They go*.]

Now back to our festival.

The Trial

ACT I

Khiri *the maid servant.*

Khiri. Some people have the means to be good in gorgeous comfort, and others like us groan under the burden of their goodness. Their charity grows fat in their easy chairs, while we carry out their mission with the sweat of our brows. They reap undying fame and we early death.

[*A voice from without: Khiri! Khiri!*]

Khiri. There she calls! No time for poor me even to nurse my grievance!

[*Enters Rani* Kalyani.]

Kalyani. Sulky as usual!

Khiri. That proves I am made of flesh and blood.

Kalyani. What is your latest grievance?

Khiri. That I made a wrong choice when I chose you for my mistress. Why should I come to a Rani's house, if I must serve a whole world of ragged riffraffs, cook for a needy neighbourhood bred in dirt, and wear out my fingers washing their dishes? And all this with nobody to help me!

Kalyani. Help you could have enough if your tongue did not sting out all the servants I brought to my house.

Khiri. You are right. I have a sensitive mind, and cannot bear the least wrong around me. This fastidious delicacy of mine dooms me to solitude. The servants you had were pure-blooded robbers, blessed with a dangerously innocent look.

Kalyani. And what about yourself?

Khiri. Holy Mother! I never claim to be an exception. I freely take all that I can lay my hands on. Yet I have but a single pair of them. The Creator made these to grab and to hold; therefore if you multiply hands about you, you divide your possessions.

Kalyani. But your solitude seems to be bursting with a crowd of nephews and nieces and a miscellaneous brood of cousins.

Hasn't each of them a pair of hands for their share? You anger me and yet make me laugh.

Khiri. If only you laughed less and got angered more, possibly you could have changed my nature.

Kalyani. Your nature change! Not even when you are dead.

Khiri. This is encouragingly true. It makes me hope that death will be cautious about claiming me. There! look at that lazy crowd waiting at your gate. Some of them have the story of a sick husband, who obligingly never dies, and some of an uncle, whose death remains for ever fresh with its endless claim to funeral rites. They bring their bags full of lies, to exchange them for solid silver. I never cease to wonder how certain people can have a special relish for being cheated.

Kalyani. The poor cheat because wealth is often meaner than poverty. However, tell me why, last evening, when I fed the poor, sweets were scarce and also milk.

Khiri. Very likely the pastryman and the milk-vendor like to give you a fair chance to be cheated.

[*Enter neighbouring* Women.]

Women [*they shout*]. Long live Rani Kalyani!

Khiri. Listen to that! If their stomachs had missed their fill of good fare yesterday, their lungs would show it this morning.

Kalyani. Who is that girl with you, Piari? I never saw her before.

Second Woman. It is the new bride come to our house. I have brought her for your blessing.

Khiri. It is easy to guess what you mean by blessing.

Kalyani. She has a sweet face.

Second Woman. But not a particle of jewelry has she brought from her father's house.

Khiri. 'They are all safely stored in your own chest,' whisper those who are in the secret.

Kalyani. Come with me into my room.

[Kalyani *goes with the* woman *and the bride.*]

First Woman. The uncommon cheek of that woman.

Khiri. It is tiresomely common.

Third Woman. But this surpasses anything that we know.

Khiri. Because it benefits somebody else but you.

Third Woman. Your wit makes our sides burst with laughter.

First Woman. Whatever we may say, our Rani has the biggest heart in the world.

Khiri. In other words, she is the biggest fool under the Sun.

Fourth Woman. That is true. You remember how blind Andi was loaded with money, merely for fun, it seemed to me.

Third Woman. And that old witch of a potter woman took away from her a real woolen rug as a reward for her facility in weeping.

Fourth Woman. There is no harm in charity, but must it be foolish?

First Woman. But she has such a sweet nature.

Khiri. A great deal of one's sweetness belongs to one's pocket.

Fourth Woman. What I object to in her is her familiarity with vulgar people.

Third Woman. She could easily have a better companion, to say the least, than Kedar's mother.

Fourth Woman. It is simply courting the applause of the vulgar.

Khiri. Such is the way of the world. It is all give and take. She supplies food to our mouths, to gather back praise from them. She gets the best of the bargain. For food is vulgar, but praise is for the great.

Fourth Woman. There they, come back from the Rani's room, that woman with the bride.

First Woman. Show us what you have got.

Second Woman. Nothing but a pair of bracelets.

Third Woman. It sounds like a practical joke.

Fourth Woman. You remember Piari got for her newly married daughter a gold chain besides a pair of earrings.

Second Woman. Pity is not for the poor, but fortunate are they who have the reputation for it.

Fourth Woman. The generosity of the rich is a mere hobby, it is only to please themselves.

Khiri. If only Lakshmi, the Goddess of Luck, were kind to me, I would show how to be kind in proper style.

Second Woman. We pray that your wish may be fulfilled.

First Woman. Stop your chatter! I hear the Rani's footsteps!

Fourth Woman [*loudly*]. Our Rani is an angel of mercy.

Third Woman. Wealth has been blessed by the touch of her hands.

[*Enters* Kalyani.]

Kalyani. What are you all so busy talking about?

Khiri. They have been furiously ploughing the ground of your good fame, harrowing, hoeing and raking, weeding out every green thing that bore flowers.

Kalyani. Before you go home remember that if gifts had to flow parallel with expectations they would have run dry and disappeared from the world within a few days of creation.

[*She leaves the room.*]

Fourth Woman. Isn't that spiteful? She must have been eavesdropping.

Khiri. No need for that. She is old enough to know by this time that the praise that grows to excess before her face is generally pruned thin behind her back.

Fourth Woman. Really, you people ought to control your tongues.

Third Woman. If only you can do it, it won't matter much if the rest of us fail.

Khiri. Enough for the day's work of detraction. Now you can go home with eased hearts and try to forget the smart of receiving favours. [*The women go.—she calls*] Kini, Bini, Kashi! [*The girls come.*]

Kashi. Yes, Granny.

Kini and Bini. Yes, aunt.

Khiri. Come and take your meal.

Girls. We are not hungry.

Khiri. For eating hunger is not essential, but opportunity is. You will find some milk in the cupboard and some sweets.

Kashi. You are doing nothing but eat all day. Appetite has its limits.

Khiri. But good things are immensely more limited. Bini, why don't I see the silver comb you had in your hair?

Bini. Poor Khetu's girl—

Khiri. I understand. Benevolence! The plague is in the air in this house! It is fatal for a girl of your circumstances. Our Rani indulges in wasting her means only to prove that they can never be exhausted. But for you to give is to lose for ever, do you not see the difference? Now then, off to bed.

[*They go.*]

[*Enters* Kalyani.]

Khiri. Life has become a burden to me, Rani.

Kalyani. You seem to bear it with wonderful ease.

Khiri. I swear by your feet, I am serious. I have news from home, that my aunt, my father's youngest sister, is on her death-bed.

Kalyani. A year is hardly past since I paid you the funeral expenses of this very same aunt, the youngest one.

Khiri. What a pity! But you seem to have a keen memory only about my poor aunts.

Kalyani. Does it choke you to ask from me? Must you lie?

Khiri. Lies are necessary to give dignity to begging. Truth would be monotonous and mean.

Kalyani. But, have I ever denied you, when you asked?

Khiri. To neglect our weapons, when not needed, is the sure way to miss them in the time of need. But I must tell you that you encourage lies by believing them.

Kalyani. They will fail this time.

Khiri. I shall not despair about my next chance. Till then, my father's youngest sister shall never be mentioned again.

[Kalyani *goes out laughing.*]

Mother Goddess of Luck, your favourite bird, the owl, must have daily carried you to this house. Could it by mistake alight on my shoulder, I would feed it with choice morsels of mice flesh till it became languid and lay at my door.

[*Enters Goddess* Lakshmi.]

Khiri. Visitors again!

Lakshmi. I am willing to leave, if I am not wanted.

Khiri. I must not be rash. That seems to be a regular crown on your head. And yet you don't look ridiculous with it as a real queen would do. Tell me who you are.

Lakshmi. I am Lakshmi.

Khiri. Not from the stage?

Lakshmi. No, from my heaven.

Khiri. You must be tired. Do take your seat, and do not be in a hurry to leave. I know full well you have no mercy for those who have brains. It is, I suppose, because the clever ones need never die of starvation and only fools need your special favour.

Lakshmi. Are you not ashamed to make your living by cheating your mistress?

Khiri. It is because you are perverse in your choice that those who have minds live upon those who have money.

Lakshmi. Intellect I never despise, only the crooked minds I avoid.

Khiri. The intellect, which is too straight, is only another name for stupidity! But if you promise me your favour, I give you my solemn word that henceforth my dullness will delight your heart. I shall be content to remain a perfect bore shunned by all intelligent people.

Lakshmi. Do you think you will ever be able to spend a farthing in charity?

Khiri. With pleasure. For when charity grazes only at the fringe of one's surplus, it adds to the beauty of the view—and it can also be made paying by good management. Only change our mutual position, and you will find the Rani developing a marvellous talent for devising means to get what is not her own. On the other hand, I shall become perfectly silly in swallowing lies and parting with my possessions, and my temper will grow as insipid as that of an egregious saint.

Lakshmi. Your prayer is granted. I make you a Rani. The world will forget that you ever were a servant unless you yourself help it to remember.

ACT II

Khiri *the Queen.*

Khiri. Where is Kashi?

Kashi. Here I am.

Khiri. Where are your four attendants?

Kashi. It is a perfect misery to be dogged by servants day and night.

Khiri. Should the elephant ever complain of the weight of its tusks? Malati!

Malati. Yes, Your Highness!

Khiri. Teach this girl why she must be followed by attendants.

Malati. Remember that you are a Rani's grand-daughter. In the Nawab's house, where I used to serve, the Begum had a litter of pet mongooses; each of them had four maids for their attendants, and sepoys besides.

Khiri. Kashi, do you hear?

Attendant. Moti of our neighbourhood craves audience.

Khiri. Malati!

Malati. Yes, Your Highness!

Khiri. What is the form of salutation expected from visitors in your Begum's house?

Malati. They have to walk forward, salaaming by touching the earth at each step, and then retire walking backward, salaaming again.

Khiri. Let Moti come before me in proper style.

[Malati *brings in* Moti.]

Malati. Bend your head low. Touch the floor, and then touch the tip of your nose. Once again—not so fast—step properly.

Moti. Ah my poor back! How it aches!

Malati. Take dust on the tip of your nose three times.

Moti. I am rheumatic.

Malati. Once again.

Moti. Long live Rani Mother. Today, being the eleventh day of the moon, is for fasting and for almsgiving.

Khiri. Your Rani Mother can ascertain the phases of the moon even without your help, if she finds it profitable.

Moti. Let me receive alms from our Rani and take leave singing her praises.

Khiri. The first part of your prayer I prefer to ignore; the rest I graciously grant. You may leave immediately singing my praises. Malati!

Malati. Yes, Your Highness!

Khiri. Let this woman take her leave in proper style.

Moti. Then I go.

Malati. Not so easily. Bend your head down. Take up the dust of the floor on the tip of your nose. Once again. Once more.

[Moti *goes.*]

Khiri. Bini, what happened to the ring you had on your forefinger? Has it been stolen?

Bini. Not stolen.

Khiri. Then lost?

Bini. Not lost.

Khiri. Then someone has cheated you of it?

Bini. No.

Khiri. You must admit that a thing either remains, or is stolen, or lost, or....

Bini. I have given it away.

Khiri. Which plainly means that someone has cheated you of it. Tell me, who has it?

Bini. Mallika. She is the poorest of all your servants, with her children starving. I have such a heap of rings, I thought....

Khiri. Listen to her! Only those of moderate means earn fame by spending in charity, while the rich in doing it earn ingratitude. Charity has no merit for those who possess too much. Malati!

Malati. Yes, Your Highness.

Khiri. Mallika must be dismissed at once.

Malati. She shall be driven away.

Khiri. But not with the ring on her. What music is that outside my palace?

An Attendant. A marriage procession.

Khiri. A marriage procession in front of the Rani's house! Suppose I happen to object, what is there to prevent me? Malati!

Malati. Yes, Your Highness!

Khiri. What do they do in a Nawab's house in such a case?

Malati. The bridegroom is taken to the prison, and, for three days and nights two amateur flute players practice their scales at each of his ears, and then he is hanged if he survives.

Khiri. Ask my guards to give everyone of the party ten strokes with a shoe.

First Attendant. Only ten strokes! It almost sounds like a caress.

Second Attendant. They ought to rejoice at this happy ending.

Third Attendant. Our Rani has the gift of humour, for which God be praised.

[*Enters a* Maid.]

Maid. My pay has been in arrears for the last nine months. To slave and yet to borrow money to feed oneself is not to my taste. Either pay up my wages or allow me leave and go home.

Khiri. To pay up your wages is tolerably good, but it saves a lot of trouble to allow you to leave. Malati!

Malati. Yes, Your Highness.

Khiri. What is your advice?

Malati. Let her be fined at least a hundred rupees.

Khiri. As she is poor I remit fifty rupees out of her fine.

First Attendant. Rani, you are kind.

Second Attendant. How lucky for her to get fifty rupees for nothing.

Third Attendant. You can as well count it nine hundred and fifty rupees out of a thousand.

Fourth Attendant. How few are there whose charity can be such a drain.

Khiri. You do make me blush. [*To the* Maid] Now you may go away with proper ceremony and finish the rest of your weeping at leisure outside my palace.

[Malati *takes away the* Maid *making her walk backwards with salaams.*]

[*Re-enters* Malati.]

Malati. Rani Kalyani is at your door.

Khiri. Has she come riding on her elephant?

Malati. No, walking. She is dusty all over.

Khiri. Must I admit her in?

First Attendant. She should sit at a proper distance.

Second Attendant. Let her stand behind your back.

Third Attendant. She can be dismissed by saying that. Your Highness is tired.

Khiri. Malati!

Malati. Yes, Your Highness!

Khiri. Advise me what to do.

Malati. Let all other seats be removed but your own.

Khiri. You are clever. Let my hundred and twenty slave girls stand in a row outside that door. Sashi, hold the state umbrella over my head. Malati!

Malati. Yes, Your Highness!

Khiri. Is it all right?

Malati. Perfect! like a picture!

Khiri. Bring her into my presence.

[Malati *goes out and returns with* Kalyani.]

Kalyani. Are you well?

Khiri. My desire is to keep well, but the rest of the world tries its best to wreck me.

Kalyani. I must have a talk with you in private.

Khiri. Nothing can be more private than this. Only yourself and I. These are mere servants. Malati!

Malati. Yes, Your Highness!

Khiri. Is it possible to send them away?

Malati. I shudder to think of it.

Kalyani. Then let me tell you briefly. Our Pathan King has forcibly robbed me of my lands.

Khiri. You are not joking? Then those villages Gopalnagar, Kanaiganj and....

Kalyani. They no longer belong to me.

Khiri. That's interesting. Haven't you some cash left?

Kalyani. Nothing whatever.

Khiri. How funny! That sapphire necklace and those wonderful diamonds and that chain of rubies, seven rows deep....

Kalyani. They are all taken away.

Khiri. Doesn't our scripture say that wealth is unstable like a water drop on a lotus leaf? And your jewelled umbrella, and that throne with its canopy—I suppose they also have followed the rest.

Kalyani. Yes.

Khiri. This is instructive. Our sages truly say that prosperity is like a beautiful dream that makes the awakening all the more dismal. But have they left you your palace?

Kalyani. The soldiers are in possession.

Khiri. It does sound like a story—a Rani yesterday and today a beggar in the street. Malati!

Malati. Yes, Your Highness!

Khiri. What do you say?

Malati. Those who grow too high must have their fall.

Kalyani. If I may have shelter here for a short time I can try to recover my lost fortune.

Khiri. How unfortunate! My palace is crowded with my servants—no space left where a needle can be dropped. Of course I could leave you my room and try to rough it in my country-house.

First Attendant. Absurd!

Second Attendant. It will simply break our hearts.

Kalyani. I cannot dream of putting you to such inconvenience. I take my leave.

Khiri. Must you go so soon? By the by if you still have some jewelry left, you may leave it with me for permanent safe keeping.

Kalyani. Nothing has been saved.

Khiri. How late it is. It gives me a headache if I am made to talk too much I feel it already coming on. [Kalyani *goes.*] See that my State chair and footstool are carefully put back in the storeroom. Malati!

Malati. Yes, Your Highness!

Khiri. What do you think of this?

Malati. It makes one laugh to see the frog turning into a tadpole again.

An Attendant. A woman craves your audience. Shall I send her away.

Khiri. No, no, call her in. I am in a delightful mood today.

[*Enters the* Woman.]

The Woman. I am in trouble.

Khiri. You want to pass it on to others?

The Woman. Robbers came to my room last night.

Khiri. And you must take your revenge on me!

The Woman. I ask for your pity.

Khiri. Pity for what you have lost yourself and nothing for what you ask me to lose?

The Woman. If you must reject my prayer, tell me where I may get it granted.

Khiri. Kalyani is the proper person to suit you. My men will go and show you her place.

The Woman. Her place is well known to me,—I go back to her! [*Revealing herself*] I am the Goddess Lakshmi!

Khiri. If you must leave me, do it in proper style.—Malati, Malati, Tarini! Where are my maids?

[*Enters* Kalyani.]

Kalyani. Have you gone mad? It is still dark, and your shouts bid fair to wake the whole neighbourhood.

Khiri. What ugly dreams I have had all night! It is a new life to wake up from them. Stay a while, let me take the dust of your feet. You are my Rani, and I am your servant for ever.

The Waterfall

Scene. A mountainous country, with a road leading to the temple of Bhairava. The scene remains the same throughout the play.*

In the background is represented the upper framework of a big iron machine; opposite to this is the spire of the Bhairava temple, with its trident.

Ranajit, the king of Uttarakut, has his royal tent in the mango grove by the side of the road. He is resting there on the way to celebrate the evening festival, on the dark night of the moon. After twenty-five years of strenuous effort, his royal engineer, Bibhuti, has succeeded in building up an embankment across the waterfall called Muktadhārā.**

The inhabitants of Uttarakut are seen visiting the temple with their offerings and preparing to hold in the temple courtyard the festival, which is to celebrate the achievement of the royal engineer, Bibhuti.

The temple *devotees* of Bhairava are in the foreground. They are seen making a long circuit in religious procession round the temple. As they sing the praises of the god Bhairava, some are swinging their censers, some are beating the gongs, some are blowing the conch shells.

[*The* Devotees *sing, in procession,—*]

Victory to Him, the Terrible,
The Lord of Destruction,
The uttermost Peace,
The Dissolver of doubts,
The Breaker of fetters,
Who carries us beyond all conflicts,
The Terrible, the Terrible!

[*They go in.*]

[*A* Stranger *comes with his offerings of worship and meets* a Citizen *of Uttarakut.*]

---

* One of the names of the God Shiva, meaning 'Terrible'.
** 'Free Current'.

Stranger. What's that there put up against the sky? It is frightful!

Citizen. Don't you know? You're a stranger, I see,—It's the Machine.

Stranger. Machine! What Machine?

Citizen. The Royal Engineer, Bibhuti, has been working at it for the last twenty-five years. It's just been finished. A festival is now being held in honour of the occasion.

Stranger. What's the object of the Machine?

Citizen. It has bound up the waterfall of Muktadhārā.

Stranger. What a monster! It looks like a dragon's skull with its fleshless jaws hanging down! The constant sight of it would make the life within you withered and dead.

Citizen. The life within *us* has got a thick hide to protect it! You needn't have any fear for *us*!

Stranger. All the same, this isn't a thing to put up nakedly before the sun and stars. Can't you see how it seems to irritate the whole sky by its obtrusion?

Citizen. But aren't you going to attend the evening worship of Bhairava?

Stranger. Yes, I've come out for that object. Every year I bring my offering at this time. But I've never seen such a monstrous obstruction in the sky before. Don't you think it's a sacrilege to allow it to overtop the spire of the Temple?

[*He goes.*]

[*Enters a woman named* Amba, *with a white veil which covers her head and body and trails in the dust.*]

Amba. My Suman! My Suman! Won't my son Suman come back to me? *You've* all returned, but where is he?

Citizen. Who are you?

Amba. I'm Amba of Janai village. Suman, my son, is the light of my eyes, the breath of my life,—my Suman!

Citizen. What's happened to him?

Amba. I don't know where they've taken him. I'd gone to worship Bhairava, in the Temple; and when I came back, I found that he had been taken away.

Citizen. Then he must have been recruited for the work of building up the embankment.

Amba. I've heard that they've taken him along this road to the west of the Hill of Gauri; and my eyesight doesn't reach so far. I can't see the way across it.

Citizen. What's the use of grieving! We're going to the Temple. It's a great day for us. You also must come.

Amba. No, no! From that day, when I lost my son, I've dreaded going to the Temple. Let me tell you our worship never reaches Him. Someone filches it away, as it's carried to the shrine.

Citizen. Who's that?

Amba. The one who's taken my Suman away from me! I don't know who it is, Suman! My Suman! My darling!

[*They go.*]

[*The* messenger *from Abhijit, the Crown Prince of Uttarakut, meets* Bibhuti, *while he is on his way to the Temple.*]

Messenger. Bibhuti! The Crown Prince has sent me to you.

Bibhuti. What is his wish?

Messenger. You have been for a long time building up an embankment across the waterfall of Muktadhārā. Over and over again it gave way, and men perished smothered with sand and earth; and others got washed away by the flood at last, to-day—

Bibhuti. My object is accomplished and the sacrifice of their lives has met with its fulfilment.

Messenger. The inhabitants of Shiu-tarai are still ignorant of this fact. They cannot believe, that any man can deprive them of the water, which has been to them the gift of God.

Bibhuti. God has given them the water; but He has given me the power to bind that water.

Messenger. They don't know that, within a week, their fields—

Bibhuti. Why talk about their fields? What have I to do with their fields?

Messenger. Wasn't it your object to devastate their fields with drought?

Bibhuti. My object was to make Man triumphant over the sands and water and stones, which conspired against him. I had not the time to trouble my mind about what would happen to some wretched maize fields of some wretched cultivator in some place or other.

Messenger. The Crown Prince asks you, if the time has not come at last for you to trouble your mind about it.

Bibhuti. No! My mind is occupied with the contemplation of the majesty of the Machine.

Messenger. Cannot the cry of hunger interrupt that contemplation?

Bibhuti. No! the pressure of water cannot break my embankment; the cry of hunger cannot sway my Machine.

Messenger. Aren't you afraid of curses?

Bibhuti. Curses?—When labourers became scarce in Uttarakut, I had all the young men of over eighteen years of age from every house of Pattana village brought out by the King's command, and a great number of them never returned to their homes. My Machine has triumphed against the storm of mothers' curses. He who fights God's own power, is not afraid of man's malediction.

Messenger. The Crown Prince says that you have already attained the glory of a creation; and now it is time for you to attain a greater glory by demolishing that creation.

Bibhuti. So long as my work remained unfinished, it was mine. But now that it is finished, it belongs to all Uttarakut. I have no longer the right to demolish it.

Messenger. The Crown Prince declares, that he will take this right into his own hands.

Bibhuti. Are these words from our own Crown Prince himself? Does he not belong to us?

Messenger. He says, that it has yet to be proved, whether God's Will has found its entrance into the Government of Uttarakut; the Machine must not stand between.

Bibhuti. It is my mission to prove, by the force of the Machine, that God's throne is ours. Tell the Crown Prince, that no road is left open to make the Machine slacken its grip.

Messenger. The God, who breaks, does not need the broad road for his passage. The smallest holes, which escape our notice, are enough for him.

Bibhuti. Holes! What do you know about them?

Messenger. Nothing. But He knows, who makes use of them.

[Messenger *goes.*]

[Citizens *of Uttarakut, on their way to the Temple, meet* Bibhuti.]

First Citizen. Engineer, you're a wonderful fellow! We never noticed when you got ahead of us!

Second Citizen. That's ever been his habit. Nobody knows how he wins in the race. That shaven-headed Bibhuti of our Chabua village got his ears pulled along with ourselves at the village school. And yet he's done such wonders, surpassing us all!

Third Citizen. Hallo, Gobru! why'd you stand there, basket in hand, with your mouth wide open? Is this the first time you've seen Bibhuti? Bring out the garlands. Let's garland him.

Bibhuti. No, no! What's the use of doing that?

Third Citizen. Why do you say 'no'? If the length of your neck could keep pace with your greatness, it'd grow like a camel's and we'd load it up to the tip of your nose with garlands.

Second Citizen. Harish, our drummer, hasn't yet arrived.

First Citizen. That man's the very prince of the sluggards! He needs a good beating on the drum of his back.

Third Citizen. Nonsense, he can beat the drum far better than we can.

Fourth Citizen. The idea came to me, that we might borrow the chariot from Samanta, to drive Bibhuti on it to the Temple. But we hear that the king himself 'll go walking to the temple. Let's carry him on our shoulders.

Bibhuti. No, no! This is too much!

Fifth Citizen. Not at all! You were born in the lap of Uttarakut, and now you've got to be raised on its shoulders.

[*They all take him up and sing.*]

The Song of the Machine.

We salute the Machine, the Machine!
Loud with its rumbling of wheels,
Quick with its thunder flame,
Fastening its fangs
into the breast of the world.
Hurling against obstructions
its fiery defiance
That melts iron, crushes rocks,
And drives the inert from its rest.
We salute the Machine, the Machine!
Now stolidly stable, with timber and stones.
Now light and free, like a storm cloud.
Sailing across earth, water and sky.
The Machine, whose claws wrench bare.
The entrails of the earth.
Whose magic net captures in its meshes.
The elements elusive and subtle.
We salute the Machine, the Machine!

[*They all go out.*]

[*Enter King* Ranajit *and his* Minister *from the Camp.*]

Ranajit. You ever failed thoroughly to subdue our subjects in Shiu-tarai. And now, Bibhuti has made it possible at last by controlling the waterfall, Muktadhārā. But how is it, that you do not show any sign of elation? Is it jealousy!

Minister. Pardon me, Your Majesty. It is not our business to wrestle with the clay and stones by the help of spades and pickaxes. Our weapon is diplomacy. We deal with men's minds. It was I who advised you to send the Crown Prince to Shiu-tarai; and the embankment, which could have been built up by this policy, would have controlled a turbulent force with greater security and permanence than this one before us.

Ranajit. Yet what was the result? They have not paid taxes for two years. Famines are not unusual among them, yet in former days they had never left their dues unpaid.

Minister. Something more valuable than taxes was being realised at the very moment when you ordered the Crown Prince back. It is not a sound policy to despise the small. When things are intolerable, then the small becomes great with the power of their suffering.

Ranajit. You change the tune of your advice, time after time. I distinctly remember how you have often said to me that it is easiest to put pressure upon those, who are down below you, from the vantage ground of the higher position; and that foreign subjects must always be under that pressure.

Minister. Yes, I did say that; but the circumstances then were different; therefore my advice was timely. But now,—

Ranajit. It was against my wish to send the Crown Prince to Shiu-tarai.

Minister. Why, Sire?

Ranajit. Distance has its dignity. Familiarity diminishes it. You can win the hearts of your own people through love; but aliens must be won over by fear.

Minister. You forget, Sire, what was the real reason for sending the Crown Prince to Shiu-tarai. For some days, we had noticed in him a spirit of restlessness, had we suspected that, by some chance, he had come to know that he was not born to the royal house, but picked up near the source of this waterfall. Therefore in order to keep his mind engaged,—

Ranajit. Yes, I know. He began to visit the source of the waterfall alone, in the night. Once I surprised him, and asked him what was the matter, and why he was there. He said, 'I find my mothcr's tongue in the murmurs of this water.'

Minister. Once I asked him what had come over him, and why he was so often absent from the palace. He answered, that he had come into the world to open out roads: this was the inner meaning of his life which he must fulfil.

Ranajit. The prophecy, that he would be the ruler of a great empire, is no longer credible.

Minister. But, Sire, it was the *guru* of your *guru* who came here specially for the purpose of telling you this. *He* made that prediction.

Ranajit. He must have been mistaken. The Crown Prince, in all his moods, has always made me suffer loss. By his last fit of folly, wantonly destroying the wall across the Nandi Pass, he has undone the work in a few days which our forefathers took years to complete. And now there will be nothing to prevent the wool and other products of Shiu-tarai from finding their outlet in markets beyond our own kingdom. This will raise the price of food and clothing in Uttarakut.

Minister. You must remember that he is young and takes an one-sided view of his duty, having only the good of Shiu-tarai in view.

Ranajit. But that is what I call rebellion against his own people. I am sure that Vairagi* Dhananjai, of Shiu-tarai, whose business it is to incite our subjects against us, must

*A mendicant ascetic singer.

have had a hand in this business. We must throttle this man with his own rosary. We must capture him.

Minister. I dare not contradict. But I am sure you know, that there are dangers which are better left free, than captured.

Ranajit. You need not trouble yourself about it.

Minister. No Sire! I want *you* to trouble about it.

[*Enters* Warder.]

Warder. Sire, your uncle, Viswajit, of Mohangarh, has come.

Ranajit. There is another of them! He is the worst of all those, who have acted their part in spoiling the Crown Prince. The man, who is a relation and yet an alien, is like a hump on the back of a bunch-back. It always follows you. You cannot cut it off, and yet it is a trouble to bear it. What is that?

Minister. The devotees have come out, and are going round the temple in procession.

[*The* Devotees *come and sing the rest of their song.*]

Victory to the fearful flame.
That tears the heart of darkness,
That burns to ashes things that are dead,
Victory to him, whose voice thunders forth truth,
Whose right arm smites the unrighteous,
Whose guidance leads mortals across death.
The Terrible!

[*They go away.*]

[Viswajit, *the uncle of* Ranajit, *enters.*]

Ranajit. My greeting to you! I never expected the good fortune of your coming and joining with us to-night in our worship.

Viswajit. I have come to warn you that the God Bhairava will reject the worship you bring to him to-night.

Ranajit. Such words from you are an insult to our great Festival.

Viswajit. Festival? For what? For shutting up the water, that has ever poured forth from the cup of the God of Gods, so that all who thirst may drink? Why did you do it?

Ranajit. To defeat our enemies!

Viswajit. Are you not afraid of making an enemy of your God himself?

Ranajit. Our victory is His. He is the Patron God of Uttarakut. Therefore, He has allowed His own boon to be withdrawn for our sake. He will bring Shiu-tarai to the feet of Uttarakut, piercing its heart with the spear of thirst.

Viswajit. If that is true, then the worship you offer to Him is no worship at all, but merely wages.

Ranajit. Uncle, you are partial to the outsiders, and against your own kith and kin. It is through *your* lessons that Abhijit has failed fully to accept the duties of the kingdom of Uttarakut which are to be his hereafter.

Viswajit. Through *my* lessons!—Was there not a time when I belonged to your party? After your actions had caused a rebellion in Pattana, was it not I who crushed it, desolating the whole place? Then came that boy Abhijit into my heart. He came like a flash to light; and those whom I had struck, blinded by the darkness of my heart—I could see them for the first time in their full humanity. You accepted him into your home, because you found in him the signs of a World Emperor; and now you try to keep him tied to the limits of the throne of Uttarakut.

Ranajit. I am sure that it was you who divulged to him the secret, it was you, who told him that he was a foundling picked up at the source of the waterfall, Muktadhārā.

Viswajit. Yes, I did. It was on the night of the Lamp Festival in my palace I found him standing alone in the balcony, gazing at the summit of Gauri. I asked him, what he was looking at. He said that he saw the vision of the roads of the future,—the roads which had not yet been built across the difficult passes of the mountains; the roads that would bring the distant near. When I heard him, I said to myself, that nothing could keep such a child captive, whom some homeless mother had given birth to near the waterfall, which seeks its home in the Unknown. I could not contain myself and I said to him,—'My child, that bare mountain accepted you in its arms when you were born by the roadside. The welcome music of the home was not for you at your birth.'

Ranajit. Now, I understand.

Viswajit. What do you understand?

Ranajit. Abhijit has lost his feeling? attachment for our royal house ever since the time he heard this news from you. In order to show this disaffection the first thing he did was to break the wall of the fort of Nandi and open out the road of Nandi Pass.

Viswajit. What harm was there in that? The open road belongs to all,—as much to Uttarakut as to Shiu-tarai.

Ranajit. Uncle, I have borne with you for long, but no more of this! You must leave my kingdom!

Viswajit. I have not the power to leave you. But if you leave me, I shall merely suffer it. [*Goes.*]

[*Enters* Amba.]

Amba. Who are you there? The sun is about to set, but my Suman hasn't yet come back.

Ranajit. Who are you?

Amba. I'm nobody. He, who was my all in all, has been taken away from me along this path. And has this path no end? Does my Suman walk and ever walk on, into the West, across the peak of Gauri, where the sun is sinking, the light is sinking, and everything is sinking?

Ranajit [*to his* Minister]. It seems that—

Minister. Yes, Sire, it must be connected with the building up of the embankment.

Ranajit [*to* Amba]. Set your mind free from all grief. I assure you, your son has received the last great gift of life.

Amba. If that were true, he would have brought it to my hands in the evening. For I'm his mother.

Ranajit. He will bring it. That evening time has not yet come.

Amba. May your words turn out to be true! I shall wait for him on this road leading to the temple. [*She goes*.]

[*A* Schoolmaster *enters, with a group of* Boys.]

Schoolmaster. These wretched boys are in for a good caning, I can see. Shout, with your loudest voices boys: 'Salve Imperator.'

Boys. 'Salve Im—'

Schoolmaster. '—perātor!'

Boys. '—perātor!'

Schoolmaster. 'Salve Imperātor Imperātorum!'

Boys. 'Salve Imperātorum!—'

Schoolmaster. —'Imperātorum!'

Boys. 'Imperātorum!'

Ranajit. Where are you going?

Schoolmaster. Your Majesty is about to confer special honour on the Royal Engineer, Bibhuti; and I am taking my boys to the festival, in order to share in the rejoicing. I do not want my boys to miss any opportunity of participating in the glory of Uttarakut.

Ranajit. Do these boys know what Bibhuti has done?

The Boys [*clapping their hands and jumping*]. Yes! Yes! We know. He has shut up the drinking water of the Shiu-tarai people!

Ranajit. Why has he shut it up?

Boys. To give them a good lesson.

Ranajit. What for?

Boys. To make them smart!

Ranajit. Why?

Boys. Because they are bad!

Ranajit. Why bad?

Boys. Oh they are terribly bad. Everybody knows it!

Ranajit. Then, *you* do not know why they are bad?

Schoolmaster. Certainly, they know it, Your Majesty. [*To the* Boys] What's happened to you, you blockheads? Haven't you—Haven't you,—in your books?—Haven't you—in your books?—[*In a low voice, whispering*] Their religion is rotten!

Boys. Yes! Yes! Their religion is rotten!

Schoolmaster. And they are not like us,—come, answer, boys,—don't you remember [*pointing to his nose*].

Boys. Yes, they haven't got high-bridged noses.

Schoolmaster. Good! Of course you know what has been proved by our Professor. What does a high-bridged nose denote?

Boys. The greatness of the race!

Schoolmaster. Good! Good! And what is the mission of the greater races?—Speak out! They conquer—speak out!—They conquer,—the world,—for themselves. Is not that so?

Boys. Yes! They conquer the world for themselves.

Schoolmaster. Is there a single case in which Uttarakut has been defeated in a war?

Boys. No, never!

Schoolmaster. You all know how the grandfather of our king, with only 293 soldiers, put to fight 31,700 barbarians from the South. Isn't that true, boys?

Boys. Yes!

Schoolmaster. Your Majesty may rest assured that these very boys will one day be a terror to all those who have the misfortune to be born outside our boundaries. I shall be false to my vocation as a schoolmaster if this does not happen. I never allow myself to forget for one moment the great responsibility which we teachers have. We build up *men*! Your statesmen merely use them.—And yet Your

Majesty should take the trouble to compare the pay which *they* draw, with what *we* get.

Minister. But those very students are your best reward.

Schoolmaster. Wonderfully uttered! Indeed, they are our best reward! Beautiful! But, Sir, food is becoming so dear now-a-days. For instance, the butter from cow's milk was once—

Minister. You needn't go on. I shall ponder over this question of the butter from cow's milk. Now you may take your leave.

[*The* Schoolmaster, *with his* Boys, *departs.*]

Ranajit. Inside the skull of this schoolmaster of yours, there is nothing but the butter made of cow's milk.

Minister. Nevertheless, Sire, such people are useful. He loyally repeats the lesson, day after day, according to the instruction that he has received. If he had more brains, such a thing as this would not be possible.

Ranajit. What is that in the sky?

Minister. Have you forgotten about it? That is the top of Bibhuti's Machine.

Ranajit. I have never seen it so clear as it is today.

Minister. The storm this morning has cleared the sky. That is why it is so distinct.

Ranajit. Don't you see how the sun from behind it looks red with anger, and the Machine appears like the menacing fist of a giant. It has not been at all proper to raise it so high.

Minister. The thing appears like a spasm of agony in the heart of the sky.

Ranajit. It is time for us to go to the temple. [*They go.*]

[*A second group of* Citizens *of Uttarakut enters.*]

First Citizen. Don't you notice, how Bibhuti seeks to evade us now-a-days? He tries to rub off from his skin the fact that he was bred up along with ourselves. One day he'll realize, that it's not good for the sword to grow longer than the sheath.

Second Citizen. Whatever you may say, Bibhuti has upheld the reputation of Uttarakut.

First Citizen. Stop that nonsense! You're making too much of him! This embankment, which has cost him all his resources, has given way ten times at least.

Third Citizen. Who knows that it won't give way once again?

First Citizen. Have you noticed the mound on the northern side.

Second Citizen. What about it?

First Citizen. Don't you know? Everybody, who has seen it, says—

Second Citizen. What? Tell me.

First Citizen. You *are* a simpleton! Don't you know, that from one end to the other, it's—Oh, rubbish!

Second Citizen. Do explain it to me a little more clearly.

First Citizen. Wait a while. It'll explain itself, when all of a sudden—[*Ends with a gesture.*]

Second Citizen. Terrible! All of a sudden?

First Citizen. Yes! Jagru will be able to tell you all about it. He has measured every inch of it.

Second Citizen. That's the best thing about Jagru. He has a wonderfully cool head. When everybody's delirious with admiration, he quietly brings out his measuring tape.

Third Citizen. Some people say that all the science of Bibhuti—

First Citizen. Yes, yes! It's stolen from Benkot Varma. *He* was a great man, indeed! Yes indeed, *he* was great! There was nobody like *him*. What brains! What prodigious brain power!—And yet Bibhuti gets all the rewards, and that poor man,—he actually died of starvation.

Third Citizen. Only of starvation?

First Citizen. Whether from starvation or from some food from some hand,—who knows? But what's the use of discussing it? Someone may overhear what we're saying. There are all kinds of scandal-mongers in this land. Our people can't bear to hear good of others.

Second Citizen. Whatever you may say, he's a—

First Citizen. What wonder is there in that. Just consider in what soil he flourished. That Chabua village of ours,—don't you realize, it has given birth to my great grandfather?—Of course you, know his name.

Second Citizen. Of course! Everybody in Uttarakut knows him. He's that—what do you call it?

First Citizen. Bhāskar. There was none in the whole kingdom of Uttarakut, who could come near to him in making snuff. The great Rajah Satrujit couldn't pass a day without buying snuff from him.

Third Citizen. Let's hurry to the temple now. We belong to the same village as Bibhuti. Our place will be on his right side.

[Batu *from behind the screen cries out: 'Don't go, friend! Don't go! Turn away from this path!'*]

Second Citizen. There he is,—old Batu!

[Batu *enters with a torn blanket on his back and a crooked stick in his hand.*]

First Citizen. Where are you going, Batu?

Batu. I warn you, friends! Don't take that path! Go back, while there's time!

Second Citizen. Why?

Batu. They'll sacrifice,—sacrifice human beings! They've taken away by force two of my grandsons, who never returned.

Third Citizen. Sacrifice? Before whom?

Batu. Before the Demon Thirst!

Second Citizen. Who's that?

Batu. The Demon whose dry tongue grows and grows, like a flame of fire fed by the oil.

First Citizen. Madman! We're going to Bhairava's temple. Where's your Demon Thirst there?

Batu. Haven't you heard the news? They're going to dethrone Bhairava today, and the Demon Thirst will occupy his altar.

Second Citizen. Hold your tongue madman! The people of Uttarakut will cut you to pieces, if they hear you talk like this.

Batu. They're throwing mud at me, and the children are pelting me with stones. Everybody's saying, that my grandsons were fortunate in being able to give up their lives.

First Citizen. That's true!

Batu. True? If the offer of life does not bring life in return,—if with death you gain death itself,—then Bhairava will never allow such an utter loss! I warn you, friends, never take that path! [*He goes.*]

Second Citizen. I must confess his words seem to send a shiver of cold through my blood.

First Citizen. Ranju, you're a great coward. Let's go!

[*They all go.*]

[*Enter the Crown Prince* Abhijit *and the Prince* Sanjay.]

Sanjay. I cannot understand why you are leaving our palace.

Abhijit. You will not fully understand it. For how are you to know that my life is a stream which must have its free course over the stones of the king's house.

Sanjay. We all have noticed that you have been feeling restless for some time past. It seemed as if the bond that kept you tied to us was slackening every day. Has it snapped at last?

Abhijit. Sanjay! Look at that image of the sunset over the peak of Gauri. Some bird of fire has spread its wings and is flying towards the night, the setting sun has drawn in the sky the picture of my own life's adventure.

Sanjay. To me the picture is different. Look how the top of that Machine has pierced the heart of this evening. It seems like a stricken bird falling head foremost into the valley of night! I do not like this omen! Now is the time for rest. Come into the palace.

Abhijit. Where there is an obstruction, there can be no rest.

Sanjay. How have you discovered, after all these days, this obstruction of which you are speaking?

Abhijit. I discovered it when I heard that they had bound the waters of Muktadhārā.

Sanjay. I do not understand the meaning of these words.

Abhijit. Every man has the mystery of his inner life somewhere written in the outer world. The secret of my own life has its symbol in that waterfall of Muktadhārā. When I saw its movements shackled I received a shock at the very root of my being; I discovered that this throne of Uttarakut is an embankment built up across my own life's current. And I have come out into the road to set free its course.

Sanjay. Take me with you as your companion!

Abhijit. No! You have to find out your own course. If you follow me, then I shall only obscure it—your own true path.

Sanjay. Do not be so hard! You hurt me!

Abhijit. You know my heart; and you will understand me even when I pain you.

Sanjay. I do not wish to question you as to the source from which your call has come. But, Prince, now it is evening, and the music of the nightfall comes floating from the palace tower. Has not this also its call? All that is stern and strenuous may have its glory. But all that is sweet has also its value.

Abhijit. The pursuit of the hard is for paying the price of the sweet.

Sanjay. Do you remember, the other day, you were surprised to find a white lotus before your seat, where you have your prayer? Some one had gathered that lotus early in the morning before you were awake, and you were not told who it was. Can you ignore, at a moment like this, the divine gift which lies hidden in the heart of that little incident? Does not the face of that timid creature haunt your memory, who hid herself, but not her worship?

Abhijit. Yes, it does! And for the sake of that very love, which is in this world, I cannot tolerate this hideousness. It kills the music of the earth, and laughs its sinister laughter, displaying its rows of steel teeth in the sky. Because I love the paradise of the gods, I am ready to fight the Titans who menace it.

Sanjay. Cannot you see the picture of an infinite sorrow in the twilight glow, clinging to that purple hill?

Abhijit. Yes, my heart fills with tears. I never boast of harshness as heroic. Look at that tiny bird, sitting on the topmost branch of the pine tree, all alone. I do not know whether it will go to its nest, or take its journey across the night to a distant forest; but the sight of that lonely bird gazing at the last ray of the setting sun fills my heart with a sadness which is sweet. How beautiful is this world! Here is my salutation to all that has made my life sweet.

[*Enters* Batu.]

Batu. They wouldn't let me go on, but turned me back with blows.

Abhijit. What has happened to you, Batu? There is a wound on your forehead, from which blood flows.

Batu. I came out to warn them; I cried out to them to leave that path and go back.

Abhijit. Why?

Batu. Don't you know, Prince? They're going to instal, upon the altar of the Machine, the Demon Thirst. They will sacrifice human beings to this Demon.

Sanjay. What is this wild talk?

Batu. They're already poured out the blood of my own two grandsons at the foundation of this altar. I'd hoped that this shrine of sin would break into pieces with its own load of evil. But that has not yet come to pass; and the God Bhairava has not yet awakened out of sleep.

Abhijit. Yes, the shrine will break in pieces. The time has come!

Batu [*coming close to him, whispers*]. Then you must have heard,—heard the call of Bhairava?

Abhijit. Yes, I have heard.

Batu. Then there is no escape for you?

Abhijit. No escape for me!

Batu. Don't you see how the blood flows from my wound? Will you be able to bear it, Prince, when your heart bleeds?

Abhijit. By the grace of Bhairava, I shall bear it.

Batu. When everybody becomes your enemy? When your own people renounce you?

Abhijit. I must bear it!

Batu. Then there's no fear!

Abhijit. No fear for me.

Batu. Good! Keep me in your mind I'm also bound for that path. You'll be able to recognize me, even in the dark, by this mark of blood, which Bhairava Himself has painted on my forehead. [Batu *goes*.]

[*Enters the King's Guard,* Uddhab.]

Uddhab [*to the Crown Prince*]. Sire, what made you open out the road along the Nandi Pass?

Abhijit. To save the people of Shiu-tarai from perpetual famine.

Uddhab. Our King is kind! Is he not always ready to help them?

Abhijit. When the right hand in its miserliness shuts out the path of plenitude the generosity of the left hand is no help at all. For this I have freed the passage of provisions in Shiu-tarai. I have no respect for that mercy, which keeps poverty dependent on it.

Uddhab. The King says, that you have taken the bottom out of *Uttarakut's* food vessel by breaking down the fort of the Nandi Pass.

Abhijit. I have set Uttarakut free from remaining for all time a parasite of Shiu-tarai.

Uddhab. It was extremely rash of you. the King has heard the news. I dare not say any more. Leave this place at once, if you can do so. It's not safe for me to be seen talking with you on the road. [Uddhab *goes*.]

[*Enters* Amba.]

Amba. Suman, my darling! Have none of you followed that path, along which they took my Suman?

Abhijit. Have they taken your son away?

Amba. Yes, towards the West, where the sun sinks, where the days come to their end.

Abhijit. My journey is also along that path.

Amba. Then remember an unfortunate woman like me. When you meet him, tell him that mother is waiting.

Abhijit. Yes, I shall tell him. [Amba *goes out*.]

[*The Devotees of Bhairava enter singing*.]

Victory to Him, who is Terrible!
The Lord of Destruction!
The uttermost Peace!
The Dissolver of doubts,
The Breaker of fetters!
Who carries us beyond all conflicts.
The Terrible! The Terrible!

[*They go*.]

[*Enters a General*, Bijaypal.]

Bijaypal. Princes, accept my humble salutation. I come from the King.

Abhijit. What is his command?

Bijaypal. I must tell it to you in secret.

Sanjay (*holding* Abhijit *by his hand*). Why in secret?—Secret even from me?

Bijaypal. Such is my instruction. I beg you, Crown Prince, to enter the tent.

Sanjay. I must accompany him. [*Attempts to do so*.]

Bijaypal. No! That will be against the wishes of the King.

Sanjay. Then I shall wait for him at this road side.

[Abhijit, *followed by* Bijaypal, *goes towards the tent*.]

[*Enters a* Flower-seller.]

Flower-seller [*to* Sanjay]. Sir, who is this man, Bibhuti, of Uttarakut?

Sanjay. Why do you seek him?

Flower-seller. I'm a stranger coming from Deotali, and I've heard that they are throwing flowers on his path in Uttarakut. He must be some saint. So I've brought these flowers from my own garden to offer to him.

Sanjay. He is not a saint, but a clever man.

Flower-seller. What has he done?

Sanjay. He has bound up our waterfall.

Flower-seller. Is all this worship for *that*? Will the binding of the waterfall serve *God's* purpose?

Sanjay. No. It will fetter God's own designs.

Flower-seller. I don't understand.

Sanjay. It is good for you not to understand it. Go back again! [*She starts to go*.] Stay, hear me! Will you sell that white lotus to me?

Flower-seller. I can't sell this flower, which I had already offered in my mind to some saint.

Sanjay. The saint, whom I venerate more than any one else, shall have this.

Flower-seller. Then take it. [*He offers money*.] No! No price for this! Give the Father my salutation, and tell him that I'm the poor woman of Deotali, who sells flowers.

[*She goes*.]

[*Enters* Bijaypal.]

Sanjay. Where is the Crown Prince?

Bijaypal. He is a captive in the tent.

Sanjay. The Crown Prince a captive! What arrogance!

Bijaypal. Here is the warrant from the King.

Sanjay. Whose conspiracy is this? Let me go to him for a moment.

Bijaypal. Pardon me, I cannot.

Sanjay. Then arrest me, also! I am a rebel!

Bijaypal. I have not the instructions.

Sanjay. I go myself to force from him the instructions. [*He goes some way, and then returns.*] Give this white lotus to the Crown Prince, in my name. [*They go out.*]

[*Enters the Bairagi,* Dhananjay *of Shiu-tarai with* Citizens *who are his followers from Shiu-tarai.*]

Dhananjay [*to one of his followers*]. You look as pale as a ghost! Why? What's the matter?

First Shiu-tarai Citizen. Master, the blows from Chandapal, the King's brother-in-law, have become intolerable!

[*The Shiu-tarai Leader,* Ganesh, *enters.*]

Ganesh. Father, give me your orders! Let me snatch away the baton from that scoundrel, Chandapal, and prove to him what a blow can really mean.

Dhananjay. You had better try to prove what a 'no blow' can really mean! The helm's not for beating the waves, but for conquering them by keeping itself steady.

Second Shiu-tarai Citizen. Then, what's your wish?

Dhananjay. Raise your head! Say that nothing hurts you, and then the hurt will receive its death blow.

Third Shiu-tarai Citizen. It's difficult to say that nothing hurts *me*!

Dhananjay. The true man within us is a flame of fire. He consumes all hurts in light. Only the brute beast is hurt. The brute beast is flesh, and it goes whining when it is struck.—Why do you stand with your mouths gaping wide open? Cannot you follow my words!

Second Shiu-tarai Citizen. Father, we understand *you*! It doesn't matter if we fail to understand your words.

Dhananjay. Then it's past cure.

Ganesh. It takes a most tedious time to understand words. But when we understand *you,* we are saved at once.

Dhananjay. Saved at once? But what about later on?

Ganesh. We know that we must come to you for our shelter, and that shows that we understand.

Dhananjay. No, not in the least. That's why your eyes are still red with passion, and your voice lacks music. Shall I give you the proper tune? [*He sings*.]

Let your hurts come upon me, Master!
More, if you wish, and yet more!

You cowards! In order to avoid being hurt, you either hurt others, or else run away. Both are the same. Both are for the brute beasts. [*He sings again*.]

I hide myself, I run away.
I try to avoid you in fear.
Capture me, and take all that I have.

Look here, children! I am going to make my final reckoning with the great god, Mrityunjay the Conqueror of death I want to say to him, 'Try me, and see if blows hurt me, or not.' I must not in this voyage burden my boat with those who fear and those who frighten others. [*He sings again*.]

May this be my last stake at the game.
Let me see whether I win or thou!
In the markets, in the highways, among the crowds,
I had my mirth and I laughed.
Let me see if at last you can make me weep!

All [*crying out together*]. Bravo, Father—'Let me see if at last you can make me weep.'

Second Shiu-tarai Citizen. Tell us where are you going?

Dhananjay. To the King's Festival.

Third Shiu-tarai Citizen. But the King's Festival is not for you. Why do you go there at all?

Dhananjay. I must make my name known in the King's Court.

Fourth Shiu-tarai Citizen. When once he catches you then he'll—. But, no! that must never be!

Dhananjay. Let it be, man! Let it be to the full!

First Shiu-tarai Citizen. *You're* not afraid of the King, Master. But we dread him!

Dhananjay. That's only because, in your secret hearts, you want to hurt. But I don't want to hurt, and therefore never fear.

Second Shiu-tarai Citizen. Very well then. We also shall accompany you!

Third Shiu-tarai Citizen. Yes! We shall got to the King's Court.

Dhananjay. What will you ask the King?

Third Shiu-tarai Citizen. There are so many things to *ask*. But the question is, which of them will be granted.

Dhananjay. Why not ask for the kingdom?

Third Shiu-tarai Citizen. Father, you're joking!

Dhananjay. Not at all! If the kingdom belonged to the king alone and not also to the subjects, then the hopping about of that one-legged kingdom might make you jump with fright; but it would bring tears to the eyes of God!—You must claim the kingdom for the sake of the king himself.

Second Shiu-tarai Citizen. But when they come to push us out?

Dhananjay. The push from the king will come back upon the king himself, if your claim has truth. [*He sings*.]

I forget, and forget again, my Lord,
That Thou callest us to Thine own seat.—

Shall I tell you the truth, children? So long as you don't recognize the seat to be His, your claim to the throne will be futile. [*He sings again*.]

Thy door-keepers do not know us,
They shut the gate against our face. We stand outside Thy house.

How are the door-keepers to recognize us? The dust has settled upon the mark of royalty on our foreheads. We can show nothing to prove our claim. [*He sings once more.*]

Thou hast given us life with Thine own hand,
And with it Thy crown of honour, But greed, fear
and shame smudge it with grimy touch,
And Thy gift is obscured day by day.

First Shiu-tarai Citizen. Whatever you may say, we don't understand why you're going to the King's Court.

Dhananjay. Shall I tell you why? It's because I have misgivings in my mind about you.

First Shiu-tarai Citizen. Why, Father?

Dhananjay. The more you cling to me, while trying to swim, the more you forget your lessons in swimming, and also keep dragging me down. I must take my leave of you and go where nobody follows me.

First Shiu-tarai Citizen. But the king won't easily let you go!

Dhananjay. Why should he let me go?

Second Shiu-tarai Citizen. We can never remain quiet, if they molest you!

Dhananjay. If He, to whom I have dedicated this body of mine, chooses to suffer through me, you also will have to be patient.

First Shiu-tarai Citizen. Very well, then, Father! Let us also go, and then let happen what may!

Dhananjay. You must wait here for me. This is a strange place and I must get to know something about the neighbourhood. [*He goes.*]

First Shiu-tarai Citizen. Have you noticed the features of these men of Uttarakut? They look as if the Creator, when He made them, had begun with a big lump of flesh and had had no time to finish His work.

Second Shiu-tarai Citizen. And do you see how they dress themselves in tight clothes.

Third Shiu-tarai Citizen. They pack themselves up tightly in bundles as though to prevent the least leakage.

First Shiu-tarai Citizen. They're born to drudgery. They spend their lives in going from market to market, and from one landing place to another.

Second Shiu-tarai Citizen. They've no culture worth speaking of. The books that they have are worth nothing.

First Shiu-tarai Citizen. Nothing at all. Haven't you noticed the letters in them like lines of white ants creeping across the page.

Second Shiu-tarai Citizen. Well said! White ants indeed! Their culture gnaws everything to pieces.

Third Shiu-tarai Citizen. And heaps up earth mounds. They kill life with their arms and destroy mind with their books.

Second Shiu-tarai Citizen. Sin! Sin! Our *guru* says that even to cross their shadow is a sin. Do you know why?

Third Shiu-tarai Citizen. Tell me, why.

Second Shiu-tarai Citizen. After the nectar had been churned up by the Gods and Titans from the sea, some drops of it were spilt from the Gods' cups. From the clay thus formed the ancestor of the Shiu-tarai was made. And when the Titans licked the nearly empty cups of the Gods and threw them into the ditch, the broken pieces of the cups were fashioned into the ancestor of the Uttarakut people. That's why they are so hard, and faugh!—so unclean!

Third Shiu-tarai Citizen. Where did you learn all this?

Second Shiu-tarai Citizen. From our own *guru*!

Third Shiu-tarai Citizen [*reverently bowing his head*]. *Guru,* you're truth itself!

[*A group of* Uttarakut Citizens *enters.*]

First Uttarakut Citizen. Everything has passed off so happily, excepting the admission of that blacksmith, Bibhuti into the Kshatriya order by our king.

Second Uttarakut Citizen. That's all a domestic question. We shall deal with that, later on. Meanwhile let's cry 'Long live the Royal Engineer, Bibhuti.'

Third Uttarakut Citizen. He who has united the Kshatriya's weapons with the tools of the Vaishya! 'Long live Bibhuti.'

First Uttarakut Citizen. Hallo! There are some men from Shiu-tarai.

Second Uttarakut Citizen. How d' you know?

First Uttarakut Citizen. Don't you see their ear-cups. How queer they look! They seem like people suddenly thumped on the head and thus stopped in their growth.

Second Uttarakut Citizen. Of all head dresses, why have they chosen this? Do they think that ears are a mistake of the Creator?

First Uttarakut Citizen. They have put an embankment over their ears, lest the precious little intelligence which they have should ooze out.

Third Uttarakut Citizen. No, it's rather to prevent any common sense entering in to trouble them.

First Uttarakut Citizen. Some ear-pulling ghost of Uttarakut might haunt them!

[*They all laugh.*]

First Uttarakut Citizen. Hallo! You clodhoppers from Shiu-tarai! What's the matter with you?

Third Uttarakut Citizen. Don't you know that today's our festival? Come and join us in our cry—'Long live the Royal Engineer Bibhuti!'

First Uttarakut Citizen. Are your throats dry? Shout 'Long live Bibhuti.'

Ganesh. Why should we cry 'Long live Bibhuti'! What has he done?

First Uttarakut Citizen. Just hark at him! 'What has he done?' The tremendous news has not reached them yet! That's all the result of their ear-caps!

[*The* Uttarakut Citizens *laugh.*]

Third Uttarakut Citizen. Do you ask what he has done? Why! The water to quench your thirst is in his hands! If he withholds it, then you will dry up, like toads in a time of drought!

Second Shiu-tarai Citizen. Our water in Bibhuti's hands! Has he suddenly become a God?

Second Uttarakut Citizen. He has dismissed God from service. He'll take up God's work himself.

First Shiu-tarai Citizen. Is there any specimen of his work?

First Uttarakut Citizen. Yes! That embankment across Muktadhārā.

[Shiu-tarai Citizens *laugh loudly.*]

Second Uttarakut Citizen. D'you take this to be a joke?

Ganesh. Why! What else can it be? That son of a blacksmith to snatch away from us the gift that comes from Bhairava Himself!

First Uttarakut Citizen. See with your own eyes there in the sky!

Second Shiu-tarai Citizen. Great heavens! What on earth is that?

Third Shiu-tarai Citizen. Good God! It looks like a gigantic grasshopper just going to jump towards the stars!

First Uttarakut Citizen. That grasshopper is going to stop, with his legs, your water supply!

Ganesh. Leave off that foolery, won't you? Some day you will be saying that the son of this blacksmith is riding the grasshopper in order to catch the moon!

First Uttarakut Citizen. That's the beauty of their ear-caps. They refuse to listen and thus they perish!

First Shiu-tarai Citizen. We refuse to perish!

Third Uttarakut Citizen. That sounds well! But who is to save you?

Ganesh. Haven't you seen our God, our Vairagi Dhananjay? One of his bodies is in the temple, and one outside.

Third Uttarakut Citizen. Listen to these men with their ear-caps on! Nobody can save them from utter destruction.

[*The* Uttarakut Citizens *go out*.]

[*Enters* Dhananjay.]

Dhananjay. Fools! What have you been saying? Is it in my hand to save you from death?—Then you're dead thrice over!

Ganesh. The Uttarakut people said to us that Bibhuti has stopped the water of Mukta-dhārā.

Dhananjay. Did they say that an embankment had been raised?

Ganesh. Yes, Father!

Dhananjay. You haven't listened to them carefully!

Ganesh. It is not worth listening to!

Dhananjay. Have you kept all your ears with me alone? Must I hear for all of you?

Third Shiu-tarai Citizen. What is there to hear at all, Father?

Dhananjay. Is it a small thing, to control the turbulent power, whether it is outside us or within us?

Ganesh. That may be; but what about this stoppage of—

Dhananjay. That's a different matter; and Bhairava will never suffer it to be done. I must go and find out all about it. This world is full of voices. To stop listening to them is to perish. [Dhananjay *goes out*.]

[*Another* Citizen *from Shiu-tarai enters*.]

Fourth Shiu-tarai Citizen. Bishan, what's the news?

Bishan. The Crown Prince has been recalled from Shiu-tarai.

All. Impossible!

Bishan. What are you to do?

All. We shall take him back.

Bishan. How?

All. By force.

Bishan. What about our King?

All. We defy him.

[*Enter King* Ranajit *and* Minister.]

Ranajit. Whom do you defy?

All [*to the King*]. Long live your Majesty!

Ganesh. We have come to you with our prayer.

Ranajit. What is it?

All. We want the Crown Prince for ourselves.

Ranajit. You are modest in your demand.

First Shiu-tarai Citizen. Yes, we must take him back to Shiu-tarai.

Ranajit. And then triumphantly forget to pay the taxes?

All. But we're starving.

Ranajit. Where is your leader?

Second Shiu-tarai Citizen [*pointing to* Ganesh]. Here's our leader, Ganesh.

Ranajit. No. Where is the Vairagi.

Ganesh. There he comes.

[*Enters* Dhananjay.]

Ranajit. It is you who make these people forget themselves.

Dhananjay. Yes, Sir. And I forget myself also.

Ranajit. Don't parry words with me! Tell me, are you for paying taxes?

Dhananjay. No, Sir! Decidedly no!

Ranajit. You are insolent.

Dhananjay. I must not give you what is not yours.

Ranajit. Not mine?

Dhananjay. A part of our excess food belongs to you, but not the food which belongs to our hunger.

Ranajit. Do you prevent my people from paying me my dues?

Dhananjay. Yes, they are timid and ready to submit. But I tell them. 'Give your life only to Him, whose gift it is.'

Ranajit. Their timidity you merely repress with your own assurance; but when that bloated assurance is pricked somewhere, the fear will burst out with double force, and then they will be lost. You have trouble written on the tablet of your fate.

Dhananjay. I have taken that tablet to my heart. There dwells He, who is above all trouble.

Ranajit [*to* Shiu-tarai Citizens]. All of you go back to your place, and the Vairagi will remain here.

All. No, that cannot be!

Dhananjay [*sings*].

'Remain!' You cry.
But, strain hard as you may,
Only that will remain which must.

King! You can keep nothing by straining. He who gives all, keeps all. That which your greed tries to keep, is a stolen thing. It will have to be given up. [*sings*.]

You are wilful, you are strong, in the injuries you inflict,
There is one who suffers,
And only what he chooses to bear,
Shall be borne.

You make a mistake, King, when you think that the world, which you take by force is your world. What you keep free, you gain. But seize it, and it eludes you! [*sings*.]

You dream that you make the world dance,
to the tune of your own desire;
Suddenly your eyes open; you see,
That things happen which you never wish.

Ranajit. Minister, keep this Vairagi under custody.

Minister. Sire,—[*pauses*.]

Ranajit. This command of mine is not agreeable to you?

Minister. A terrible engine of punishment is made ready. You merely weaken it, by trying to add to its fierceness.

Shiu-tarai Citizens. We shall never allow this.

Dhananjay. Leave me, I tell you! Leave me and go!

First Shiu-tarai Citizen. Haven't you heard, Father, that we have also lost our Crown Prince?

Second Shiu-tarai Citizen. Who is there to sustain our strength if we lose both of you?

Dhananjay. I am defeated! Let me retire.

All. Why, Father?

Dhananjay. You rejoice to think, that you gain me, and take no heed that you lose yourself! I cannot make good that loss! You put me to shame!

First Shiu-tarai Citizen. Don't say that! We shall do whatever you wish.

Dhananjay. Then leave me and go.

Second Shiu-tarai Citizen. But have you the heart to keep away from us? Do you not love us?

Dhananjay. It is better to love you and keep you free, than to love you and smother you by my love. Go! No more of this! Go, and leave me!

Second Shiu-tarai Citizen. Very well, Father, we go. But—

Dhananjay. No 'but! Hold your heads high and go!'

All. Very well, father, we go! [*They move slowly away.*]

Dhananjay. Is *that* what you call going? Quick! Begone!

Ganesh. As you wish. But you must know, that all our hopes and thoughts remain with you. [*They go.*]

Ranajit. What are you thinking of, Vairagi? Why are you so silent?

Dhananjay. They have made me anxious, King!

Ranajit. For what?

Dhananjay. I am afraid that I have succeeded in doing what your own Chandapāl has failed to accomplish with his baton.

Ranajit. What makes you think so?

Dhananjay. Once I chuckled to myself and said,—'I am strengthening their hopes and thoughts.' But today they brutally threw it in my face, that it was I who had robbed them of their hopes and thoughts.

Ranajit. How has that been made possible?

Dhananjay. The more I excited them, the less I matured their minds. By making people run and rush, you do not lighten their load of debts.—They believe me to be greater even than their Providence, and to have the power to write off the debt, which they owe to their God. And therefore they shut their eyes and cling to me with all their might.

Ranajit. They have taken *you* to be their God.

Dhananjay. And thus they stop at *me,* and never reach their true God. He, who could have guided them from within, has been obscured by me, who forced them from outside.

Ranajit. You prevent them, when they come to pay their dues to their king. But do not *you* suffer in *your* mind, when they come to pay *you* the offering which is for their God?

Dhananjay. I do indeed! I feel as if I could sink through the ground. They become bankrupt in their minds by spending on me all their worship. The responsibility for their debt will be mine; and I shall not be able to escape from it.

Ranajit. What is your duty now?

Dhananjay. To remain away from them. If it is true that I have raised an embankment across the freedom of their minds, then I am afraid the God Bhairava will take both your Bibhuti and me to account at the same time.

Ranajit. Then why delay? Why not move away?—[*To* Uddhab.] Take this Vairagi to my tent and keep him there.

[Uddhab *takes* Dhananjay *to the tent*.]

Ranajit. Minister! Go and see Abhijit in the guard house. If you find him in a repentant mood, then—

Minister. Sire, is it not right, that you yourself should personally—

Ranajit. No, no! He is a traitor against his own people. I shall not see his face, until he confesses his guilt I go back to my palace. Send me the news there! [*The King goes.*]

[*Enter the* Devotees, *who sing.*]

Victory to the fearful Flame,
That tears the heart of Darkness
That burns to ashes things which are dead
Victory to Him, whose voice thunders forth Truth
Whose right arm smites the unrighteous
Whose guidance leads mortals across Death

[*They go.*]

[Uddhab *re-enters.*]

Uddhab. What is this? The King goes away without seeing the Crown Prince!

Minister. He was afraid, lest his resolution should fail him. He was prolonging his talk with the Vairagi, because the conflict was going on in his mind. He could not decide to go into the tent or to leave the tent. I must go and see the Crown Prince. [*They go out.*]

[*Some* Citizens *from Uttarakut enter.*]

First Citizen. We must be firm. Let's go to the King.

Second Citizen. What's the good of it? The Crown Prince is the jewel of his heart. We will never be able to judge him; he will only be angry with us.

First Citizen. That doesn't matter. We must give him a piece of our mind, whatever may happen after. The Crown Prince made such a fine display of his love for us, and is this the end? Shiu-tarai has become greater in importance to him than Uttarakut.

Second Citizen. If this can come to pass, then there's no justice in the world!

Third Citizen. It's impossible to trust anybody merely by his appearance.

First Citizen. If our king doesn't punish him, we must do it ourselves.

Second Citizen. What will you do?

First Citizen. He'll not find his place here. He must be sent off along the very path he has opened out at Nandi Pass.

Third Citizen. But that man at Chabua village says, that he's not at Shiu-tarai at this moment. And he cannot be found in the palace here.

First Citizen. I am sure that our King has been hiding him from us.

Third Citizen. Hiding him? We'll break down the palace walls and drag him out!

First Citizen. We'll set fire to the palace.

[*Enter the* Minister *and* Uddhab.]

First Citizen [*to the* Minister]. Don't you try to play the game of hide and seek with us! Bring out the Crown Prince!

Minister. Who am I, to bring him out?

Second Citizen. It must have been by your advice.—But, I tell you—it won't do! We'll drag him out from his hiding place.

Minister. Then take the reins of this government in your own hands, and release him from the King's prison.

Third Citizen. From the King's prison!

Minister. The King has imprisoned him.

All. Long live the King! Victory to Uttarakut!

Second Citizen. Come, let's go to the prison, and there—

Minister. What?

Second Citizen. We'll take the flowers from the garland that Bibhuti has cast off, and put the string of it on the Crown Prince's neck.

Minister. The Crown Prince is guilty, you say, because he has broken the Fort. But is there no guilt in it, when *you* break the laws of the realm?

Second Citizen. That's altogether a different affair.

Third Citizen. But if we *do* break the laws?

Minister. You may jump into the void because you are not in love with the ground underneath your feet. But I can assure you, that you won't find yourself in love with that void.

Third Citizen. Then let's go and stand before the Palace and shout, 'Long live the King.'

First Citizen. Look there! The sun has set, and the sky's growing dark. But that framework of Bibhuti's machine is still glowing. It looks as if it had got red with drunkenness.

Second Citizen. And on that trident, the last sinking light of the day is held aloft. It looks a kind of,—I don't know how to describe it. [*The* Citizens *of Uttarakut go out.*]

Minister. Now I understand, why the King has kept the Crown Prince captive in his own camp.

Uddhab. Why?

Minister. To save him from the hands of his people. But things look ugly. The excitement is growing wilder every moment.

[*Enters* Sanjay.]

Sanjay. I dare not show my eagerness to the King, because that only helps to make his determination stronger.

Minister. Prince, try to keep quiet. Do not add to the complications which are already too great.

Sanjay. I went to talk to the people. I knew that they loved the Crown Prince more than life itself; that they would not tolerate his imprisonment. But I found them flaming with anger at the news of the opening out of Nandi Pass.

Minister. Then you ought to understand, that the Crown Prince's safety lies in his imprisonment itself.

Sanjay. I have ever followed him, from my childhood. Let me follow him into the prison.

Minister. What good will that do?

Sanjay. Every man is but half a man by himself. He finds his unity only when he is truly united with someone else. My ... unity I find in my union with the Crown Prince.

Minister. But where the union is true, a mere outward meeting is superfluous. The cloud in the sky, and the water in the sea, are truly one, in spite of their distance from each other. Our Crown Prince must manifest himself through you, where he is absent.

Sanjay. These words do not seem like your own. They sound like his.

Minister. His words are everywhere in the air of this place. We make use of them, and yet forget that they are his.

Sanjay. You have done well to remind me of this. I shall serve him by living away from him. I must now go to the King.

Minister. Why?

Sanjay. I shall ask the King to give me the Governorship of Shiu-tarai.

Minister. But the times are very critical.

Sanjay. And therefore, this is the best time. [*They go.*]

[*Enters* Vishwajit, *the King's uncle.*]

Vishwajit. Who is there? Is that Uddhab?

Uddhab. Yes, Sire!

Vishwajit. I was waiting for it to grow dark. Have you received my letter?

Uddhab. I have.

Vishwajit. Have you followed my advice?

Uddhab. You will know within a short time. But—

Vishwajit. Have no misgiving in your mind. The King is not ready to give him freedom: but if, by some chance, someone without his knowledge effects it, it will be a great relief to the King.

Uddhab. But he will never forgive the man who does it.

Vishwajit. My soldiers will take you and your guards captive. The responsibility is mine.

[*A voice from outside,* 'Fire! Fire!']

Uddhab. There it is! They have set on fire the kitchen tent, which is near the guard-room. This is the opportunity for me to release Dhananjay and the Crown Prince.

[*He goes out, and* Abhijit *comes in later.*]

Abhijit [*to* Vishwajit]. Why are you here?

Vishwajit. I have come to capture you. You must come to Mohangarh.

Abhijit. Nothing will be able to keep me captive today,—neither anger, nor affection. You think that you are the agents who set this tent on fire? No! This fire has been waiting for me! The leisure has not been granted to me to remain in captivity.

Vishwajit. Why, child! What work have you to do?

Abhijit. I must pay off the debt of my birthright. The current of the waterfall has been my first nurse and I must set her free.

Vishwajit. There is time enough for that, but not today!

Abhijit. All that I know is this, that the time has come! And no one knows when that time will ever come again.

Vishwajit. We also shall join you.

Abhijit. No, the quest is mine; it has never reached you.

Vishwajit. The people of Shiu-tarai, who love you and are eagerly waiting to join hands in your work,—will you not call them to your side.

Abhijit. If my call had come to them also, they would never sit waiting for me. My call will only lead them astray.

Vishwajit. It is growing dark, my child.

Abhijit. The light comes from that direction, from whence comes the call.

Vishwajit. I have not the power to turn you from your own path. Though you are taking a plunge into the darkness, I will trust in God to guide you. I must leave you in His hands. Only let me hear one word of hope. Tell me, that we shall meet again.

Abhijit. Keep it ever in your mind, that we can never be separated. [*They go in opposite directions.*]

[*Enter* Batu *and* Dhananjay.]

Batu. Father, the day is ended and it grows dark.

Dhananjay. My son, we have formed the habit of depending upon the light which is outside us, and therefore we are blinded when it is dark.

Batu. I had thought that the dance of the God, Bhairava, would commence from to-day. But has the Engineer, Bibhuti, bound up even His hands and feet with the machine?

Dhananjay. When Bhairava begins His dance, it is not visible. Only when it comes to its end, is it revealed.

Batu. Give us confidence, Master. We are afraid! Awake Bhairava! Awake! The light has gone out! The path is dark! We find no response! Lord of all conquering Life! Kill our fear with something still more dread! Bhairava, awake! Awake! [*He goes.*]

[*Enter* Citizens *of Uttarakut.*]

First Citizen. It was a lie! He's not in the prison house! They have hidden him somewhere.

Second Citizen. We shall see how they can hide him.

Dhananjay. No! They will never be able to hide him. The walls will break down; the gate will be shattered. The light will rush into the dark corner, and everything will be revealed.

First Citizen. Who's this?—He gave me such a start.

Third Citizen. All's right! We must have some victim! This Vairagi will serve us quite well. Bind him!

Dhananjay. What is the use of catching one, who has always surrendered himself?

First Citizen. Leave your saintliness behind you! We are not your followers.

Dhananjay. You are fortunate! I know some miserable wretches, who have lost their teacher by following him.

First Citizen. Who is their teacher?

Dhananjay. Their true teacher is he, from whom they get their blows.

[*Enter the* Devotees, *who sing.*]

Victory to the fearful Flame,
That tears the heart of Darkness,
That burns to ashes things which are dead,
Victory to Him, whose voice thunders forth Truth,
Whose right arm smites the unrighteous,
Whose guidance leads mortals across death,
Victory to Him!

Third Citizen. Look there! Look at that! The evening is darkening and that machine is looking blacker and blacker.

First Citizen. In the day time, it tried to outmatch the sunlight, and now it's rivalling the night itself in blackness. It looks like a ghost!

Second Citizen. I can't understand why Bibhuti built it in that fashion. Wherever we are in the town, we cannot help looking at it. It's like a shriek rending the sky.

[*Enters* Fourth Citizen.]

Fourth Citizen. Our King's uncle has carried away by force the Crown Prince along with the guards who guarded his prison.

First Citizen. What's the meaning of that?

Third Citizen. It shows he has the blood of Uttarakut in his veins. He must have done it, for fear lest the Crown Prince should fail to get his proper punishment from our King.

First Citizen. Outrageous! Think of it! To encroach upon our right to punish our own Prince ourselves!

Second Citizen. The best thing to do, friend, is to—you understand?

First Citizen. Yes, Yes. The gold mine which he has in his territory,—

Third Citizen. And I've heard from a most reliable source that he has at least fifty thousand head of cattle in his stall. We must take possession of them, counting every head. This is insufferable!

Fourth Citizen. And then again, the yearly yield of his saffron field must amount at least to—

Second Citizen. Yes! yes! His state must be made to disgorge it. What an affront!

First Citizen. Come! Let us inform the King about it.

[*They all go.*]

[*Enters a* Traveller, *who shouts out.*]

First Traveller. Budhan! Sambhu! Budha-an! Sambhu-u-u! What a nuisance! They sent me in advance, saying they'd overtake me, following the short cut. But there's no sign of them.—[*Looking up*] That black iron monster over there! It's making grimaces at me! It makes me shiver with fear.—

[*Enters another* Traveller.]

Who's there? Why don't you answer? Are you Budhan?

Second Traveller. I'm Nimku, the lamp-seller. They've got in all night festival in the Capital, and lamps will be needed.—Who are you?

First Traveller. I'm Hubba. I belong to a band of strolling players. Did you meet with our party on the way, and their leader Andu?

Nimku. There are crowds of men coming up. How could I recognize them?

Hubba. But our Andu is an entire man by himself. You don't have to put on glasses to pick him out of the crowd. He's not a mere fraction.—I say! What a quantity of lamps you have in your basket! Can't you spare one for me? Those who are out in the street have greater need of lamps than those who are in their houses.

Nimku. How much will you pay for it?

Hubba. If I could afford to *pay,* I should order you in a loud voice, and not waste my sweet tones on you!

Nimku. You seem to be a humorist! [*He goes.*]

Hubba. I failed to get my lamp; but I got my recognition as a humorist! That's something! Humorists have the knack of making themselves felt, even in the dark. Confound this chirping of the crickets! It is like pins and needles in the limbs of the sky, made audible.—I wish I had used my muscle with that lamp-seller, instead of displaying my humour.

[*Enters a* Recruiter.]

Recruiter. Up! up!

Hubba. Oh, goodness! Why on earth d'you go and frighten me in that way?

Recruiter. Get ready to start!

Hubba. That was exactly my intention, my friend. And now I am trying to digest the lesson how to get stuck, when one tries to go ahead.

Recruiter. Your party is ready. Only you are wanting.

Hubba. What do you say? We, inhabitants of Tin Mohāna are remarkably inept at understanding words, when their meaning is not clear. What do you mean by *my* party?

Recruiter. We inhabitants of Chabua village have become wonderful adepts in making our meaning clear by other means than words. [*Gives him a push.*] Now you understand!

Hubba. H'm! Yes! The simple meaning is, I must start, whether I wish it or not. But for what place? Please make your answer a little more gentle this time. That first push of your talk has cleared my mind greatly.

Recruiter. You have to go to Shiu-tarai.

Hubba. To Shiu-tarai? On this dark night? What is the subject of the play there?

Recruiter. The subject is 'The rebuilding of the fort of Nandi Pass'.

Hubba. You mean to rebuild the Fort with *my* help? My dear friend, it's only because you can't get a good sight of me, in this darkness, that you could ever utter such an absurdity as that! I'm—

Recruiter. I don't care who you are! You've got your two hands.

Hubba. That's only because I could not help it. But can you call these—

Recruiter. The proof of the use of your hands doesn't come from your mouth. We shall discover it at the right time. Come now! Get up!

[*Enters* Second Recruiter.]

Second Recruiter. Here's another man, Kankar.

Kankar. Who is he?

Wayfarer. I'm nobody, Sir! I am Lachman. I sound the gong in the Temple of Bhairava.

Kankar. That means your hands are strong. Come to Shiu-tarai!

Lachman. But the gong?

Kankar. Bhairava will sound His own gong himself.

Lachman. Pray, have pity on me! My wife's ailing!

Kankar. She'll either be cured or dead, when you're absent. And the same thing'll happen if you're present.

Hubba. Lachman, my good fellow! Don't make a fuss. The work has its risk, I know. But your objection also has its own risk, and I've had some taste of it already.

Kankar. Listen! I can hear the voice of Narsingh.

[Narsingh *enters with a gang of men*.]

Kankar. Is the news good, Narsingh?

Narsingh. I've gathered these men for our purpose. And some have already been despatched.

One of the Party. I refuse to go.

Kankar. Why? What's the matter with you?

One of the Party. Nothing. But I'm not going.

Kankar. What's his name, Narsingh?

Narsingh. His name's Banwari. He makes rosaries out of lotus seeds.

Kankar. Let me settle with him. [*To* Banwari] Why do you refuse to go?

Banwari. I've no quarrel with the Shiu-tarai people. They're not our enemies.

Kankar. But let's suppose that we are *their* enemies! Hasn't *that* also its responsibility?

Banwari. I'd hate to take part in wrong-doing.

Kankar. Wrong's only wrong where you've the right to judge. Uttarakut is a great body, you're only a part. Whatever you do as a part of it—you can have no responsibility for that!

Banwari. There's a greater body, whose part's Uttarakut as well as Shiu-tarai.

Kankar. I say, Narsingh! This man argues! Nobody's a greater nuisance for the country than the man who argues!

Narsingh. Hard work is the best cure for that! This is why I'm taking him along with us.

Banwari. I'll be only a burden to you and of no use for your work.

Kankar. You're a burden to Uttarakut, and we're trying to get rid of you.

Hubba. My dear friend Banwari, you seem to belong to that class of men who are rational and you won't accept the fact that there's another class of men who are powerful. And you two always clash! Either learn their method, or else give up your own and keep quiet.

Banwari. What's *your* method?

Hubba. I usually sing. But that would only be useless now, and therefore I keep silence.

Kankar [*to* Banwari]. Now tell me what you're going to do.

Banwari. I shan't move a step further.

Kankar. Oh! Then we'll have to make you move. I say, there! Bind him with this rope.

Hubba [*intervening*]. My dear sir, please let me say one word. Don't be angry with me! The force you spend in carrying this man can be better used, if you save it.

Kankar. Those who are unwilling to serve Uttarakut—we've got our unpleasant duty towards them, and we can't neglect it. D'you understand?

Hubba. H'm, yes! Very clearly indeed!

[*They all go out except* Narsingh *and* Kankar.]

Narsingh. Here comes Bibhuti. Long live Bibhuti!

[*Enters* Bibhuti.]

Kankar. We've made great progress. Our party's grown strong. Why are you here? They're waiting for you at their Festival.

Bibhuti. I have no heart for this Festival.

Narsingh. Why?

Bibhuti. The news about the Nandi Pass has deliberately been sent to us to-day, in order to take away from the glory of my reception. There is a rivalry against me.

Kankar. Who's the rival?

Bibhuti. I do not want to utter his name. You all know it. The problem has become acute with him,—whether he shall have more honour in this country than I. I have not told you one fact. A messenger came to me from the other party, to lure me away, and he also gave me a hint that they are ready to break the embankment.

Narsingh. What impudence!

Kankar. How could you bear it, Bibhuti?

Bibhuti. It is useless to contradict the ravings of madness.

Kankar. But is it right to feel too secure? I remember how you said once that there are one or two weak spots, which can easily be—

Bibhuti. Those who have any information about these weak spots also know, that they themselves will be carried away by the flood, if they meddle with them.

Narsingh. Wouldn't it be wise to keep guards at those places?

Bibhuti. Death itself is keeping guard there. There is not the least fear for my embankment. If only I can shut up once again the Nandi Pass, I shall die happy.

Kankar. It's not at all difficult for you to do that.

Bibhuti. My appliances are ready. Only the Pass is so narrow, that it can be defended by a very few men.

Kankar. That means we shall require men who must die.

[*From behind the scene, the cry comes, 'Awake, Bhairava! Awake!'*]

[*Enters* Dhananjay.]

Kankar. This is an evil sight for us at the moment of starting for our adventure.

Bibhuti. Vairagi, saints like you have never succeeded in awakening Bhairava. But men like myself, whom you call infidels, are on our way to give Him a good rousing up.

Dhananjay. I have no doubt in my mind, that it's for you to awaken Him.

Bibhuti. Our process of awakening Him is not through sounding temple gongs and lighting temple lamps.

Dhananjay. No! When you bind Him with your fetters, he will wake up to break them.

Bibhuti. *Our* fetters are not easy to break. The evils are innumerable, and there are an infinite number of knots.

Dhananjay. *His* time comes when the obstacle becomes insurmountable.

[*The* Devotees *come, singing.*]

Victory to Him, the Terrible,
The Lord of Destruction,
The Uttermost Peace,
The Dissolver of doubts,
The Breaker of fetters,
Who carries us beyond all conflicts,
The Terrible! The Terrible!

[*Enter* Ranajit *and* Minister.]

Minister. Sire, the camp is deserted and a great part of it is burnt away. The few guards, who were there—

Ranajit. Never mind about them. Where is Abhijit? I *must* know!

Kankar. King! We claim punishment for the Crown Prince.

Ranajit. Do I ever wait for your claim, in order to punish the one who deserves it?

Kankar. The people harbour suspicions in their minds, when they cannot find him.

Ranajit. Suspicions? Against whom?

Kankar. Pardon me, Sire! You must understand the state of mind of your subjects. Owing to the delay in finding the Crown Prince, their impatience has grown to such a degree, that they will never wait for your judgment, when he is discovered.

Bibhuti. Of our own accord we have taken in hand the duty of building up again the Fort of Nandi Pass.

Ranajit. Why could you not leave it in my hands?

Bibhuti. We have the right to suspect your secret sanction to this outrage done by the Crown Prince.

Minister. Sire, the mind of the public is excited by their self-glorification on the one hand and by their anger on the other. Do not add to *their* impatience, and make it still more turbulent by *your* impatience.

Ranajit. Who is there? Is it Dhananjay?

Dhananjay. I am happy to find that you have not forgotten me!

Ranajit. You certainly know where Abhijit is.

Dhananjay. I can never keep secret what I know for certain.

Ranajit. Then what are you doing here?

Dhananjay. I am waiting for the appearance of the Crown Prince.

[*From outside, the voice is heard of* Amba.]

Amba. Suman! Suman, my darling! It's dark. It's so dark!

Ranajit. Who is that calling?

Minister. It is that mad woman, Amba.

[*Enters* Amba.]

Amba. He has not yet come back.

Ranajit. Why do you seek him? The time came, and Bhairava called him away.

Amba. Does Bhairava only call away and never restore,—secretly? In the depth of the night?—My Suman!

[Amba *goes out*.]

[*Enters a* Messenger.]

Messenger. A multitude of men from Shiu-tarai is marching up.

Bibhuti. How is that? We had planned to disarm them, by falling on them suddenly. There must be some traitor among us! Kankar! Very few people knew, except your party. Then how was it,—?

Kankar. Bibhuti! You suspect even us!

Bibhuti. Suspicion knows no limits.

Kankar. Then we also suspect you.

Bibhuti. You have the right! But when the time comes, there will be a reckoning.

Ranajit [*to the* Messenger]. Do you know, why they are coming?

Messenger. They have heard that the Crown Prince is in prison, and they have come to seek him out and rescue him.

Bibhuti. We are also seeking him, as well as they. Let us see who can find him!

Dhananjay. Both of you will find him. He has no favourites.

Messenger. There comes Ganesh, the leader of Shiu-tarai.

[*Enters* Ganesh.]

Ganesh [*to* Dhananjay]. Father, shall we find him?

Dhananjay. Yes.

Ganesh. Promise us!

Dhananjay. Yes, you shall find him.

Ranajit. Whom are you seeking?

Ganesh. King! You must release him.

Ranajit. Whom?

Ganesh. Our Crown Prince! You do not want him, but we do! Would you shut up everything that we need for our life,—even him?

Dhananjay. Fool! Who has the power to shut *him* up?

Ganesh. We shall make him our King.

Dhananjay. Yes, you shall! He is coming with his King's crown.

[*Enter the* Devotees, *singing.*]

Victory to the fearful Flame,
That tears the heart of Darkness,
That burns to ashes things which are dead.
Victory to Him whose voice thunders forth Truth.
Whose right arm smites the unrighteous.
Whose guidance leads mortals across Death.

[*From outside is heard the cry of* Amba.]

Amba. Mother calls, Suman! Mother calls! Come back, Suman! come back!

[*A sound is heard in the distance.*]

Bibhuti. Hark! What is that? What is that sound?

Dhananjay. It is laughter, bubbling up from the heart of the darkness.

Bibhuti. Hush! Let me find out from what direction the sound comes.

[*In the distance, the cry is faintly heard, 'Victory to Bhairava!'*]

Bibhuti [*listening with his head bent towards the ground*]. It is the sound of water.

Dhananjay. The first beat of the drum before the dance—

Bibhuti. The sound grows in strength!

Kankar. It seems—

Narsingh. Yes! It certainly seems—

Bibhuti. My God! There is no doubt of it. The water of Muktadhārā is freed!—Who has done it?—Who has broken the embankment? He shall pay the price! There is no escape for him! [*He rushes out.*]

[Kankar *and* Narsingh *rush out, following him.*]

Ranajit. Minister! What is this!

Dhananjay. It is the call to the Feast of the Breaking of Bondage— [*Sings.*]

The drum beats;
It beats into the beatings of my heart.

Minister. Sire, it is—

Ranajit. Yes, it must be his!

Minister. It can be no other man than—

Ranajit. Who is so brave as he?

Dhananjay [*sings*].

His feet dance,
They dance in the depth of my life.

Ranajit. I shall punish him, if punished he must be. But these people, maddened with rage,—Only Abhijit! He is favoured of the Gods! May the Gods save him!

Ganesh. I do not understand what has happened, Master!

Dhananjay [*sings*].

The night watches,
And watches also the Watchman.
The silent stars throb with dread.

Ranajit. I hear some steps!—Abhijit! Abhijit!

Minister. It must be he, who comes.

Dhananjay [*sings*].

My heart aches and aches,
While the fetters fall to pieces.

[*Enters* Sanjay.]

Ranajit. Here comes Sanjay!—Where is Abhijit?

Sanjay. The waterfall of Muktadhārā has borne him away, and we have lost him.

Ranajit. What say you, Prince?

Sanjay. He has broken the embankment.

Ranajit. I understand! And with this he has found his freedom! Sanjay! Did he take you with him?

Sanjay. No! But I was certain he would go there. And so I preceded him, and waited in the dark.—But there it ends. He kept me back. He would not let me go.

Ranajit. Tell me more!

Sanjay. Somehow he had come to know about a weakness in the structure, and at that point he gave his blow to the monster Machine. The monster returned that blow against him. Then Muktadhārā, like a mother, took up his stricken body into her arms and carried him away.

Ganesh. We came to seek our Prince! Shall we never find him again!

Dhananjay. You have found him for ever!

[*Enter the* Devotees *of Bhairava, singing.*]

Victory to Him, who is Terrible,
The Lord of Destruction,
The Uttermost Peace!
The Dissolver of doubts,
The Breaker of fetters,
Who carries us beyond all conflicts,
The Terrible! the Terrible!
Victory to the fearful Flame,
That tears the heart of Darkness!
That Turns to ashes things that are dead!
Victory to Him, whose voice thunders forth Truth.
Whose right arm smites the unrighteous,
Whose guidance leads mortals across death!
The Terrible! the Terrible!

Red Oleanders

A DRAMA IN ONE ACT

The curtain rises on a window covered by a network of intricate pattern in front of the Palace.

[Nandini *and* Kishôr, *a digger boy, come in.*]

Kishôr. Have you enough flowers, Nandini? Here, I have brought some more.

Nandini. Run away, Kishôr, do,—back to your work, quick! You'll be late again.

Kishôr. I must steal some time from my digging and digging of nuggets to bring out flowers to you.

Nandini. But they'll punish you, my boy, if they know.

Kishôr. You said you *must* have red oleanders. I am glad they're hard to find in this place, Only one tree I discovered after days of search, nearly hidden away behind a rubbish heap.

Nandini. Show it me. I'll go and gather the flowers myself.

Kishôr. Don't be cruel, Nandini. This tree is my one secret which none shall know. I've always envied Bishu, he can sing to you songs that are his own. From now I shall have flowers which you'll have to take only from my hands.

Nandini. But it breaks my heart to know that those brutes punish you.

Kishôr. It makes these flowers all the more preciously mine. They come from my pain.

Nandini. It pains me to accept anything which brings you hurt.

Kishôr. I dream of dying one day for your sake, Nandini.

Nandini. Is there nothing I can give you in return?

Kishôr. Promise that you will accept flowers only from me every morning.

Nandini. I will. But do be careful.

Kishôr. No, no, I shall be rash and defy their blows. My homage shall be my daily triumph. [*Goes.*]

[Professor *comes in.*]

Professor. Nandini!

Nandini. Yes, Professor!

Professor. Why do you come and startle one, now and again, and then pass by? Since you awaken a cry in our hearts, what harm if you stop a moment in answer to it? Let us talk a little.

Nandini. What need have you of me?

Professor. If you talk of need, look over there! —You'll see our tunnel-diggers creeping out of the holes like worms, with loads of things of need. In this Yaksha Town all our treasure is of gold, the secret treasure of the dust. But the gold which is you, beautiful one, is not of the dust, but of the light which never owns any bond.

Nandini. Over and over again you say this to me. What makes you wonder at me so, Professor?

Professor. The sunlight gleaming through the forest thickets surprises nobody, but the light that breaks through a cracked wall is quite a different thing. In Yaksha Town, you are this light that startles. Tell me, what d'you think of this place?

Nandini. It puzzles me to see a whole city thrusting its head underground, groping with both hands in the dark. You dig tunnels in the underworld and come out with dead wealth that the earth has kept buried for ages past.

Professor. The *Jinn* of that dead wealth we invoke. If we can enslave him the whole world lies at our feet.

Nandini. Then again, you hide your king behind a wall of netting. Is it for fear of people finding out that he's a man?

Professor. As the ghost of our dead wealth is fearfully potent so is our ghostly royalty, made hazy by this net, with its inhuman power to frighten people.

Nandini. All you say is a kind of made-up talk.

Professor. Of course made-up. The naked is without a credential, it's the made-up clothes that define us. It delights me immensely to discuss philosophy with you.

Nandini. That's strange! You who burrow day and night in a mass of yellow pages, like your diggers in the bowels of the earth,—why waste your time on me?

Professor. The privilege of wasting time proves one's wealth of time. We poor drudges are insects in a hole in this solid toil, you are the evening star in the rich sky of leisure. When we see you, our wings grow restless. Come to my room. For a moment allow me to be reckless in my waste of time.

Nandini. No, not now. I have come to see your king, in *his* room.

Professor. How can you enter through the screen?

Nandini. I shall find my way through the net-work.

Professor. Do you know, Nandini, I too live behind a net-work of scholarship. I am an unmitigated scholar, just as our king is an unmitigated king.

Nandini. You are laughing at me, Professor. But tell me, when they brought me here, why didn't they bring my Rañjan also?

Professor. It's their way to snatch things by fractions. But why should you want to drag your life's treasure down amongst this dead wealth of ours?

Nandini. Because I know he can put a beating heart behind these dead ribs.

Professor. Your own presence is puzzling enough for our governors here; if Rañjan also comes they will be in despair.

Nandini. They do not know how comic they are,—Rañjan will bring God's own laughter in their midst and startle them into life.

Professor. Divine laughter is the sunlight that melts ice, but not stones. Only the pressure of gross muscle can move our governors.

Nandini. My Rañjan's strength is like that of your river, Sankhini,— it can laugh and yet it can break. Let me tell you a little secret news of mine. I shall meet Rañjan to-day.

Professor. Who told you that?

Nandini. Yes, yes, we shall meet. The news has come.

Professor. Through what way could news come and yet evade the Governor?

Nandini. Through the same way that brings news of the coming Spring.

Professor. You mean it's in the air,—like the rumours which flush in the colour of the sky, or flutter in the dance of the wind?

Nandini. I won't say more now. When Rañjan comes you'll see for yourself how rumours in the air come down on earth.

Professor. Once she begins to talk of Rañjan there's no stopping Nandini's mouth! Well, well, I have my books, let me take my shelter behind them,—I dare not go on with this. [*Coming back after going a little way.*] Nandini. Let me ask you one thing. Aren't you frightened of our Yaksha Town?

Nandini. Why should I feel afraid?

Professor. All creatures fear an eclipse, not the full sun. Yaksha Town is a city under eclipse. The Shadow Demon, who lives in the gold caves, has eaten into it. It is not whole itself, neither does it allow any one else to remain whole. Listen to me, don't stay here. When you go, these pits will yawn all the wider for us, I know,—yet I say to you, fly; go and live happily with Rañjan where people in their drunken fury don't tear the earth's veil to pieces. [*Going a little way and then coming back.*] Nandini, will you give me a flower from your chain of red oleanders?

Nandini. Why, what will you do with it?

Professor. How often have I thought that there is some omen in these ornaments of yours.

Nandini. I don't know of any.

Professor. Perhaps your fate knows. In that red there is not only beauty, but also the fascination of fear.

Nandini. Fear! Even in me?

Professor. I don't know what event you have come to write with that crimson tint. There was the gardenia and the tuberose, there was white jasmine,—why did you leave them all and choose this flower? Do you know, we often choose our own fate thus, without knowing it!

Nandini. Rañjan sometimes calls me Red Oleander. I feel that the colour of his love is red,—that red I wear on my neck, on my breast, on my arms.

Professor. Well, just give me one of those flowers,—a moment's gift,—let me try to understand the meaning of its colour.

Nandini. Here, take it. Rañjan is coming to-day,—out of my heart's delight I give it to you. [Professor *goes.*]

[Gôkul, *a digger, comes in.*]

Gôkul. Turn this way, woman! Who are you? I've never yet been able to understand you.

Nandini. I'm nothing more than what you see. What need have you to understand me?

Gôkul. I don't trust what I can't understand. For what purpose has the King brought you here?

Nandini. Because I serve no purpose of his.

Gôkul. You know some spell, I'm sure. You're snaring everybody here. You're a witch! Those who are bewitched by your beauty will come to their death.

Nandini. That death will not be yours, Gôkul, never fear! You'll die digging.

Gôkul. Let me see, let me see, what's that dangling over your forehead?

Nandini. Only a tassel of red oleanders.

Gôkul. What does it mean?

Nandini. It has no meaning at all.

Gôkul. I don't believe you, one bit! You're up to some trickery. Some evil will befall us before the day is out. That's why you have got yourself up like this. Oh you terrible, terrible witch!

Nandini. What makes you think me so terrible?

Gôkul. You're looking like an ominous torch.

Nandini. The autumn song:

> *Hark, 'tis Autumn calling:*
> *'Come, O, come away!'—*
> *Her basket is heaped with corn.*

Don't you see the September sun is spreading the glow of the ripening corn in the air?

> *Drunken with the perfumed wine of wind,*
> *the sky seems to sway among the*
> *shivering corn,*
> *its sunlight trailing on the fields*

You too come out, King!—out into the fields.

Voice. Fields! What could I do there?

Nandini. The work there is much simpler than your work in Yaksha Town.

Voice. It's the simple which is impossible for me. A lake cannot run out dancing, like a frolicsome waterfall. Leave me now, I have no time.

Nandini. The day you let me into your store-house the blocks of gold did not surprise me,—what amazed me was the immense strength with which you lifted and arranged them. But can blocks of gold ever answer to the swinging rhythm of your arms in the same way as fields of corn? Are you not afraid, King, of handling the dead wealth of the earth?

Voice. What is there to fear?

Nandini. The living heart of the earth gives itself up in love and life and beauty, but when you rend its bosom and disturb the dead, you bring up with your booty the curse of its dark demon, blind and hard, cruel and envious.

Don't you see everybody here is either angry, or suspicious, or afraid?

Voice. Curse?

Nandini. Yes, the curse of grabbing and killing.

Voice. But we bring up strength. Does not my strength please you, Nandini?

Nandini. Indeed it does. Therefore I ask you, come out into the light, step on the ground, let the earth be glad.

Voice. Do you know, Nandini, you too are half-hidden behind an evasion,—you mystery of beauty! I want to pluck you out of it, to grasp you within my closed fist, to handle you, scrutinise you,—or else to break you to pieces.

Nandini. Whatever do you mean?

Voice. Why can't I strain out the tint of your oleanders and build a dream out of it to keep before my eyes? Those few frail petals guard it and hinder me. Within you there is the same hindrance, so strong because so soft. Nandini, will you tell me what you think of me?

Nandini. Not now, you have no time. Let me go.

Voice. No, no, don't go. Do tell me what you think of me.

Nandini. Have I not told you often enough? I think you are wonderful. Strength swelling up in your arms, like rolling clouds before a storm,—it makes my heart dance within me.

Voice. And when your heart dances to see Rañjan, is that also—

Nandini. Let that be,—you have no time.

Voice. There is time,—for this; only tell me, then go.

Nandini. That dance rhythm is different, you won't understand.

Voice. I will, I must understand.

Nandini. I can't explain it clearly. Let me go.

Voice. Tell me, at least, whether you like me.

Nandini. Yes, I like you.

Voice. The same as Rañjan?

Nandini. Again the same question! I tell you, you don't understand these things.

Voice. I *do* understand, a little. I know what the difference is between Rañjan and me. In me there is only strength, in Rañjan there is magic.

Nandini. What d'you mean by magic?

Voice. Shall I explain? Underground there are blocks of stone, iron, gold,—there you have the image of strength. On the surface grows the grass, the flower blossoms,—there you have the play of magic. I can extract gold from the fearsome depths of secrecy, but to wrest that magic from the near at hand I fail.

Nandini. You have no end of things, yet why always covet?

Voice. All I possess is so much dead weight. No increase of gold can create a particle of a touchstone, no increase of power can ever come up to youth. I can only guard by force. If I had Rañjan's youth I could leave you free and yet hold you fast. My time is spent in knotting the binding rope, but, alas, everything else can be kept tied, except joy.

Nandini. It is you who entangle yourself in your own net, then why keep on fretting?

Voice. You will never understand. I, who am a desert, stretch out my hand to you, a tiny blade of grass, and cry: I am parched, I am bare, I am weary. The flaming thirst of this desert licks up one fertile field after another, only to enlarge itself,—it can never annex the life of the frailest of grasses.

Nandini. One would never think you were so tired.

Voice. One day, Nandini, in a far off land, I saw a mountain as weary as myself. I could not guess that all its stones were aching inwardly. One night I heard a noise, as if some giant's evil dream had moaned and moaned and suddenly snapped asunder. Next morning I found the mountain had disappeared in the chasm of a yawning earthquake. That made me understand how overgrown power crushes itself inwardly by its own weight. I see in you something quite opposite.

Nandini. What is it you see in me?

Voice. The dance rhythm of the All.

Nandini. I don't understand.

Voice. The rhythm that lightens the enormous weight of matter. To that rhythm the bands of stars and planets go about dancing from sky to sky, like so many minstrel boys. It is that rhythm, Nandini, that makes you so simple, so perfect. How small you are compared to me, yet I envy you.

Nandini. You have cut yourself off from everybody and so deprived yourself.

Voice. I keep myself apart, that it may become easy for me to plunder the world's big treasure-houses. Nevertheless there are gifts that your little flower-like fingers can easily reach, but not all the strength of my body,—gifts hidden in God's closed hand. That hand I must force open some day.

Nandini. When you talk like that, I don't follow you. Let me go.

Voice. Go then; but here, I stretch out this hand of mine from my window, place your hand on it for a moment.

Nandini. Only a hand, and the rest of you hidden? It frightens me!

Voice. Everybody flies from me because they only see my hand. But if I wished to hold you with all of me, would you come to me, Nandini?

Nandini. Why talk like this when you wouldn't even let me come into your room?

Voice. My busy time, overloaded with work, dragged along against obstruction, is not for you. On the day when you can arrive, full sail before the wind, into the bosom of my full.

Phágulal. Isn't it our holiday? Yesterday was the fast day of the War Goddess. To-day they worship the Flag.

Chandrá. Must you drink just because it's a holiday? In our village home, on feast days, you never—

Phágulal. Freedom itself was enough for the holidays in our village. The caged bird spends its holiday knocking against the bars. In Yaksha Town holidays are more of a nuisance than work.

Chandrá. Let's go back home, then.

Phágulal. The road to our home is closed for ever.

Chandrá. How's that?

Phágulal. Our homes don't yield them any profit.

Chandrá. But are we closely fitted to their profits only,—like husks to grains of corn,—with nothing of us left over?

Phágulal. Our mad Bishu says: to remain whole is useful only for the lamb itself; those who eat it prefer to leave out its horns and hooves, and even object to its bleating when butchered.

There's the madcap, singing as he goes.

Chandrá. It's only the last few days that his songs have burst forth.

Phágulal. That's true.

Chandrá. He's been possessed by Nandini. She draws his heart and his songs too.

Phágulal. No wonder.

Chandrá. Indeed! You'd better be careful. She'll next be bringing out songs from *your* throat,—which would be rough on our neighbours. The witch is up to all kinds of tricks, and is sure to bring misfortune.

Phágulal. Bishu's misfortune is nothing recent, he knew Nandini long before coming here.

Chandrá [*calling out*]. I say, Bishu, come this way. Maybe you'll find somebody here also to listen to your singing,—it won't be altogether thrown away.

[Bishu *comes in, singing*.]

Bishu [*sings*].

Boatman of my dreams,
The sail is filled with a boisterous breeze
and my mad heart sings
to the lilt of the rocking of thy boat,
at the call of the far away landing.

Chandrá. I know who the boatman of your dreams is.

Bishu. How should you know from outside? You haven't seen from inside my boat.

Chandrá. Your boat is going to get wrecked one of these days, let me tell you,—by that pet Nandini of yours.

[Gôkul, *the digger, comes in.*]

Gôkul. I say, Bishu, I don't quite trust your Nandini.

Bishu. Why, what has she done?

Gôkul. She does nothing, that's the rub. I don't understand the way she goes on.

Chandrá. To see her flaunting her prettiness all over the place makes me sick.

Gôkul. We can trust features that are plain enough to understand.

Bishu. I know the atmosphere of this place breeds contempt for beauty. There must be beauty even in hell; but nobody there can understand it, that's their cruellest punishment.

Chandrá. Maybe we are fools, but even our Governor here can't stand her—d'you know that?

Bishu. Take care, Chandrá, lest you catch the infection of our Governor's eyes—then perhaps yours too will redden at the sight of us. What say you, Phágulal?

Phágulal. To tell you the truth, brother, when I see Nandini, I feel ashamed to think of myself. I can't utter a word when she's there.

Gôkul. The day will come when you'll know her to your cost,—perhaps too late. [*Goes.*]

Phágulal. Bishu, your friend Chandrá wants to know why we drink.

Bishu. God in his mercy has everywhere provided a liberal allowance of drink. We men with our arms supply the output of our muscles, you women with yours supply the wine of embraces. In this world there is hunger to force us to work; but there's also the green of the woods, the gold of the sunshine, to make us drunk with their holiday-call.

Chandrá. You call these things *drink?*

Bishu. Yes, drinks of life, an endless stream of intoxication. Take my case. I come to this place; I am set to work burgling the underworld; for me nature's own ration of spirits is stopped; so my inner man craves the artificial wine of the market place. [*Sings.*]

> *My life, your sap has run dry,*
> *Fill then the cup with the wine of death,*
> *That flushes all emptiness with its laughter.*

Chandrá. Come, brother, let us fly from here.

Bishu. To that boundless tavern, underneath the blue canopy? Alas, the road is closed, and we seek consolation in the stolen wine of the prison house. No open sky, no leisure for us; so we have distilled the essence of all the song and laughter, all the sunlight of the twelve hours' day into one draught of liquid fire. [*Sings.*]

> *Thy sun is hidden amid a mass of murky cloud.*
> *Thy day has smudged itself black in dusty toil.*
> *Then let the dark night descend*
> *the last comrade of drunken oblivion,*
> *Let it cover thy tired eyes with the mist*
> *that will help thee desperately to lose thyself.*

Chandrá. Well, well, Bishu, you men have gone to the dogs in Yaksha Town, if you like, but we women haven't changed at all.

Bishu. Haven't you? Your flowers have faded, and you are all slavering for gold.

Chandrá. No, never!

Bishu. I say, yes. That Phágulal toils for hours over and above the twelve,—why? For a reason unknown to him, unknown even to you. But I know. It's your dream of gold that lashes him on to work, more severely than the foreman's whip.

Chandrá. Very well. Then why don't we fly from here, and go back home?

Bishu. Your Governor has closed the way as well as the will to return. If you go there to-day you will fly back here to-morrow, like a caged bird to its cage, hankering for its drugged food.

Phágulal. I say, Bishu, once upon a time you came very near spoiling your eyesight poring over books; how is it they made you ply the spade along with the rest of us stupid boors?

Chandrá. All this time we've been here, we haven't got from Bishu the answer to this particular question.

Phágulal. Yet we all know it.

Bishu. Well, out with it then!

Phágulal. They employed you to spy on us.

Bishu. If you knew that, how is it you let me off alive?

Phágulal. But, we knew also, that game was not in your line.

Chandrá. How is it you couldn't stick to such a comfortable job, brother?

Bishu. Comfortable job? To stick to a living being like a carbuncle on his back?

I said: 'I must go home, my health is failing.'

'Poor thing,' said the Governor, 'how can you go home in such a state? However, there's no harm in your trying.'

Well, I did try. And then I found that, as soon as one enters the maw of Yaksha Town, its jaws shut fast, and the one road that remains open leads withinwards. Now I am swamped in that interior without hope and without light, and the only difference between you and me is, that the Governor looks down upon me even worse than upon you. Man despises the broken pot of his own creation more than the withered leaf fallen from the tree.

Phágulal. What does that matter, Bishu? You have risen high in our esteem.

Bishu. Discovery only means death. Where you favour falls there falls the Governor's glance. The more noisily the yellow frogs welcome the black toad, the sooner their croaking points him out to the boa-constrictor.

Chandrá. But when will your work be finished?

Bishu. The calendar never records the last day. After the first day comes the second, after the second the third. There's no such thing as getting finished here. We're always digging—one yard, two yards, three yards. We go on raising gold nuggets,—after one nugget another, then more and more and more. In Yaksha Town figures follow one another in rows and never arrive at any conclusion. That's why we are not men to them, but only numbers.—Phágu, what's yours?

Phágulal. I'm No. 47 V.

Bishu. I'm 69 Ng.

Chandrá. Brother, they've hoarded such heaps of gold, can't they stop digging now?

Bishu. There's always an end to things of need, no doubt; so we stop when we've had enough to eat. But we don't need drunkenness, therefore there's no end to it. These nuggets are the drink—the solid drink—of our Gold King. Don't you see?

Chandrá. No, I don't.

Bishu. Cups in hand, we forget that we are chained to our limits. Gold blocks in hand, our master fancies he's freed from the gravitation of the commonplace, and is soaring in the rarest of upper heights.

Chandrá. In this season the villages are preparing for their harvest festival. Let's go home.

Phágulal. Don't worry me, Chandrá. A thousand times over have I told you that in these parts there are high roads to the market, to the burning ground, to the scaffold,—everywhere except to the homeland.

Chandrá. If we were to go to the Governor, and just tell him—

Bishu. Hasn't your woman's wit seen through the Governor yet?

Chandrá. Why, he seems to be so nice and—

Bishu. Yes, nice and polished, like the crocodile's teeth, which fit into one another with so thorough a bite that the King himself can't unlock the jaw, even if he wants to.

Chandrá. There comes the Governor.

Bishu. Then it's all up with us. He's sure to have overheard—

Chandrá. Why, we haven't said anything so very—

Bishu. Sister, we can only say the words,—they put in the meaning.

[*The* Governor *comes in.*]

Chandrá. Sir Governor!

Governor. Well, my child?

Chandrá. Grant us leave to go home for a little.

Governor. Why, aren't the rooms we have given you excellent, much better than the ones at home? We have even kept a state watchman for your safety.

Hullo, 69 Ng, to see you amongst these people reminds one of a heron come to teach paddy birds how to cut capers.

Bishu. Sir, your jesting does not reassure me. Had my feet the strength to make others dance, would I not have run away from here, first thing? Especially after the striking examples I've seen of the fate that overtakes dancing masters in this country. As things are, one's legs tremble even to walk straight.

Chandrá. Give us leave, Sir Governor, do give us leave. Let us go just for once, and see our waving fields of barleycorn in the ear, and the ample shade of our banian tree with its hanging roots. I cannot tell you how our hearts ache.

Don't you see that your men here work all day in the dark, and in the evening steep themselves in the denser dark of drunkenness? Have you no pity for them?

Governor. My dear child, surely you know of our constant anxiety for their welfare. That is exactly why I have sent for our High Preacher, Kenarám Gosain himself, to give moral talks to the men. Their votive fees will pay for his upkeep. Every evening the Gosain will come and—

Phágulal. That won't do, sir! Now, at worst, we get drunk of an evening, but if we are preached to every night, there'll be manslaughter!

Bishu. Hush, hush, Phágulal.

[*Preacher* Gosain *comes in*.]

Governor. Talk of the Preacher and he appears. Your Holiness, I do you reverence. These workmen of ours sometimes feel disturbed in their weak minds. Deign to whisper in their ears some texts of peace. The need is urgent.

Gosain. These people? Are they not the very incarnation of the sacred Tortoise of our scripture, that held up the sinking earth on its back? Because they meekly suppress themselves underneath their burden, the upper world can keep its head aloft. The very thought sends a thrill through my body!

Just think of it, friend 47 V, yours is the duty of supplying food to this mouth which chants the holy name. With the sweat of your brow have you woven this wrap printed with the holy name, which exalts this devoted body. Surely that is no mean privilege. May you remain for ever undisturbed, is my benediction, for then the grace of God will abide with you likewise.

My friends, repeat aloud the holy name of Hari, and all your burdens will be lightened. The name of Hari shall be taken in the beginning, in the middle, and at the end,—so say the scriptures.

Chandrá. How sweet! It's long since I have heard such words! Give, oh give me a little dust off your feet!

Phágulal. Stop this waste of money, Governor. If it's our offerings you want, we can stand it, but we're fairly sick of this cant.

Bishu. Once Phágulal runs amok it's all over with the lot of you. Hush, hush, Phágulal!

Chandrá. Are you bent on spoiling your chances both in this world and the next, you wretched man? You were never like this before. Nandini's ill wind has blown upon you,—and no mistake.

Gosain. What charming naiveté, Sir Governor! What's in their heart is always on their lips. What can we teach them?—it's they who'll teach us a lesson. You know what I mean.

Governor. I know where the root of the trouble is. I'll have to take them in hand myself, I see. Meanwhile, pray go to the next parish and chant them the holy name,—the sawyers there have taken to grumbling, somewhat.

Gosain. Which parish did you say?

Governor. Parish T-D. No. 71 T is headman there. It ends to the left of where No. 65 of Row M lives.

Gosain. My son, though Parish T-D may not yet be quieted, the whole Row of M's have lately become steeped in a beautiful spirit of meekness. Still it is better to keep an extra police force posted in the parish some time longer. Because, as you know our scripture says,—pride is our greatest foe. After the strength of the police has helped to conquer pride, then comes our turn. I take my leave.

Chandrá. Forgive these men, Your Holiness, and give them your blessing, that they may follow the right path.

Gosain. Fear not, good woman, they'll all end thoroughly pacified. [*The* Gosain *goes.*]

Governor. I say, 69 Ng, the temper of your parish seems to be somewhat strained.

Bishu. That's nothing strange. The Gosain called them the incarnation of the Tortoise. But, according to scripture, incarnations change; and, when the Tortoise gave place to the Boar, in place of hard shell came out aggressive teeth, so that all-suffering patience was transformed into defiant obstinacy.

Chandrá. But, Sir Governor, don't forget my request.

Governor. I have heard it and will bear it in mind. [*He goes.*]

Chandrá. Ah now, didn't you see how nice the Governor is? How he smiles every time he talks!

Bishu. Crocodile's teeth begin by smiling and end by biting.

Chandrá. Where does his bite come in?

Bishu. Don't you know he's going to make it a rule not to let the workmen's wives accompany them here.

Chandrá. Why?

Bishu. We have a place in their account book as numbers, but women's figures do not mate with figures of arithmetic.

Chandrá. O dear! but have they no women-folk of their own?

Bishu. Their ladies are besotted with the wine of gold, even worse than their husbands.

Chandrá. Bishu, you had a wife at home,—what's become of her?

Bishu. So long as I filled the honoured post of spy, they used to invite her to those big mansions to play cards with their ladies. Ever since I joined Phágulal's set, all that was stopped, and she left me in a huff at the humiliation.

Chandrá. For shame! But look, brother Bishu, what a grand procession! One palanquin after another! Don't you see the sparkle of the jewelled fringes of the elephant-seats? How beautiful the out-riders on horseback look, as if they had bits of sunlight pinned on the points of their spears!

Bishu. Those are the Governor's and Deputy Governor's ladies, going to the Flag-worship.

Chandrá. Bless my soul, what a gorgeous array and how fine they look!

I say, Bishu, if you hadn't given up that job, would you have gone along with that set in this grand style?—and that wife of yours surely—

Bishu. Yes, we too should have come to just such a pass.

Chandrá. Is there no way going back,—none whatever?

Bishu. There is,—through the gutter.

A Distant Voice. Bishu, my mad one!

Bishu. Yes, my mad girl!

Phágulal. There's Nandini. There'll be no more of Bishu for us, for the rest of the day.

Chandrá. Tell me, Bishu, what does she charm you with?

Bishu. The charm of sorrow.

Chandrá. Why do you talk so topsy-turvy?

Bishu. She reminds me that there are sorrows, to forget which is the greatest of sorrow.

Phágulal. Please to speak plainly, Bishu, otherwise it becomes positively annoying!

Bishu. The pain of desire for the near belongs to the animal, the sorrow of aspiration for the far belongs to man. That far away flame of my eternal sorrow is revealed through Nandini.

Chandrá. Brother, we don't understand these things. But one thing I do understand and that is,—the less you men can make out a girl, the more she attracts you! We simple women,—our price is not so high, but we at least keep you on the straight path. I warn you, once for all, that girl with her noose of red oleanders will drag you to perdition.

[Chandrá *and* Phágulal *go.*]

[Nandini *comes in.*]

Nandini. My mad one, did you hear their autumn songs this morning?

Bishu. Is my morning like yours that I should hear singing? Mine is only a swept-away remnant of the weary night.

Nandini. In my gladness of heart I thought I'd stand on the rampart and join in their song. But the guards would not let me, so I've come to you.

Bishu. I am not a rampart.

Nandini. You are *my* rampart. When I come to you I seem to climb high, I find the open light.

Bishu. Ever since coming to Yaksha Town the sky has dropped out of my life. I felt as if they had pounded me in the same mortar with all the fractions of men here, and rolled us into a solid lump.

Then you came and looked into my face in a way that made me sure some light could still be seen through me.

Nandini. In this closed fort a bit of sky survives only between you and me, my mad one.

Bishu. Through that sky my songs can fly towards you. [*Sings.*]

> *You keep me awake that I may sing to you,*
> *O Breaker of my sleep!*
> *And so my heart you startle with your call,*
> *O Waker of my grief!*
> *The shades of evening* fall,
> *the birds come to their nest.*
> *The boat arrives ashore,*
> *yet my heart knows no rest,*
> *O Waker of my grief!*

Nandini. The waker of your grief, Bishu?

Bishu. Yes, you are my messenger from the unreachable shore. The day you came to Yaksha Town a gust of salt air knocked at my heart.

Nandini. But I never had any message of this sorrow of which you sing.

Bishu. Not even from Rañjan?

Nandini. No, he holds an oar in each hand and ferries me across the stormy waters; he catches wild horses by the mane and rides with me through the woods; he shoots an arrow between the eyebrows of the tiger on the spring, and scatters my fear with loud laughter. As he jumps into our Nagai river and disturbs its current with his joyous splashing, so he disturbs me with his tumultuous life. Desperately he stakes his all on the game and thus has he won me.

You also were there with us, but you held aloof, and at last something urged you one day to leave our gambling set. At the time of your parting you looked at my face in a way I could not quite make out. After that I've had no news of you for long. Tell me where you went off to then.

Bishu. My boat was tied to the bank; the rope snapped; the wild wind drove it into the tackles unknown.

Nandini. But who dragged you back from there to dig for nuggets here in Yaksha Town?

Bishu. A woman. Just as a bird on the wing is brought to the ground by a chance arrow, so did she bring me down to the dust. I forgot myself.

Nandini. How could she touch you?

Bishu. When the thirsty heart despairs of finding water it's easy enough for it to be deluded by a mirage, and driven in barren quest from desert to desert.

One day, while I was gazing at the sunset clouds, she had her eye upon the golden spire of the Governor's palace. Her glance challenged me to take her over there. In my foolish pride I vowed to do so. When I did bring her here, under the golden spire, the spell was broken.

Nandini. I've come to take you away from here.

Bishu. Since you have moved even the king of this place, what power on earth can prevent you? Tell me, don't you feel afraid of him?

Nandini. I did fear him from outside that screen. But now I've seen him inside.

Bishu. What was he like?

Nandini. Like a man from the epics,—his forehead like the gateway of a tower, his arms the iron bolts of some inaccessible fortress.

Bishu. What did you see when you went inside?

Nandini. A falcon was sitting on his left wrist. He put it on the perch and gazed at my face. Then, just as he had been stroking the falcon's wings, he began gently to stroke my hand. After a while he suddenly asked: 'Don't you fear me, Nandini?'

'Not in the least,' said I.

Then he buried his fingers in my unbound hair and sat long with closed eyes.

Bishu. How did you like it?

Nandini. I liked it. Shall I tell you how? It was as if he were a thousand-year-old banyan tree, and I a tiny little bird; when I lit on a branch of his and had my little swing, he needs must have felt a thrill of delight to his very marrow. I loved to give that bit of joy to that lonely soul.

Bishu. Then what did he say?

Nandini. Starting up and fixing his spear-point gaze on my face, he suddenly said: 'I want to know you.'

I felt a shiver run down my body and asked: 'What is there to know?—I am not a manuscript!'

'I know all there is in manuscripts,' said he, 'but I don't know you.' Then he became excited and cried: 'Tell me all about Rañjan. Tell me how you love him.'

I talked on: 'I love Rañjan as the rudder in the water might love the sail in the sky, answering its rhythm of wind in the rhythm of waves.'

He listened quietly, staring like a big greedy boy. All of a sudden he startled me by exclaiming: 'Could you die for him?'

'This very moment,' I replied.

'Never,' he almost roared, as if in anger.

'Yes, I could,' I repeated.

'What good would that do you?'

'I don't know,' said I.

Then he writhed and shouted: 'Go away from my room, go, go at once, don't disturb me in my work.'

I could not understand what that meant.

Bishu. He gets angry when he can't understand.

Nandini. Bishu, don't you feel pity for him?

Bishu. The day when God will be moved to pity for him, he will die.

Nandini. No, no, you don't know how desperately he wants to live.

Bishu. You will see this very day what his living means. I don't know whether you'll be able to bear the sight.

Nandini. There, look, there's a shadow. I am sure the Governor has secretly heard what we've been saying.

Bishu. This place is dark with the Governor's shadow, it is everywhere. How do you like him?

Nandini. I have never seen anything so lifeless,—like a cane stick cut from the cane bush,—no leaves, no roots, no sap in the veins.

Bishu. Cut off from life, he spends himself in repressing life.

Nandini. Hush, he will hear you.

Bishu. He hears even when you are silent, which is all the more dangerous. When I am with the diggers I am careful in my speech, so much so that the Governor thinks I'm the sorriest of the lot, and spares me out of sheer contempt. But, my mad girl, when I am with you my mind scorns to be cautious.

Nandini. No, no, you must not court danger. There comes the Governor.

[*The* Governor *comes in.*]

Governor. Hallo, 69 Ng! you seem to be making friends with everybody, without distinction.

Bishu. You may remember that I began by making friends even with you, only it was the distinction that stood in the way.

Governor. Well, what are we discussing now?

Bishu. We are discussing how to escape from this fortress of yours.

Governor. Really? So recklessly, that you don't even mind confessing it?

Bishu. Sir Governor, it doesn't need much cleverness to know that when a captive bird pecks at the bars it's not in the spirit of caress. What does it matter whether that's openly confessed or not?

Governor. The captives' want of love we were aware of, but their not fearing to admit it has become evident only recently.

Nandini. Won't you let Rañjan come?

Governor. You will see him this very day.

Nandini. I knew that; still, for your message of hope I wish you victory. Governor, take this garland of *kunda* flowers.

Governor. Why throw away the garland thus, and not keep it for Rañjan?

Nandini. There is a garland for him.

Governor. Aha, I thought so! I suppose it's the one hanging round your neck. The garland of victory may be of *kunda* flowers, the gift of the hand; but the garland of welcome is of red oleanders, the gift of the heart. Well, let's be quick in accepting what comes from the hand, for that will fade; as for the heart's offering, the longer it waits the more precious it grows. [*The* Governor *goes.*]

Nandini [*knocking at the window*]. Do you hear? Let me come into your room.

Voice [*from behind the scenes*]. Why always the same futile request? Who is that with you? A pair to Rañjan?

Bishu. No, King, I am the obverse side of Rañjan, on which falls the shadow.

Voice. What use has Nandini for you?

Bishu. The use which music has for the hollow of the flute.

Voice. Nandini, what is this man to you?

Nandini. He's my partner in music. My heart soars in his voice, my pain cries in his tunes,—that's what he tells me. [*Sings.*]

'I love, I love,'— 'Tis the cry that breaks out
from the bosom of earth and water.

Voice. So that's your partner! What if I dissolved your partnership this very minute?

Nandini. Why are you so cross? Haven't you any companion yourself?

Voice. Has the mid-day sun any companion?

Nandini. Well, let's change the subject. What's that? What's that in your hand?

Voice. A dead frog.

Nandini. What for?

Voice. Once upon a time this frog got into a hole in a stone, and in that shelter it existed for three thousand years. I have learnt from it the secret of continuing to exist, but to live it does not know. To-day I felt bored and smashed its shelter. I've thus saved it from existing for ever. Isn't that good news?

Nandini. Your stone walls will also fall away from around me to-day,— I shall meet Rañjan.

Voice. I want to see you both together.

Nandini. You won't be able to see from behind your net.

Voice. I shall let you sit inside my room.

Nandini. What will you do with us?

Voice. Nothing, I only want to know you.

Nandini. When you talk of knowing, it frightens me.

Voice. Why?

Nandini. I feel that you have no patience with things that cannot be known, but can only be felt.

Voice. I dare not trust such things lest they should play me false. Now go away, don't waste my time.—No, no, wait a little. Give me that tassel of red oleanders which hangs from your hair.

Nandini. What will you do with it?

Voice. When I look at those flowers it seems to me as if the red light of my evil star has appeared in their shape. At times I want to snatch them from you and tear them to pieces. Again I think that if Nandini were ever to place that spray of flowers on my head, with her own hands, then—

Nandini. Then what?

Voice. Then perhaps I might die in peace.

Nandini. Some one loves red oleanders and calls me by that name. It is in remembrance of him that I wear these flowers.

Voice. Then, I tell you, they're going to be *his* evil star as well as *mine*.

Nandini. Don't say such things for shame! I am going.

Voice. Where?

Nandini. I shall go and sit near the gate of your fort.

Voice. Why?

Nandini. When Rañjan comes he'll see I am waiting for him.

Voice. I should like to tread hard on Rañjan and grind him in the dust.

Nandini. Why pretend to frighten me?

Voice. Pretend, you say? Don't you know I am really fearsome?

Nandini. You seem to take pleasure in seeing people frightened at you. In our village plays Srikantha takes the part of a demon; when he comes on the stage, he is delighted if the children are terrified. You are like him. Do you know what I think?

Voice. What is it?

Nandini. The people here trade on frightening others. That's why they have put you behind a network and dressed you fantastically. Don't you feel ashamed to be got up like a bogeyman?

Voice. How dare you!

Nandini. Those whom you have scared all along will one day feel ashamed to be afraid. If my Rañjan were here, he would have snapped his fingers in your face, and not been afraid even if he died for it.

Voice. Your impudence is something great. I should like to stand you up on the top of a heap of everything I've smashed throughout my life. And then—

Nandini. Then what?

Voice. Then, like a squeezed bunch of grapes with its juice running out from between the gripping fingers, if I could but hold you tight with these two hands of mine,—and then—go, go, run away, at once, at once!

Nandini. If you shout at me so rudely, I'll stay on, do what you will!

Voice. I long savagely to prove to you how cruel I am. Have you never heard moans from inside my room?

Nandini. I have. Whose moaning was it?

Voice. The hidden mystery of life, wrenched away by me, bewails its torn ties. To get fire from a tree you have to burn it. Nandini, there is fire within you too, red fire. One day I shall burn you and extract that also.

Nandini. Oh, you are cruel!

Voice. I must either gather or scatter. I can feel no pity for what I do not get. Breaking is a fierce kind of getting.

Nandini. But why thrust out your clenched fist like that?

Voice. Here, I take away my fist. Now fly, as the dove flies from the shadow of a hawk.

Nandini. Very well, I will go, and not vex you any more.

Voice. Here, listen, come back, Nandini!

Nandini. What is it?

Voice. On your face, there is the play of life in your eyes and lips; at the back of you flows your black hair, the silent fall of death. The other day when my hands sank into it they felt the *soft calm of dying*. I long to sleep with my face hidden inside those thick black clusters. You don't know how tired I am!

Nandini. Don't you ever sleep?

Voice. I feel afraid to sleep.

Nandini. Let me sing you the latest song that I've learnt.

[*Sings.*]

'I love, I love' is the cry that breaks out from
the bosom of earth and water.
The sky broods like an aching heart, the horizon is
tender like eyes misted with tears.

Voice. Enough! Enough! stop your singing!

Nandini [*sings on*].

A lament heaves and bursts
on the shore of the sea.
The whispers of forgotten days
are born in new leaves to die again.

See, Bishu, he has left the dead frog there and disappeared. He is afraid of songs.

Bishu. The old frog in his heart yearns to die when it hears singing, that's why he feels afraid. My mad girl, why is there a strange light on your face to-day, like the glow of a distant torch in the sky?

Nandini. News has reached me, Rañjan is coming to-day.

Bishu. How?

Nandini. Let me tell you. Every day a pair of blue-throats come and sit on the pomegranate tree in front of my window. Every night, before I sleep, I salute the pole star and say: Sacred star of constancy, if a feather from the wings of the blue-throats finds its way into my room, then I will know my Rañjan is coming. This morning, as soon as I woke, I found a feather on my bed. See, here it is under my breast-cloth. When I meet him I shall put this feather on his crest.

Bishu. They say blue-throats' wings are an omen of victory.

Nandini. Rañjan's way to victory lies through my heart.

Bishu. No more of this; let me go to my work.

Nandini. I shan't let you work to-day.

Bishu. What must I do then.

Nandini. Sing that song of waiting.

Bishu [*sings*].

He who ever wants me through the ages,—
is it not he who sits to-day by my wayside?
I seem to remember a glimpse I had of his face,
in the twilight dusk of some ancient year.
Is it not he who sits to-day by the wayside?

Nandini. Bishu, when you sing I cannot help feeling that I owe you much, but have never given anything to you.

Bishu. I shall decorate my forehead with the mark of your never-giving, and go my way. No little-giving for me, in return for my song! Where will you go now?

Nandini. To the wayside by which Rañjan is coming.

[*They go.*]

[*The* Governor *and a* Headman *come in.*]

Governor. No, we can't possibly allow Rañjan to enter this parish.

Headman. I put him to work in the tunnels of Vajragarh.

Governor. Well, what happened?

Headman. He said he was not used to being made to work. The Headman of Vajragarh came with the police, but the fellow doesn't know what fear is. Threaten him, he bursts out laughing. Asked why he laughs, he says solemnity is the mask of stupidity and he has come to take it off.

Governor. Did you set him to work with the diggers?

Headman. I did, I thought that pressure would make him yield. But on the contrary it seemed to lift the pressure from the diggers' minds also. He cheered them up, and asked them to have a digger's dance!

Governor. Digger's dance! What on earth is that?

Headman. Rañjan started singing. Where were they to get drums?—they objected. Rañjan said, if there weren't any drums, there were spades enough. So they began keeping time with the spades, making a joke of their digging up of nuggets.

The Headman himself came over to reprimand them. 'What style of work is this?' he thundered.

'I have unbound the work,' said Rañjan. 'It won't have to be dragged out by main force any more, it will run along of itself, dancing.'

Governor. The fellow is mad, I see.

Headman. Hopelessly mad. 'Use your spade properly,' shouted I. 'Much better give me a guitar,' said he, smiling.

Governor. But how did he manage to escape from Vajragarh and come up here?

Headman. That I do not know. Nothing seems to fasten on to him. His boisterousness is infectious. The diggers are getting frisky.

Governor. Hallo, isn't that Rañjan himself,—going along the road, thrumming on an old guitar? Impudent rascal! He doesn't even care to hide.

Headman. Well, I never! Goodness alone knows how he broke through the wall!

Governor. Go and seize him instantly! He must not meet Nandini in this parish, for anything.

[*Enters* Assistant Governor.]

Governor. Where are you going?

Assistant Governor. To arrest Rañjan.

Governor. Where is the Deputy Governor?

Assistant Governor. He is so much amused by this fellow that he doesn't want to lay hands on him. He says the man's laugh shows us what queer creatures we governors have grown into.

Governor. I have an idea. Don't arrest Rañjan. Send him on to the King's sanctum.

Assistant Governor. He refuses to obey our call, even in the King's name.

Governor. Tell him the King has made a slave-girl of his Nandini.

Assistant Governor. But if the King—

Governor. Don't you worry. Come on, I'll go with you myself. [*They go.*]

[*Enter* Professor *and* Antiquarian.]

Antiquarian. I say, what is this infernal noise going on inside?

Professor. The King, probably in a temper with himself, is engaged in breaking some of his own handiwork.

Antiquarian. It sounds like big pillars crashing down one after another.

Professor. There was a lake, at the foot of our hill over there, in which the waters of this Sankhini river used to gather. One day, suddenly, the rock to its left gave way, and the stored-up water rushed out laughing like mad. To see the King now-a-days, it strikes me that his treasure lake has grown weary of its rock wall.

Antiquarian. What did you bring me here for, Professor?

Professor. Latterly he has begun to get angry with my science. He says it only burgles through one wall to reveal another behind it, and never reaches the inner chamber of the Life spirit. I thought that, perhaps in the study of antiquity, he might explore the secret of Life's play. My knapsack has been rifled empty, now he can go on pocket-picking history.

Antiquarian. A girl wearing a grass-green robe.

Professor. She has for her mantle the green joy of the earth. That is our Nandini. In this Yaksha Town there are governors, foremen, headmen, tunnel-diggers, scholars like myself; there are policemen, executioners, and undertakers,—altogether a beautiful assortment! Only *she* is out of element. Midst the clamour of the market place she is a tuned-up lyre. There are days when the mesh of my studies is torn by the sudden breeze of her passing by, and through that rent my attention flies away *swish,* like a bird.

Antiquarian. Good heavens, man! Are even your well-seasoned bones subject to these poetic fits?

Professor. Life's attraction, like the tidal wave, tears away mind from its anchorage of books.

Antiquarian. Tell me, where am I to meet the King.

Professor. There's no means of meeting him. You'll have to talk to him from outside this network.

Antiquarian. We're to converse with this net between us?

Professor. Not the kind of whispered talk that may take place through a woman's veil, but solidly concentrated conversation. Even the cows in his stall don't dare to give milk, they yield their butter straight off.

Antiquarian. Admirable! To extract the essential from the diluted, is what scholars aim at.

Professor. But not what God in His creation aims at. He respects the fruit stones that are hard, but rejoices in the pulp that is sweet.

Antiquarian. Professor, I see that your grey science is galloping fast towards grass-green. But I wonder how you can stand this King of yours.

Professor. Shall I tell you the truth? I love him.

Antiquarian. You don't mean to say so?

Professor. He is so great that even what is wrong with him will not be able to spoil him.

[*The* Governor *comes in.*]

Governor. I say, man of science, so this is the person you volunteered to bring here. Our King flew into a passion at the very mention of his special subject.

Antiquarian. May I ask why?

Governor. The King says there is no age of history which may be called old. It is always an eternal extension of the present.

Antiquarian. Can the front exist without the back?

Governor. What he said was: 'Time proceeds by revealing the new on his front; but the men of learning, suppressing that fact, will have it that Time ever carries the burden of the old on his back.'

[Nandini *comes in hurriedly.*]

Nandini. What is happening? Who are they?

Governor. Hallo, Nandini, is that you? I shall wear your *kunda* chain late in the evening. When three-quarters of me can hardly be seen for the dark, then perchance a flower garland might become even me.

Nandini. Look over there—what a piteous sight! Who are those people, going along with the guards, filing out from the backdoor of the King's apartments?

Governor. We call them the King's leavings.

Nandini. What does that mean?

Governor. Some day you too will know its meaning; let it be for today.

Nandini. But are these men? Have they flesh and marrow, life and soul?

Governor. Maybe they haven't.

Nandini. Had they never any?

Governor. Maybe they had.

Nandini. Where then is it all gone now?

Governor. Man of science, explain it if you can, I'm off.

[*He goes.*]

Nandini. Alas, alas! I see amongst these shadows faces that I know. Surely that is our Anup and Upamanyu?

Professor, they belong to our neighbouring village. Two brothers as tall as they were strong. They used to come and race their boats in our river on the fourteenth day of the moon in rainy June. Oh, who has brought them to this miserable plight?

See, there goes Shaklu,—in sword play he used to win the prize garland before all the others. Anu-up! Sha-klu-u! look this way; it's I, your the principle underlying all rise to greatness.

Nandini. It's a fiendish principle!

Professor. It's no use getting annoyed with a principle. Principles are neither good nor bad. That which happens *does* happen. To go against it, is to knock your head against the law of being.

Nandini. If this is the way of man's being, I refuse to *be,* I want to depart with those shadows,—show me the way.

Professor. When the time comes for showing us out, the great ones themselves will point the way. Before that, there's no such nuisance as a way at all! You see how our Antiquarian has quietly slipped off, thinking he'll fly and save himself. After going a few steps, he'll soon discover that there's a wire network stretched from post to post, from country to country.

Nandini, I see, your temper is rising. The red oleanders against your flaming cheek are beginning to look like evening storm clouds gathering for a night of terror.

Nandini [*knocking at the net window*]. Listen, listen!

Professor. Whom are you calling?

Nandini. That King of yours, shrouded in his mist of netting.

Professor. The door of the inner room has been closed. He won't hear you.

Nandini [*calling out*]. Bishu, mad brother mine!

Professor. What d'you want with *him?*

Nandini. Why hasn't he come back yet? I feel afraid.

Professor. He was with you only a little while ago.

Nandini. The Governor said he was wanted to identify Rañjan. I tried to go with him, but they wouldn't let me. Whose groaning is that?

Professor. It must be that wrestler of ours.

Nandini. What wrestler?

Professor. The world-famous Gajju, whose brother, Bhajan, had the bravado to challenge the King to a wrestling match, since when not even a thread of his loin cloth is anywhere to be seen. That put Gajju on his mettle, and he came on with great sound and fury. I told him at the outset that, if he wanted to dig in the tunnels underneath this kingdom, he was welcome,—he could at least drag on a dead and alive existence for some time. But if he wanted to make a show of heroics, that would not be tolerated for a moment.

Nandini. Does it at all make for their well-being thus to keep watch and ward over these man-traps night and day?

Professor. Well-being! There's no question of 'well' in it at all,—only 'being'. That *being* of theirs has expanded so terribly that, unless millions of men are pressed into service, who's going to support its weight? So the net is spreading farther and farther. They must exist, you see.

Nandini. Must they? If it is necessary to die in order to live like men, what harm in dying?

Professor. Again that anger, the wild cry of red oleander? It is sweet, no doubt, yet what is true is true. If it gives you pleasure to say that one must die to live, well, say so by all means; but those who say that others must die that they themselves may live,—it's only they who are actually alive. You may cry out that this shows a lack of humanity, but you forget, in your indignation, that this is what humanity itself happens to be. The tiger does not feed on the tiger, it's only man who fattens on his fellow-man.

[*The* Wrestler *totters in.*]

Nandini. Oh poor thing, see how he comes, staggering. Wrestler, lie down here. Professor, do see where he's hurt.

Professor. You won't see any outward sign of a wound.

Wrestler. All-merciful God, grant me strength once more in my life, if only for one little day!

Professor. Why, my dear fellow?

Wrestler. Just to wring that Governor's neck!

Professor. What has the Governor done to you?

Wrestler. It's he who brought about the whole thing. I never wanted to fight. Now, after egging me on, he goes about saying it's my fault.

Professor. Why, what interest had he in your fighting?

Wrestler. They only feel safe when they rob the whole world of strength. Lord of Mercy, grant that I may be able to gouge his eyes out some day, to tear asunder his lying tongue!

Nandini. How do you feel now, Wrestler?

Wrestler. Altogether hollowed out! These demons know the magic art of sucking away not only strength but hope.

If only once I could somehow,—O good God, but once,—everything is possible to Thy mercy,—if only I could fasten my teeth for once in the Governor's throat!

Nandini. Professor, help me to raise him.

Professor. That would be a crime, Nandini, according to the custom of this land.

Nandini. Wouldn't it be a crime to let the man perish?

Professor. That which there is none to punish may be a sin, but never a crime. Nandini, come away, come right away out of this. The tree spreads its root-fingers and does its grabbing underground, but there it does not bring forth its flowers. Flowers bloom on the branches which reach towards the light. My sweet Red Oleander, don't try to probe our secrets in the depths of their dust. Be for us swaying in the air above, that we may gaze upwards to see you.

There comes the Governor. He hates to see me talk to you. So I must go.

Nandini. Why is he so dead against me?

Professor. I can guess. You have touched his heart-strings. The longer it takes to tune them up, the more awful the discord meanwhile.

[*The* Professor *goes, the* Governor *comes in.*]

Nandini. Sir Governor!

Governor. Nandini, when our Gosain saw that *kunda* garland of yours in my room, both his eyes,—but here he comes— [*The* Gosain *comes in.*]

Your Holiness, accept my reverence. That garland was given to me by our Nandini here.

Gosain. Ah indeed! the gift of a pure heart! God's own white *kunda* flowers! Their beauty remains unsullied even in the hands of a man of the world. This is what gives one faith in the power of virtue, and hope for the sinners' redemption.

Nandini. Please do something for this man, Your Reverence. There's very little life left in him.

Gosain. The Governor is sure to keep him as much alive as it is necessary for him to be. But, my child, these discussions ill become your lips.

Nandini. So in this kingdom you follow some calculation in apportioning life?

Gosain. Of course,—for mortal life has its limits. Our class of people have their great burden to bear, therefore we have to claim a larger portion of life's sustenance for our share. That's according to Almighty God's own decree.

Nandini. Reverend Sir, may I know what good God has so heavily charged you to do to these people?

Gosain. The life that is unlimited gives no provocation to fight for its distribution. We Preachers have the charge of turning these people towards this unlimited life. So long as they remain content with that, we are their friends.

Nandini. Let me come over to the Headman's quarters to help you.

Wrestler. No. Don't add to my troubles, I beg of you.

[*The* Wrestler *goes.*]

Nandini. Governor, stay, tell me, whither have you taken my Bishu?

Governor. Who am I that I should take him? The wind carries off the clouds,—if you think that to be a crime, make enquiries as to who is behind the wind.

Nandini. Dear me, what an awful place! You are not men, and those you drive are not men, either,—you are winds and they are clouds!

Reverend Gosain, I am sure, *you* know where my Bishu is.

Gosain. I know, for sure, that wherever he is, it's for the best.

Nandini. For whose best?

Gosain. That you won't understand—

Oh, I say, leave off, let go of that, it's my rosary.—Hallo, Governor, what wild girl is this you have—

Governor. The girl has somehow managed to ensconce herself in a niche, safe from the laws of this land, and we can't lay hands on her. Our King himself—

Gosain. Good heavens, now she'll tear off my wrap of the Holy Name too. What unspeakable outrage!

[*The* Gosain *flies.*]

Nandini. Governor, you *must* tell me where you have taken Bishu.

Governor. They have summoned him to the court of judgement. That's all that there is to tell you. Let me go.

Nandini. Because I am a woman, you are not afraid of me? God sends His thunderbolt through His messenger, the lightning spark—that bolt I have borne here with me; it will shatter the golden spire of your mastery.

Governor. Then let me tell you the truth before I go. It's you who have dragged Bishu into danger.

Nandini. I?

Governor. Yes, you! He was so long content to be quietly burrowing away underground like a worm. It's you who taught him to spread the wings of death. O fire of the gods, you'll yet draw forth many more to their fate.—

Then at length will you and I come to our understanding, and that won't be long.

Nandini. So may it be. But tell me one thing before you go. Will you not let Rañjan come and see me?

Governor. No, never.

Nandini. Never, you say! I defy you to do your worst. This very day I am sure, absolutely sure, that he and I will meet! [Governor *goes.*]

Nandini [*knocking and tugging at the network*]. Listen, listen, King! Where's your court of judgement? Open its door to me. [Kishôr *comes in.*]

Who is that? My boy, Kishôr! Do you know where Bishu is?

Kishôr. Yes, Nandini, be ready to see him. I don't know how it was, the Chief of the Guard took a fancy to my youthfulness and yielded to my entreaties. He has consented to take him along by this path.

Nandini. Guard! Take him along? Is he then—

Kishôr. Yes, here they come.

Nandini. What! Handcuffs on your wrists? Friend of my heart, where are they taking you like that?

[Bishu *comes in under arrest.*]

Bishu. It's nothing to be anxious about!—Guards, please wait a little, let me say a few words to her.—My wild girl, my heart's joy, at last I am free.

Nandini. What do you mean, Singer of my heart? I don't understand your words.

Bishu. When I used to be afraid, and try to avoid danger at every step, I seemed to be at liberty; but that liberty was the worst form of bondage.

Nandini. What offence have you committed that they should take you away thus?

Bishu. I spoke out the truth to-day, at last.

Nandini. What if you did?

Bishu. No harm at all!

Nandini. Then why did they bind you like this?

Bishu. What harm in that either? These chains will bear witness to the truth of my freedom.

Nandini. Don't they feel ashamed of themselves to lead you along the road chained like a beast? Aren't they men too?

Bishu. They have a big beast inside them, that's why their heads are not lowered by the indignity of man, rather the inner brute's tail swells and wags with pride at man's downfall.

Nandini. O dear heart! Have they been hurting you? What are these marks on your body?

Bishu. They have whipped me, with the whips they use for their dogs. The string of that whip is made with the same thread which goes to the stringing of their Gosain's rosary. When they tell their beads they don' t remember that; but probably their God is aware of it.

Nandini. Let them bind me like that too, and take me away with you, my heart's joy! Unless I share some of your punishment I shan't be able to touch food from to-day.

Kishôr. I'm sure I can persuade them to take me in exchange for you. Let me take your place, Bishu.

Bishu. Don't be silly!

Kishôr. Punishment won't hurt me. I am young. I shall bear it with joy.

Nandini. No, no, do not talk like that.

Kishôr. Nandini, my absence has been noticed, their bloodhounds are after me. Allow me to escape the indignity awaiting me by taking shelter in a punishment I joyfully accept.

Bishu. No, it won't do for you to be caught—not for a while yet. There's work for you, dear boy, and dangerous work too. Rañjan has come. You must find him out.

Kishôr. Then I bid you farewell, Nandini. What is your message when I meet Rañjan?

Nandini. This tassel of red oleanders. [*Hands it to him*.]

[Kishôr *goes*.]

Bishu. May you both be united once again.

Nandini. That union will give me no pleasure now. I shall never be able to forget that I sent you away empty-handed. And what has that poor boy, Kishôr, got from me?

Bishu. All the treasure hidden in his heart has been revealed to him by the fire you have lighted in his life. Nandini, I remind you, it's for you to put that blue-throat's feather on Rañjan's crest.— There, do you hear them singing the harvest song?

Nandini. I do, and it wrings my heart, to tears.

Bishu. The play of the fields is ended now, and the field-master is taking the ripe corn home. Come on, Guards, let's not linger anymore. [*Sings*.]

Mow the corn of the last harvest,
bind it in sheaves.
The remainder, let it return
as dust unto the dust.

[*They go*.]

[*The* Governor *and a* Doctor *come in*.]

Doctor. I've seen him. I find the King.

Governor. My wife will be driving out to-day. The post will be changed near your village, and you must see that she's not detained.

Headman. There's a plague on the cattle of our parish, and not a single ox can be had to draw the car. Never mind, we can press the diggers into service.

Governor. You know where you have to take her? To the garden-house, where the feast of the Flag-worship is to be held.

Headman. I'll see to it at once, but let me tell you one thing before I go. That 69 Ng, whom they call mad Bishu,—it's high time to cure his madness.

Governor. Why, how does he annoy you?

Headman. Not so much by what he says or does, as by what he implies.

Governor. There's no need to worry about him any further. You understand!

Headman. Really! That's good news, indeed! Another thing. That 47 V, he's rather too friendly with 69 Ng.

Governor. I have observed that.

Headman. Your Lordship's observation is ever keen. Only, as you have to keep an eye on so many things, one or two may perchance escape your notice. For instance, there's our No. 95, a distant connection of mine by marriage, ever ready to make sandals for the feet of Your Lordship's sweeper out of his own ribs,—so irrepressibly loyal is he that even his wife hangs her head for very shame,—and yet up to now—

Governor. His name has been entered in the High Register.

Headman. Ah, then his lifelong service will at last receive its reward! The news must be broken to him gently, because he gets epileptic fits, and supposing suddenly—

Governor. All right, we'll see to that. Now be off, there's no time.

Headman. Just a word about another person,—though he's my own brother-in-law. When his mother died, my wife brought him up with her own hands; yet for my master's sake—

Governor. You can tell me about him another time. Run away now.

Headman. There comes His Honour the Deputy Governor. Please speak a word to him on my behalf. He doesn't look upon me with favour. I suspect that when 69 Ng used to enjoy the favour of free entry into the palace, he must have been saying things against me.

Governor. I assure you, he never even mentioned your name.

Headman. That's just his cleverness! What can be more damaging than to suppress the name of a man, whose name is his best asset? These schemers have their different ways. No. 33 of our parish has an incurable habit of haunting Your Lordship's private chamber. One is always afraid of his inventing goodness knows what calumnies about other people. And yet if one knew the truth about his own—

Governor. There's positively no time to-day. Get away with you, quick!

Headman. I make my salute. [*Coming back.*] Just one word more lest I forget. No. 88 of our neighbouring parish started work on a miserable pittance, and before two years are out his income has run into thousands, not to speak of extras! Your Lordship's mind is like that of the gods—a few words of hypocritical praise are enough to draw down the best of your boons.

Governor. All right, all right,—that can keep for to-morrow.

Headman. I'm not so mean as to suggest taking away the bread from his mouth. But Your Lordship should seriously consider whether it's wise to keep him on at the Treasury. Our Vishnu Dutt knows him inside out. If you send—

Governor. I shall send for him this very day. But begone,—not another word!

Headman. Your Lordship, my third son is getting to be quite a big boy. He came the other day to prostrate himself at your feet. After two days of dancing attendance outside, he had to go away without gaining admission to you. He feels it very bitterly. My daughter-in-law has made with her own hands an offering of sweet pumpkin for Your Lordship—

Governor. Oh confound you! Tell him to come day after to-morrow, he will be admitted. *Now, will you*—

[Headman *goes. The* Deputy Governor *comes in.*]

Deputy Governor. I've just sent on the dancing girls and musicians to the garden.

Governor. And that little matter about Rañjan,—how far—?

Deputy Governor. That kind of work is not in my line. The Assistant Governor has taken it upon himself to do the job. By this time his—

Governor. Does the King—?

Deputy Governor. The King can't possibly have understood. Some lie told by our men has goaded Rañjan to frenzy, and he's rushing to the usual fate of—I detest the whole business. Moreover, I don't think it right to deceive the King like this.

Governor. That responsibility is mine. Now then, that girl must be—

Deputy Governor. Don't talk of all that to me. The Headman who has been put on duty is the right man,—he doesn't stick at any dirtiness whatever.

Governor. Does that man Gosain know about this affair?

Deputy Governor. I'm sure he can guess, but he's careful not to know for certain.

Governor. What's his object?

Deputy Governor. For fear of there being no way left open for saying: 'I don't believe it.'

Governor. But what makes him take all this trouble?

Deputy Governor. Don't you see? The poor man is really two in one, clumsily joined,—Priest on the skin, Governor at the marrow. He has to take precious care to prevent the Governor part of him coming up to the surface, lest it should clash too much with his telling of beads.

Governor. He might have dropped the beads altogether.

Deputy Governor. No, for whatever his blood may be, his mind, in a sense, is really pious. If only he can tell his beads in his temple, and revel in slave-driving in his dreams, he feels happy. But for him, the true complexion of our God would appear too black. In fact, Gosain is placed here only to help our God to feel comfortable.

Governor. My friend, I see the instinct of the Ruler doesn't seem to match with the colour of your own blood, either!

Deputy Governor. There's hope still. Human blood is fast drying up. But I can't stomach your No. 321 yet. When I'm obliged to embrace him in public, no holy water seems able to wash out the impurity of his touch.

Here comes Nandini.

Governor. Come away, I don't trust you. I know the spell of Nandini has fallen on your eyes.

Deputy Governor. I know that as well as you do. But you don't seem to know that a tinge of her oleanders has got mixed with the colour of duty in *your* eyes too—that's what makes them so frightfully red.

Governor. That may be. Fortunately for us, our mind knows not its own secret. Come away. [*They go.*]

[Nandini *comes in.*]

Nandini [*knocking and pushing at the network*]. Listen, listen, listen!

[*The* Gosain *comes in.*]

Gosain. Whom are you prodding like that?

Nandini. That boa-constrictor of yours, who remains in hiding and swallows men.

Gosain. Lord, lord! When Providence wishes to destroy the small, it does so by putting big words into their little mouths.

See here, Nandini, believe me when I tell you that I aim at your welfare.

Nandini. Try some more real method of doing me good.

Gosain. Come to my sanctuary, let me chant you the Holy Name for a while.

Nandini. What have I to do with the name?

Gosain. You will gain peace of mind.

Nandini. Shame, shame on me if I do! I shall sit and wait here at the door.

Gosain. You have more faith in men than in God?

Nandini. Your God of the Flagstaff,—he will never unbend. But the man who is lost to sight behind the netting, will he also remain bound in his network for ever? Go, go. It's your trade to delude men with words, after filching away their lives. [*The* Gosain *goes.*]

[*Enter* Phágulal *and* Chandrá.]

Phágulal. Our Bishu came away with you, where is he now? Tell us the truth.

Nandini. He has been made prisoner and taken away.

Chandrá. You witch, you must have given information against him. You are their spy.

Nandini. You don't really believe that!

Chandrá. What else are you doing here?

Phágulal. Every person suspects every other person in this cursed place. Yet I have always trusted you, Nandini. In my heart I used to—However, let that pass. But to-day it looks very very strange, I must say.

Nandini. Perhaps it does. It may really be even as you say. Bishu has got into trouble for coming with me. He used to be quite safe in your company, he said so himself.

Chandrá. Then why did you decoy him away, you evil-omened creature?

Nandini. Because he said he wanted to be free.

Chandrá. A precious kind of freedom you have given him!

Nandini. I could not understand all that he said. Chandrá. Why did he tell me that freedom could only be found by plunging down to the bottom of danger?—Phágulal, how could I save him who wanted to be free from the tyranny of safety?

Chandrá. We don't understand all this. If you can't bring him back, you'll have to pay for it. I'm not to be taken in by that coquettish prettiness of yours.

Phágulal. What's the use of idle bickering? Let's gather a big crowd from the workmen's lines, and then go and smash the prison gate.

Nandini. I'll come with you.

Phágulal. What for?

Nandini. To join in the breaking.

Chandrá. As if you haven't done quite enough breaking already, you sorceress!

[Gôkul *comes in.*]

Gôkul. That witch must be burnt alive, before everything else.

Chandrá. That won't be punishment enough. First knock off that beauty of hers, with which she goes about ruining people. Weed it out of her face as the grass is weeded with a hoe.

Gôkul. That I can do. Let this hammer just have a dance on her nose tip—

Phágulal. Beware! If you dare touch her—

Nandini. Stop, Phágulal. He's coward; he wants to strike me because he's afraid of me. I don't fear his blows one bit.

Gôkul. Phágulal, you haven't come to your senses yet. You think the Governor alone is your enemy. Well, I admire a straightforward enemy. But that sweet-mouthed beauty of yours—

Nandini. Ah, so you too admire the Governor, as the mud beneath his feet admires the soles of his shoes!

Phágulal. Gôkul, the time has at length come to show your prowess, but not by fighting a girl. Come along with me. I'll show you what to fight.

[Phágulal, Chandrá, *and* Gôkul *go.*]

[*A band of* Men *come in.*]

Nandini. Where are you going, my good men?

First Man. We carry the offering for the Flag-worship.

Nandini. Have you seen Rañjan?

Second Man. I saw him once, five days ago, but not since. Ask those others who follow us.

Nandini. Who are they?

Third Man. They are bearing wine for the Governors' feast.

[*The first batch goes, another comes in.*]

Nandini. Look here, red-caps, have you seen Rañjan?

First Man. I saw him the other day at the house of Headman Sambhu.

Nandini. Where is he now?

Second Man. D'you see those men taking the ladies' dresses for the feast? Ask them. They hear a lot of things that don't reach our ears.

[*Second batch goes, a third come in.*]

Nandini. Do *you* know, my men, where they have kept Rañjan?

First Man. Hush, hush!

Nandini. I am sure you know. You *must* tell me.

Second Man. What enters by our ears doesn't come out by our mouths, that's why we are still alive. Ask one of the men who are carrying the weapons.

[*They go, others come in.*]

Nandini. Oh do stop a moment and listen to me. Tell me, where is Rañjan?

First Man. The auspicious hour draws near. It's time for the King himself to come for the Flag-worship. Ask him about it when he steps out. We only know the beginning, not the end. [*They go.*]

Nandini [*shaking the network violently*]. Open the door. The time has come.

Voice [*behind the scenes*]. But not for you. Go away from here.

Nandini. You must hear *now* what I have to say. It cannot wait for another time.

Voice. You want Rañjan, I know. I have asked the Governor to fetch him at once. But don't remain standing at the door when I come out for the worship, for then you'll run great risk.

Nandini. I have cast away all fear. You can't drive me away. Happen what may, I'm not going to move till your door is opened.

Voice. To-day's for the Flag-worship. Don't distract my mind. Get away from my door.

Nandini. The gods have all eternity for their worship, they're not pressed for time. But the sorrows of men cannot wait.

King. Deceived! These traitors have deceived me,—perdition take them! My own machine refuses my sway! Call the Governor— bring him to me handcuffed—

Nandini. King, they all say you know magic. Make him wake up for my sake.

King. My magic can only put an end to waking.—Alas! I know not how to awaken.

Nandini. Then lull me to sleep,—the same sleep! Oh, why did you work this havoc? I cannot bear it any more.

King. I have killed youth. Yes, I have indeed killed youth,—all these years, with all my strength. The curse of youth, dead, is upon me.

Nandini. Did he not take my name?

King. He did,—in such a way that every vein in my body was set on fire.

Nandini [*to* Rañjan]. My love, my brave one, here do I place this blue-throat's feather in your crest. Your victory has begun from today, and I am its bearer. Ah, here is that tassel of my flowers in his hand. Then Kishôr must have met him—

But where is he? King, where is that boy?

King. Which boy?

Nandini. The boy who brought these flowers to Rañjan.

King. That absurd little child! He came to defy me with his girlish face.

Nandini. And then? Tell me! Quick!

King. He burst himself against me, like a bubble.

Nandini. King, the Time is indeed now come!

King. Time for what?

Nandini. For the last fight between you and me.

King. But I can kill you in no time,—this instant.

Nandini. From that very instant that death of mine will go on killing you every single moment.

King. Be brave, Nandini, trust me. Make me your comrade to-day.

Nandini. What would you have me do?

King. To fight against me, but with your hand in mine. That fight has already begun. There is my flag. First I break the Flagstaff,—thus! Next it's for you to tear its banner. Let your hand unite with mine to kill me, utterly kill me. That will be my emancipation.

Guards [*rushing up*]. What are you doing, King? You dare break the Flagstaff, the holiest symbol of our divinity? The Flagstaff which has its one point piercing the heart of the earth and the other that of heaven! What a terrible sin,—on the very day of the Flag-worship! Comrades, let us go and inform our Governors. [*They run off.*]

King. A great deal of breaking remains to be done. You will come with me, Nandini?

Nandini. I will.

[Phágulal *comes in.*]

Phágulal. They won't hear of letting Bishu off. I am afraid, they'll—Who is this? The King!

Oh you wicked witch,—conspiring with the King himself! O vile deceiver!

King. What is the matter with you? What is that crowd out for?

Phágulal. To break the prison gate. We may lose our lives, but we shan't fall back.

King. Why should you fall back? I too am out for breaking. Behold the first sign—my broken Flagstaff!

Phágulal. What! This is altogether beyond us simple folk.

Be merciful, Nandini, don't deceive me. Am I to believe my eyes?

Nandini. Brother, you have set out to win death. You have left no chance for deception to touch you.

Phágulal. You too come along with us, our own Nandini!

Nandini. That is what I'm still alive for, Phágulal. I wanted to bring my Rañjan amongst you. Look there, he has come, my hero, braving death!

Phágulal. Oh, horror! Is that Rañjan lying there, silent?

Nandini. Not silent. He leaves behind him in death his conquering call. He will live again, he cannot die.

Phágulal. Ah, my Nandini, my beautiful one, was it for this you were waiting all these eager days?

Nandini. I *did* await his coming, and he *did* come. I still wait to prepare for his coming again, and he *shall* come again. Where is Chandrá?

Phágulal. She has gone with her tears and prayers to the Governor, accompanied by Gôkul. I'm afraid Gôkul is seeking to take up service with the Governor. He will betray us.

King, are you sure you don't mistake us? We are out to break your own prison, I tell you!

King. Yes, it is my *own* prison. You and I must work together, for you cannot break it alone.

Phágulal. As soon as the Governor hears of it, he will march with all his forces to prevent us.

King. Yes, my fight is against them.

Phágulal. But the soldiers will not obey you.

King. *You* will be on my side!

Phágulal. Shall we be able to win through?

King. We shall at least be able to die! At last I have found the meaning of death. I am saved!

Phágulal. King, do you hear the tumult?

King. There comes the Governor with his troops. How could he be so quick about it? He must have been prepared beforehand. They have used my own power against me.

Phágulal. My men have not yet turned up.

King. They will never come. The Governor is sure to get round them.

Nandini. I had my last hope that they would bring my Bishu to me. Will that never be?

King. No hope of that, I'm afraid.

Phágulal. Then come along, Nandini, let us take you to a safe place first. The Governor will see red, if he but catches sight of you.

Nandini. You want to banish me into the solitary exile of safety? [*Calling out*] Governor! Governor!—He has swung up my garland of *kunda* flowers on his spear-head. I will dye that garland the colour of my oleanders with my heart's blood.—Governor! He has seen me! Victory to Rañjan! [*Runs off*.]

King [*calling after her*]. Nandini! [*Follows her*.]

[*The* Professor *comes in*.]

Phágulal. Where are *you* hurrying to, Professor?

Professor. Some one said that the King has at last had tidings of the secret of Life, and has gone off in quest of it. I have thrown away my books to follow him.

Phágulal. The King has just gone off to his death. He has heard Nandini's call.

Professor. The network is torn to shreds! Where is Nandini?

Phágulal. She has gone before them all. We can't reach her any more.

Professor. It is only now that we shall reach her. She won't evade us any longer.

[Professor *rushes out,* Bishu *comes in.*]

Bishu. Phágulal, where is Nandini?

Phágulal. How did you get here?

Bishu. Our workmen have broken into the prison. There they are,—running off to fight. I came to look for Nandini. Where is she?

Phágulal. She has gone in advance of us all.

Bishu. Where?

Phágulal. To the last freedom. Bishu, do you see who is lying there?

Bishu. Rañjan!

Phágulal. You see the red streak?

Bishu. I understand,—then red marriage.

Phágulal. They are united.

Bishu. Now it is for me to take my last lonely journey.—Perhaps we may meet.—Perhaps she may want me to sing.—My mad girl, O my mad girl!—

Come, brother, on to the fight!

Phágulal. To the fight! Victory to Nandini!

Bishu. Victory to Nandini!

Phágulal. Here is her wristlet of red oleanders. She has bared her arm to-day,—and left us.

Bishu. Once I told her I would not take anything from her hand. I break my word and take this. Come along!

[*They go.*]

[*Song in the distance.*]

Hark 'tis Autumn calling,—
Come, O come away!
The earth's mantle of dust is filled with ripe corn!
O the joy! the joy!

The Crown

ACT I SCENE 1

The First Trial

The Tournament

Chamber of Ishah Khan, *the General of Tipperah.*

[Ishah Khan *is seen engaged in cleaning his weapons, while the youngest Prince of Tipperah,* Rajdhar, *is speaking to him.*]

Rajdhar. I warn you once more, General, do not call me by my name.

Ishah Khan. Then how must I call you,—by pulling your ear?

Rajdhar. If you don't pay me respect, I shall repay you in your own coin.

Ishah Khan. If my respect were at your disposal, I would go and sell it in the market for a brass farthing. I can better look after my own position myself.

Rajdhar. If you wish to do that, then don't call me by my name in future.

Ishah Khan. Indeed!

Rajdhar. Yes!

Ishah Khan [*laughs aloud*]. Then how am I to call Your Highness? Shall I call you my Lord,—or my Master, or your Excellency?

Rajdhar. I may be your pupil,—yet I am a Prince! You must not forget that.

Ishah Khan. If I did forget it, then it was because you made it hard for me to remember.

Rajdhar. You are also making it hard for me to remember that you are my Tutor.

Ishah Khan. Silence! Have done!

[*Enter the Second Prince,* Indrakumar.]

Indrakumar. Khan Sahib, what is all this noise?

Ishah Khan. Listen to this! This young man here, who is the youngest of you all, imagines that unless he is called King of Kings and Emperor of Emperors his honour will be insulted. He is in such desperate straits about it!

Indrakumar. Really? [*Laughs aloud.*]

Rajdhar. Stop that laughing.

Indrakumar. Pray how must we call you?—Your Majesty [*Laughs.*]—Your Imperial Highness? [*Laughs again.*]

Rajdhar. I tell you again,—Silence.

Indrakumar. Your Highness!—[*Laughs.*] Oh, I can't contain myself—Your Majesty!—[*Laughs out loud.*] Oh, I shall break my sides with laughter.

Rajdhar. Fool!

Indrakumar. Keep your temper, Rajdhar! Keep your wisdom to yourself! I have no wish to deprive you of any of it.

Ishah Khan. His wisdom of late has grown too exalted.

Indrakumar. Yes, Khan Sahib, it has grown quite out of reach. It would take a ladder to climb up to it.

[*Enter* Maharajah Amar, *of Tipperah, and the* Jubaraj, (*the Heir Apparent*) Chandrakumar *with attendants.*]

Rajdhar. Sire, I have a complaint to make to you.

Maharajah. What is it, Rajdhar?

Rajdhar. In spite of repeated warnings, Ishah Khan takes every occasion to insult me, I ask for your protection.

Ishah Khan. The source of your insult is not any one outside; it is in yourself. There are other princes besides you. They always bear in mind that I am their tutor, and I also know that they are my pupils, and so there arises no question of honour or insult.

Maharajah. General, the Princes are grown up. We should be careful to pay them proper respect.

Ishah Khan. Maharajah, time was, when you yourself were my pupil. I cannot treat these Princes with greater respect that I did you.

Rajdhar. I have nothing to say about others but—

Ishah Khan. Child, silence! I am talking to your father.—Maharajah, pardon me if I forget myself! I am obliged to tell you that this youngest scion of your House may in time become expert in wielding his pen, but he will never take to the sword. [*Pointing to the* Jubaraj *and* second prince] Look at these, Maharajah,—those are true Princes.

Maharajah. Rajdhar, have you failed to satisfy your Tutor in your bouts at arms?

Rajdhar. If that is true, then my fate is to blame rather than my skill. I ask you to hold a Tournament in archery tomorrow.

Maharajah. Very well. Tomorrow we have leisure, and we shall test your skill. Whoever wins in the Tournament shall have this jewelled sword of mine.

[Maharajah *departs.*]

Ishah Khan. Well said, Rajdhar, well spoken! For once you have spoken as the son of a Kshatriya should speak. Even if you are defeated, it will not be inglorious. Victory and defeat are in the hands of Allah.

Rajdhar. Have done, General, keep your praises for the other Princes. If I could do without them so long, I can do without them now.

Jubaraj. Don't be angry with the General. If you win in this Tournament, then the reward you get from the Khan Sahib will exceed that from all others.

Rajdhar. Tonight is the full moon. What do you say to going out to shoot tigers at the place where they come to drink at the Gomati River?

Jubaraj. Excellent.

Indrakumar. This is astonishing!—Rajdhar shooting tigers! Hunting is not in his line.

Ishah Khan. Not in his line? Why he hunts the greater game! There is scarcely a single two footed animal in the King's Court who has never been snared in his noose.

Jubaraj. General your sword and your tongue are both terribly keen. They never return without piercing the heart.

Rajdhar. Don't pity me, Jubaraj! Let Khan Sahib whet his tongue into a knife, if he likes. It will never leave a scratch in my heart.

Indrakumar. Who can reach your heart? That is difficult indeed.

Jubaraj. Indrakumar, you are getting into the habit of hurting Rajdhar at every turn.

Rajdhar. And I have got into the habit of not getting hurt by anything he says.

Indrakumar. Have you really made up your mind to go out hunting?

Jubaraj. But, Indra Kumar, it is quite useless for us to go hunting when you are one of the party, because then for us it becomes a ridiculously vegetarian affair! While you get all the big game in the forest, we have to be content to fill our hunting bags with gourds.

Ishah Khan [*slapping* Indrakumar *on the back*]. The Jubaraj is right, who can compete with you?

Indrakumar [*to the* Jubaraj]. No. no. Joking apart, you must come with us.

Jubaraj. Very well, I will come.

[*They go out. Enter* Attendants.]

1st Attendant. It sounds suspicious, Our youngest Prince is no adept in archery. Everyone knows that. Yet, what is the meaning of his challenging our second Prince?

2nd Attendant. Some reach their aim with arrows, and some with cunning.

1st Attendant. Yes, that is the thing to be feared. When it is a trial of skill in the Tournament, if cunning is used instead of archery, it is an evil thing.

3rd Attendant. Look here, Bansi, let them use archery or cunning just as they like—but you had better keep a wise tongue in your head, if you want to live quietly, that's my advice.

2nd Attendant. Yet, Bonomali is quite right. Bansi, you become quite wild in your talk when you speak of the youngest Prince. It is not for us to judge the respective merits of the Princes,—only we can pray that our Jubaraj may live long, that our second Prince may guard him from all mischief, and as for our youngest Prince, let us keep silence.

1st Attendant. Our second Prince is absolutely simple. He has neither fear in his mind, nor crookedness in his nature. Our fear is that the one, whom we need not name, may lead him into trouble at any moment.

2nd Attendant. Ah! There they come. Let us go away.

1st Attendant. His cousin Dhurandhar comes with him. It's like the evil planet, Mars, in conjunction with the planet Saturn.

[*They go out. Enter* Rajdhar *and* Dhurandhar.]

Rajdhar. It is intolerable.

Dhurandhar. I see no sign of your tolerance wearing out. This friction has been going on almost from your birth, but it is not yet clear that the situation has become intolerable.

Rajdhar. It will be quite clear, when the time comes. I am going to get my chance. In this Tournament I shall hit the mark.

Dhurandhar. Where is your target? In Indrakumar's breast?

Rajdhar. Not his breast, but his heart. This time I shall win and pierce his pride through and through.

Dhurandhar. You expect to beat Indrakumar, and call this your opportunity?

Rajdhar. Opportunity is not always on the point of the arrow. But you must help me.

Dhurandhar. I have been helping you all along, but it has led to no result.

Rajdhar. Results ripen in time. You must get access to Indrakumar's room, where he keeps his arrows, and substitute my arrows for his in his quiver. With this change of arrows will come a change of destinies.

Dhurandhar. That is quite a simple thing to do, but what about my life? That cannot be exchanged.

Rajdhar. Have no fear. I am behind you.

Dhurandhar. You may be there behind me, but fear is there also. Do you remember when you desired to have the bow with the silver chasing belonging to Indrakumar? I got it for you and kept it hidden in your room, but when it was discovered at last, Indrakumar contemptuously made it a present to you but the insult which came to my share I shall never forget all my life. You were there also behind me,—very much behind.

Rajdhar. The time has come for you to take your own vengeance.

Dhurandhar. Yes, the time may have come, but it is difficult to divine for whom it has arrived. The best thing for weak people is to have a strong digestion for insults. Revenge may be too dangerous a luxury.

[*They go out talking*.]

ACT I SCENE 2

Door of Indrakumar's *weapon-room*.

[*Enter* Indrakumar *and* Pratap, *an attendant*.]

Indrakumar. What is it, Pratap? Why have you called me here.

Pratap. Her highness asked me to tell you that a living weapon has entered your room by some chance or other. One should make due investigation about its nature.

Indrakumar. What do you say, Pratap? Does such a thing happen even in this Iron Age?

Pratap. Yes, Prince. Only in the Iron Age can such a thing be made possible. Open the door and you will understand everything.

Indrakumar. Indeed, I hear footsteps inside!

[*The door is opened and* Rajdhar *comes out*.]

What is this, Rajdhar? [*Laughs*.] Has any stupid servant of mine mistaken you for some weapon? [*Laughs loudly*.]

Rajdhar. My sister-in-law played practical joke on me and kept me captive.

Indrakumar. This is not a room for dull, ordinary jokes. The jokes kept here are uncommonly sharp.

Rajdhar. I found out that most of my own arrows were rusty and not fit of the shooting party tonight. I have sent them to be cleaned for tomorrow's Tournament and that is why I came to borrow arrows from our sister-in-law.

Indrakumar. Is that why she has lent you the whole room? [*Laughs aloud*.]

Rajdhar [*aside*]. You may have your laugh now, but this joke will bring me my share of the laughter,—but not now.... I take me leave. I am not going out to the shooting party tonight. [*He goes out*.]

Pratap. I do not think, Sir, it was wise to jest with our youngest Prince.

[*They go out together*.]

ACT I SCENE 3

The Palace of Tourney.

[*Enter the royal princes,* Ishah Khan *and others*.]

Indrakumar [*to the* Jubaraj]. You must win. Otherwise it won't do!

Jubaraj. Who can say it won't do? Even if my arrow misses its mark, the world will go on just as it did before; and if it doesn't, yet I do not see any chance of my winning?

Indrakumar. If you miss your aim, then I shall miss mine on purpose.

Jubaraj. Don't be childish. You must keep up the reputation of your Tutor.

Ishah Khan. Jubaraj the time has come. Take your bow. Aim carefully. Steady! Now!

[*The* Jubaraj *shoots*.]

Ishah Khan. Missed!

Jubaraj. I fixed my mind, but I failed to fix my arrow.

Indrakumar. I can't believe it; If you had put your mind into it, I am sure you would have won. It gives me real pain when I find that by sheer apathy you miss your chance.

Ishah Khan. Do you know why your brother's intelligence does not shine at the point of an arrow. It is because it is blunt.

Indrakumar. General, you do him an injustice.

Ishah Khan [*to* Rajdhar]. Prince, now it is your turn. Maharajah, watch.

Rajdhar. Indrakumar must precede me.

Ishah Khan [*angrily*]. Do what I tell you.

[Rajdhar *shoots*.]

Ishah Khan. Missed!

Jubaraj. Rajdhar, you have just missed by a hair's breadth.

Rajdhar [*excitedly*]. No. I have not missed! You cannot see it plainly at this distance.

Jubaraj. No, Rajdhar, you are mistaken. Your arrow has not hit the mark.

Rajdhar. You have a prejudice against me, that is why you say it. We shall see when we examine at close quarters.

[Indrakumar *takes up his bow*.]

Jubaraj. I am useless. But do not be vexed with me, Indrakumar, for that. If your arrow misses its aim, then it will pierce my heart,—be sure of that.

[Indrakumar *shoots*.]

The Spectators. Victory to Indrakumar!

Ishah Khan. My son, may Allah give you long life. Maharajah, Indrakumar has won the prize.

Rajdhar. No, Sir! The prize is mine. It is my arrow that pierced the mark.

Maharajah. No, that cannot be.

Rajdhar. General, go and examine and see whose arrow it is that is in the mark.

Ishah Khan. I will go.

[*He comes back with the arrow.*]

Ishah Khan [*to* Indrakumar] I am an old man. Is it possible that I read the letters wrongly? The name, engraven on this arrow, seems to be that of Rajdhar.

Indrakumar. Yes, it is his name.

Maharajah. Let me see. Well,—how is it we all made the same mistake?

Rajdhar. This mistake did not start from today; it has been going on for a long while.

Ishah Khan. I do not understand.

Indrakumar. But I do.

Rajdhar. Maharajah, Give judgment.

Indrakumar [*aside to* Rajdhar]. You ask for judgment! If judgment is visited upon you, your head will be bowed to the dust. But I shall not speak a word. God will judge you.

Ishah Khan. What is the matter? There is some mystery behind it.—It is as difficult to believe that stones float in water and monkeys sink [sing]. Indrakumar, tell me truly, has there been no misplacement of arrows in the quiver?

Rajdhar. Never! Examine that for yourself.

Ishah Khan [*examining*]. Yes, the quivers are all right. Do you know if any one had access to your weapon-room lately?

Indrakumar. General, let the subject drop.

Ishah Khan. Then you accept defeat?

Indrakumar. Yes.

Ishah Khan. Well done, lad, I always felt that there was some wrong somewhere. But it remains obscure. Unless we have another Tournament it will not clear up.

Rajdhar. There is no other wrong, except my winning. But I am not going to put up with the insult of a second trial. If you think it was unfair for me to win, let the prize go to Indrakumar. I refuse to take it.

Maharajah. To that I cannot agree. When the arrow bears your name I am bound to give the prize to you. Here is the sword.

Rajdhar. I take it, with all due respect. But since I find that it offends every one, I give up my sword to Indrakumar.

[*He holds it out to* Indrakumar. Indrakumar *flings it to the ground.*]

Indrakumar. Who is going to take a prize from your hand?

Ishah Khan [*taking hold of Indrakumar's hand*]. Indrakumar! How dare you insult the Maharajah, by throwing his sword on the ground. You must be punished for this.

Indrakumar [*snatching his hand away*]. Old man! Don't touch me.

Ishah Khan. My son! You forget yourself.

Indrakumar. General, forgive me. I forgot myself. Punish me.

Jubaraj. Peace, let us return.

Indrakumar [*making obeisance to* Maharajah]. Father, pardon me for my insolence. To-day my defeat has been complete.

Ishah Khan. Maharajah, I have another request to make to you. This Tournament is over but that is mere play. Let a trail at arms be held in the proper field.

Maharajah. What field is that for Indrakumar, General?

Ishah Khan. Your intention was to fight against the Rajah of Arakan. The soldiers are ready. Let our Princes take part in this fight.

Maharajah. That is well said. I have heard that the Rajah of Arakan has come very near to the boundaries of Chittagong. He had, a while ago, repeated lessons. But the fool was never contented; nor will he be, until he has his final lesson in death. What do you say, children? Are you ready to test your manhood on the battle-field?

Indrakumar. Yes, I am; and I am sure that the Jubaraj will come also.

Rajdhar. And do you suppose that I shall remain behind?

Maharajah. Ishah Khan, do you lead these Princes to the field, and may heaven protect them!

ACT II

The Second Trial

The Battle Field

SCENE 1

Rajdhar's Camp

[*Enter* Rajdhar *and* Dhurandhar.]

Dhurandhar. You say that you will remain apart with your five thousand soldiers.

Rajdhar. Yes. I sent this proposal to Ishah Khan.

Dhurandhar. I know that, because I was present there, and they had a long talk about it.

Rajdhar. What they say?

Dhurandhar. At the very outset Indrakumar laughed aloud. He said 'Rajdhar has his own peculiar way of fighting; his warfare takes place far away from the battle-field.'

Rajdhar. Well, he was right. Thou who fight in the field are mere labourers. He who can fight from a distance is the real warrior.

Dhurandhar. You know how little he trusts you. If you go near to touch his feet he suspects that you are going to steal his shoes. Ishah Khan said,—'It is nothing very wonderful for Rajdhar to wish to be far away from battle-field; but I do not like his keeping those five thousand soldiers to himself.'

Rajdhar. Did the Jubaraj say nothing?

Dhurandhar. The Jubaraj! God has not spared him even that one spark of intelligence which is required to suspect anybody. Even you he can trust!

Rajdhar. Be careful what you say, Dhurandhar. You must not talk about the Jubaraj like that.

Dhurandhar. I understand. You have a tender spot somewhere, which I forget now and then. However, the Jubaraj said,—'No, you are doing an injustice to Rajdhar. His proposal seems to me to be a wise one. If any crisis comes in the war he will be able to help us with his reserves.'—Ishah Khan only gave his consent, after being induced to do so by the Jubaraj,—though, even then, he had his misgivings. However, I do not fully understand your intention of keeping aloof.

Rajdhar. It is because I do not see any profit in joining with them in this battle; because in case of victory no one would give me the least credit for it.

Dhurandhar. But yet, by some mistake perhaps, people may mention you; while, if you are absent, you will get no credit whether they win or lose.

Rajdhar. But I tell you, I shall win!

[*Enters* Messenger.]

Rajdhar. What is the news.

Messenger. The battle is going on. But our side has not yet been able to pierce the enemy's line. The sun is about to set and I expect that the battle will close for the day.

[*Enters* Second Messenger.]

Rajdhar. Who are you?

Second Messenger. My name is Bhola [Byomkesh]. The Jubaraj sent me about three hours ago: but, because you have moved from the place where you had your camp, it has taken all this time to find you out.

Rajdhar. What is his wish?

Second Messenger. The fight has become very hard indeed. Prince Indrakumar, with his cavalry, had attacked the enemy from the North. If he had had a little more time he could easily have driven them to the brink of the river.

Rajdhar [*somewhat sarcastically*]. Really! What is the use of guessing what might have happened, if he had had a little more time? The important thing seems to be that he never had the time.

Second Messenger. When the enemy was very nearly wavering Indrakumar heard that the Jubaraj was in difficulties, surrounded by the enemy, while Ishah Khan was engaged in some other part of the field. When Ishah Khan learnt this he said, 'I have not come here to save the Jubaraj but to win the battle. I cannot stir from this place.'

Rajdhar. Then, is the Jubaraj—

Second Messenger. No, he is out of danger. Indrakumar went to his help and because of that things have gone wrong. Messengers have been sent out in all directions to search for you. If you do not come to our help, the battle will be lost.

Rajdhar. I shall not delay.

Dhurandhar. Are you going to move forward?

[*The two* Messengers *depart.*]

Rajdhar. Yes but in another direction.

Dhurandhar. Do you mean towards home?

Rajdhar. Have you also taken your lesson in sarcasm from Ishah Khan? Let those who will show their bravery, but if any one retires home victorious, it will be myself. Dhurandhar, go and see that all the lights are extinguished in my camp.

Dhurandhar. Tell me frankly what is your intention. If you distrust me and I distrust you,—then, for us two there will remain no place in this wide world.

Rajdhar. I shall secretly cross the river with my soldiers under cover of darkness. I want to surprise the Rajah of Arakan in his camp and capture him.

Dhurandhar. But how can you manage to cross without any landing-place?

Rajdhar. I have reconnoitred. The sun has set; the moon will rise at about one o'clock at night and we must finish our work before that. Time is short; we must get ready.

ACT II SCENE 2

Ishah Khan's Camp

[*Enter* Indrakumar *and* Ishah Khan.]

Indrakumar. General, do not be angry with the Jubaraj. Let our soldiers take rest tonight. Tomorrow we shall win.

Ishah Khan. Indrakumar, you ought to understand that a fire must be put out without delay. If you give it time to spread, it may get beyond control. We should have won the battle today, but your brother like a fool entangled himself for nothing and ruined everything.

Indrakumar. Why do you say 'like a fool'. Why don't you say 'like a brave man'. With only a handful of soldiers, he—

Ishah Khan. He got into a place where only fools can go.

Indrakumar. No! Only the bravest would dare to enter there—

Ishah Khan. Very well, let it be so. Let us say that only a brave man, who is a fool withal, could get into that situation.

Indrakumar. But that did not interfere with your plans.

Ishah Khan. Yes it did! because all our soldiers got anxious and lost heart. We have not got a single man in our army who could remain unmoved at the news of any danger coming to the Jubaraj.

Indrakumar. But, General, what is the news about Rajdhar.

Ishah Khan. I have sent messengers in all directions but he cannot be found.

Indrakumar [*laughs*]. He must have run away.

Ishah Khan. It is no laughing matter.

Indrakumar. Well, I confess, I feel glad. I could never bear it,—to share our fame with him when we have won, though he did nothing to help us. It is a good thing that he has fled. This time, in the trial of the battle-field cunning would not—

Ishah Khan. You never told me what really happened at the Tournament.

Indrakumar. Don't ask me, General. I own that I was defeated.

ACT II SCENE 3

Camp of the Rajah of Arakan

[*Enter Rajah of* Arakan *and* Rajdhar.]

Arakan. Prince, it will not profit you keep me captive.

Rajdhar. Why, Sire? To gain you is the greatest profit of this war.

Arakan. This will not end the war. My brother, Hamchu, is still living. The soldiers will crown him, and the battle will continue.

Rajdhar. I will set you free; but your freedom must have its price.

Arakan. That I know. I am willing to sign the conditions of peace, acknowledging my defeat to you.

Rajdhar. No mere signing will do, Rajah, I must have some tangible proofs of your defeat to take home.

Arakan. You shall have five hundred Burmese horses from me and three elephants.

Rajdhar. No, I must take your royal crown.

Arakan. You may take my crown, but understand that along with my crown you are taking away the undying enmity of Arakan's royal house. So long as this crown remains with you there will be no peace.

Rajdhar. Peace we do not desire, Rajah. We are Kshatriyas.— One duty still remains to be done. Send a letter signed by yourself to the battle-field, commanding your General to stop the battle.

ACT II SCENE 4

The Field of Battle

[*The* Jubaraj *and* Indrakumar.]

Jubaraj. It is difficult to know which side is going to win. It seems to me that our soldiers are still despondent. They are not putting forth all their strength. Where is Ishah Khan?

Indrakumar. You can see his flag in the East.

Jubaraj. Why do you follow me today? I think you ought to go to the North.

Indrakumar. No, this is my proper place.

Jubaraj. Indrakumar, you are trying to save your brother from committing any folly. You cannot bear that the General should blame me for another blunder. But you must understand that there are limitations even to my foolishness, and possibly I shall be able to act with more circumspection today. But look—what is that?—It doesn't seem to be right! Our soldiers are already beginning to waver on the left. They may take to flight. Indrakumar, go and try to hold them. Don't be afraid about my safety. But what!— What is this? What can be the meaning of it all?

Indrakumar. I cannot understand why the enemy should stop the fight so suddenly.

Jubaraj. They have hoisted the flag of peace. But there was no cause for this, for they have been winning up to now.

[*Enters* Messenger.]

Messenger. Sire, the enemy has stopped the battle.

Jubaraj. For what reason?

Messenger. We do not know the reason, but we have heard that the Rajah of Arakan has sent word that he will no longer fight with us.

Jubaraj. That is good news! But there is something that pains me.

Indrakumar. What?

Jubaraj. Why did Rajdhar keep away with his soldiers? If only he were by our side then, we three brothers would have held the Festival of Victory together. His absence from us leaves a great gap in our glory.

Indrakumar. What harm is there, if he has fled, without claiming his share in the battle?

Jubaraj. The General is coming this way riding on his horse.

[*Enters* Ishah Khan.]

Indrakumar. General, why did the enemy stop so suddenly. Have you got the news?

Ishah Khan. Yes! Rajdhar has captured the Rajah of Arakan!

Indrakumar. Rajdhar! That can't be true!

Ishah Khan. Sometimes things, that ought to have been false, become true. I find that Allah's messengers occasionally go to sleep and Satan takes that opportunity to falsify the accounts.

Indrakumar. But could ever Satan help Rajdhar to win?

Ishah Khan. Don't you remember that Tournament—how the Devil helped him. The same Devil has helped him in this battle.

Jubaraj. General, do not be angry with Rajdhar if he has won! It is our victory. But when did it happen?

Ishah Khan. Yesterday, when we had retired from the field, in the evening he secretly crossed the river and captured the Rajah of Arakan in his camp. I had sent word to him to get ready to join us. But he had already shifted his place and had disobeyed my orders.

Indrakumar. Intolerable! He ought to be punished for this.

Ishah Khan. Not only so, but he has drawn up a peace document on his own initiative, without waiting for the Jubaraj!

Indrakumar. He must be punished for that!

Ishah Khan. Do explain this very simple matter to your elder brother.

[*Enters* Rajdhar.]

Indrakumar. Rajdhar, you have displayed cowardice!

Rajdhar. I did not come here to display my bravery like you by spoiling the battle. I came to win it.

Indrakumar. You won the battle! You won It! You have made the Goddess of Victory blush.

Rajdhar. Yes, blush with the shyness of love. This is the sign that she has accepted me. [*Holds up the crown.*]

Indrakumar. Whose crown is that?

Rajdhar. It is mine. It is the prize that I have got in this war.

Indrakumar. You who kept away from the battle,—a prize for you! No! This crown is for the Jubaraj.

Jubaraj. Rajdhar is right. The crown belongs to him.

Ishah Khan. He who shrank away from my command in the dark can never claim the prize.

Rajdhar. I should like to know, if I had not been here, what kind of a crown would have awaited you by this time and where you would all be?

Indrakumar. Wherever we might be, it is certain that we should not have kept hiding!

Jubaraj. Indrakumar, you are unjust. The truth is that Rajdhar had not been here, we should be in danger today.

Indrakumar. Danger! No danger whatever!—Danger there was, because he kept away our soldiers. If Rajdhar had not been here, I would have got this crown fighting honestly and openly,—He has stolen it like a thief. And then, further, I would have brought this crown to you. I would never have claimed it for myself.

Jubaraj. Rajdhar, you have won the victory today. Let me crown you.

Indrakumar [*with a choking voice*]. You—you crown *him*! You crown Rajdhar because he was dishonoured his knighthood. And I,—I, who was ready to sacrifice my life to save you, never get a single word of praise from you. Oh, that I should live to hear you say that if Rajdhar had not been there, nobody could have helped you!

Jubaraj. Indrakumar, I never spoke of my own danger.

Indrakumar. Enough, enough! Now that you have got such a fine ally on your side, you have no need of me, and I depart.

Jubaraj. Brother, you are again forgetting yourself—

Indrakumar. It is a disgrace to remain, where one is not needed.

[*He goes away.*]

Ishah Khan. Jubaraj, you have no right to offer this crown to anybody. I am the General in this battle, It is at my disposal.

[*He is about to put it on the* Jubaraj's *head.*]

Jubaraj. No, I cannot accept this.

Ishah Khan. Then no one else must have the crown: let it go into the river. Rajdhar has violated the laws of war and he deserved punishment.

[*Throws the crown into the river.*]

Rajdhar. Brother, you are my witness. I shall never forget this.

Jubaraj. Do you think that this is the one fact to be remembered above all others? If the crown has disappeared in the water let all shame attached to it disappear at the same moment. Do you on your part forget what you must, and let us forget what we should. Let me go and see if Indrakumar has left in anger.

[Ishah Khan *and* Jubaraj *go out.*]

ACT II SCENE 5

[*Enters* Dhurandhar.]

Rajdhar. Dhurandhar, I will offer as a sacrifice this my victor to the River, Karnafuli where my crown has vanished.

Dhurandhar. Do you mean to be defeated again?

Rajdhar. Yes, I will win through my defeat. I shall not return home till I bring Indrakumar's pride to the dust. He would not accept victory at my hands; let me see if he can earn it himself.

Dhurandhar. Don't be too certain. He may win by chance.—It is no use being angry with me for telling the truth. Indrakumar knows the art of warfare.

Rajdhar. We shall argue that out later. Meanwhile you have to do me a service. Arakan is going to start for his own country tomorrow morning. As long as he is on this side of the Chittagong boundary, all his officers will remain hostages in my camp. You have to take a message of mine to him tonight.

Dhurandhar. What message?

Rajdhar. Tell him that I have been insulted, and therefore I have seceded. I will pretend that I am taking my departure home with my five thousand soldiers. Indrakumar has already left in a fit of passion. The soldiers are getting ready to go home, knowing that the battle is over. If the Rajah of Arakan takes this opportunity to attack them, then Chittagong will be defeated.

Dhurandhar. Yes, they will be defeated,—but what then? If you must set fire to other people's houses, take care of your own.

Rajdhar. I have never been suspected of being a fool. So I need no advice from you.

ACT II SCENE 6

The Field of Battle

[*Enter* Ishah Khan *and* Jubaraj.]

Ishah Khan. Jubaraj, call upon Allah. The times are difficult.

Jubaraj. Why, Khan Sahib, when Allah wills it, it is neither difficult to live nor to die.

Ishah Khan. Because the Maharajah was confident in my strength he put you in my charge and only that troubles me. Jubaraj, try to save yourself and leave the battle to me.

Jubaraj. My tutor, this advice does not become you,—and further, the roads are all closed. Death's opportunity has become an easier one than that of flight.

Ishah Khan. Jubaraj, a fire is burning in my heart. The one regret that rankles in my mind is this, that I shall probably not live to punish Indrakumar for having deserted us.

Jubaraj. If you do not live, General, his punishment will be all the greater. He loves you as his Father.

Ishah Khan. Allah! That is true!—Jubaraj, I know that I shall not have time, but if you have the opportunity, tell him that if Ishah Khan had lived, he would have punished him; but he forgives him before he dies. No more! The time is up. I take my leave. Let me embrace you! I leave you in the hands of Allah. He will save you.

Jubaraj. Khan Sahib, I ask for your forgiveness for any wrong I might have done you.

ACT III SCENE 1

The Reward

The Battle-field

[*Enter* Soldiers.]

1st Soldier. Is it true?

2nd Soldier. Yes, that is what I have heard.

1st Soldier. What a terrible misfortune!

[*They go out. Another group enters.*]

1st Soldier. Who told you?

2nd Soldier. Our Umesh.

3rd Soldier. It stunned me completely and I could not ask him all the details.

[*They go out. A third group enters.*]

1st Soldier. We have seen his elephant, but it had not howdah and mahut. It is wandering about wildly without its master.

2nd Soldier. We are in the same condition. Has no one seen where he has fallen?

1st Soldier. No, nobody seems to know it.

2nd Soldier. But our Shibu said that when the arrow struck the Jubaraj, the driver was running away with the elephant and the driver got killed. After the Jubaraj was struck with the arrow the mahut tried to drive the elephant out of the battle, and then the driver himself got killed, and after that nobody knows where the Jubaraj fell.

[*They go out. Enter a fourth group.*]

1st Soldier. After this calamity, is there no one who can take this news to Prince Indrakumar?

2nd Soldier. Yes, messengers have been sent, but we don't know if they have found him.

3rd Soldier. Has not Prince Rajdhar heard this news?

2nd Soldier. I think he has started for Tipperah. Surely he would have come back to help the Jubaraj, if he had known it.

1st Soldier. How can we return home?

3rd Soldier. Why return?—I shall die.

[*Enters a* Man.]

Man. Why, what are you doing? Come and let us seek him.

1st Soldier. Let us go in different directions. [*Exeunt*.]

ACT III SCENE 2

[*Enter* Indrakumar *and a* Soldier.]

Indrakumar. Where, where,—where is my brother?

Soldier. We are seeking for him.

Indrakumar. And where is Ishah Khan?

Soldier. To-day, before the fourth watch, the Jubaraj with his own hand heaped earth on the grave of Ishah Khan and his own blood was mingled with that earth.

Indrakumar. Oh, shame, shame, shame to my anger! My brother, will you not grant me one moment to ask your forgiveness.

[*Enters* 2nd Soldier.]

2nd Soldier. Prince, come this way, we have found him.

Indrakumar. Where?

2nd Soldier. On the bank of the Karnaphuli river, under that *Arjun* tree.

Indrakumar. Tell me truly, is he still— [*They go out*.]

ACT III SCENE 3

On the bank of the Karnaphuli

Jubaraj. Move that branch aside a little, let me see the moon. Ah!—Nobody near me?—Is that the shadow of the tree? Or is it the shadow of death?—I can still hear the mumur of the water. Is that the last farewell greeting of the earth to me? Indrakumar, my darling brother, are you still keeping away in anger?

[*Enters* Indrakumar.]

Indrakumar. My brother!

Jubaraj. Ah, what peace! I knew you would come, and that kept me alive so long! You parted from me in anger, and I could not die without seeing you.

King and Rebel

King and Rebel Rajen *and* Hem

I am your King.

Indeed! Why should you be our King?

Because I am bigger than all of you.

You may be the biggest but certainly you are not the strongest.

Am I not? Then let us fight.

All right. Come on!

I'll smash your head.

And I will break your jaw.

I will flatten your nose.

And I will knock out your teeth.

If you value your life don't dare deny it!

If you do you will have to repent.

If these are your sentiments, of course I will not deny it.

You are a brave fellow!

We admire your courage.

Yes, you are a worthy enemy.

It will be a real pleasure to fight you.

Come, soldiers, let us prepare for this great war. Long live our King Rajen! May his enemies he confounded and victory follow his banner!

ACT II SCENE 2

Let all know that I am made Chief Justice by His Majesty King Rajen. Long live His Majesty!

Long live King Rajen!

Now I am going to hold court. Policemen!

Yes, My Lord!

Bring the prisoners before me one by one

Here is Jadu, prisoner number one.

What has he done?

He ate Bhola's lunch when Bhola was at his lessons.

Prisoner number one!

Yes, My Lord!

Did you eat Bhola's lunch without asking his leave?

Yes, My Lord!

What punishment should you have?

Let Bhola try to eat my lunch without asking me.

Bhola do you agree to this?

Yes, My Lord, I agree.

Then you may leave this court. Policemen!

Yes, My Lord!

Bring up prisoner number 2.

Here he is.

Number 2, what have you done?

I tickled Madhu's nose when he was asleep.

Indeed! and what happened?

He started up from his sleep and had a violent fit of sneezing.

Oh, how horrible! What punishment are you going to have?

I have got my punishment already. His big brother came and gave me a pretty smart slap.

Policemen!

Yes, My Lord!

This prisoner is discharged.

[*Enters* Bhola *crying.*]

What is the trouble? Haven't you eaten Jadu's lunch?

I tried to but could not.

Why, what happened?

He is too strong for me.

Policemen!

Yes, My Lord!

Bring in Jadu.

[*Enters* P *with* J.]

Jadu, what have you done to Bhola?

He tried to eat my lunch and I tried my best not to let him.

And you succeeded?

Yes, My Lord!

What a shame!

I am sure Your Lordship would do the same in similar circumstance.

I know, but you began first and were in the wrong.

What's the matter? What an awful row!

Rajen says he is our king because he is the strongest [ ] I cannot let it pass unchallenged.

Well I am not afraid of him.

You are a pair of fools. Don't forget that this is only a game. Let Rajen be our king today and possibly you will have your turn tomorrow. Long live King Rajen! Now then who is to be your Majesty's Minister?

Jiten is my Minister.

Who is your General?

You are my General.

And the Chief Justice?

Upen.

And the rest of the boys?

They are all soldiers.

Now then soldiers, form a line and salute your King. Long live King Rajen.

ACT II SCENE 2

General Moti, I am displeased with you.

Why Sire?

You are sitting idle.

Command me and I'll carry out your Majesty's wishes.

You haven't fought a single battle since your appointment.

No, sire, I haven't, because there was nothing to fight for.

You are a fine General if you have to wait for a cause to fight.

Your Majesty has no enemy.

Can' t you create enemies? You are drawing a good pay and there are my soldiers doing nothing. Some day they will kill me if they have no enemies to kill. Soldiers!

Yes sire!

What would you say if you had to go and fight somebody?

It would be great fun!

Yes, it certainly would be a great fun. General Moti!

Yes, sire!

You must get hold of some enemies and you must fight.

I will do as your majesty commands Boys! Who are there who wish to fight His Majesty the King!

None.

None! You cowards!

We are no cowards, we are His Majesty's loyal subjects.

But, Hem, you insulted our king! So there must be a war!

Oh, how jolly!

But I never insulted His Majesty.

Didn't he, my soldiers!

Of course he did. If he dare deny it we will break his head.

But how have I offended His Majesty?

You were standing at your window when His Majesty was passing by and you actually yawned!

Yawned!

Yawned!

Yawned!

Oh, how audacious!

Scandalous!

Abominable!

His Majesty never passed by my house since he was crowned!

That may be, but, sir, can you say that you never yawned!

Yes, but if what I did was wrong why did Your Lordship ask Bhola to do the same thing?

That is an intricate question of ethics, and I am not going to argue it. But you must have some punishment for what you have done. Choose your own punishment.

I won't have any lunch of my own for three days. I will manage to snatch my share from that of others.

Oh, what a brave fellow to undertake such a penance! Policeman!

Yes, My Lord!

The prisoner is discharged!

ACT III

My minister Jiten!

Yes, Sire!

Is General Moti ready for the battle?

Yes, I believe so.

The rebel Hem must be taught a good lesson.

Why is Your Majesty so severe upon him?

He is an insolent fellow.

What has he done to offend your majesty?

You are our Prime Minister and you do not know what he has done?

I confess I do not

Well, by his conduct he has shown himself to be a rebel.

Excuse my curiosity if I ask your Majesty what that conduct might be.

Well I am sure I do not remember.

General Moti knows all about it unless he also has forgotten.

Indeed! Here is the General coming.

General Moti!

Yes, sire!

Our Prime Minister does not know what the rebel Hem has done. Perhaps you will be able to tell him.

I am afraid my recollection of the matter is not very distinct.

But it was something unpardonable—was it not?

Of course, it was.

But surely General, you must have an answer ready when the people ask you why you have started the war. You must give then some reason.

Sire, I think I remember now.

I am glad to hear it. What was the matter?

When your majesty sneezed while holding court Hem did not snap his fingers.

Just imagine! He actually did not snap his fingers!

Did not snap his fingers! Oh, how atrocious!

Soldiers, never forget this insult to your Sovereign!

No, we never shall!

Remember that Hem did not snap his fingers when we sneezed.

We will give our life's blood to avenge this insult.

You will show him no mercy.

Certainly not. Not even if he begs for it on his knees.

We are pleased at your loyal zeal.

Minister Jiten, we will reward our soldiers with titles when they come back victorious.

Yes, Sire!

And they will have splendid funerals those that will die.

Certainly they will.

General, why are you silent?

I am speechless with indignation.

But you are motionless as well. Why don't you march?

Soldiers, march on!

Long live His Majesty King Rajen. May his shadow never grow less, and may his sneezes ever be attended with loyal snapping of fingers!

ACT IV

We have come to ask your Honour whether it is just on our King's part to wage war with Hem.

But he is the King.

Therefore he should be just.

But if he is not just there is no help for it.

But we maintain that he is our King only so long as he is just.

But we must submit to his wishes.

Even if they are unjust?

Yes, even so.

Why?

I am astonished at your simplicity. Why! Because he has got a powerful army.

We don't care a fig for his army. He must be just if he is to be our King.

It is very fine to hear you talk like this but what are we to do?

You ought to summon our King and let him justify himself before us.

Good Heavens! Summon our King! Some of these days you will ask me to summon the thunderbolt from heaven for having fallen on your coconut tree!

If you don't do your duty you are no longer our Chief Justice and we will put you into the prison.

I quite believe you. But there is no need of serving a summons. The King is coming himself.

[King]

Why this unlawful assembly, and what are you clamouring for?

For justice.

We have established a court of justice and you can get justice there for the mere asking.

We are asking our Chief Justice to decide whether your Majesty right to want to fight with Hem.

Right! The King is never wrong.

Because when he is wrong he is no more a king.

That is a dangerous sentiment.

And that other sentiment is far more dangerous which makes out that a king can do no wrong. We humbly ask your Majesty what has Hem done to deserve your royal displeasure?

I can't say positively because Kings as a rule have no memory for details. But, I think, when my royal elephant was being led out for a walk Hem was actually seen to spit.

If this is against the law of the realm let him be brought before the court of justice.

And so you want me to be deprived of the pleasure of waging a war—

Which happens to be unjust.

But absolutely necessary.

Why necessary?

My soldiers are in danger of forgetting the military art for want of exercise.

Is this reason why your Majesty wants this war?

Yes.

Then we are going over to Hem's side so that we may give your Majesty's soldiers good exercise. Come brothers, let us join Hem.

ACT V

General! You don't look radiantly happy.

I am sure your Majesty will also share my feeling when you know the state of affairs.

Why, what is the latest news?

Your Majesty's subjects are joining the rebels. They are not convinced of the justice of our cause.

That shows that you neglected to give them reasons.

Not at all. We gave them more reasons than were necessary, but owing to our bad memory those happened to be at variance with each other.

How unfortunate! But you must take prompt action to stop such wholesale desertion. I don't see the fun of playing the King if I lose all my subjects.

But the fight is going on. I must attend to it first.

Remember don't show mercy to the rebel. In the meanwhile my state executioner must get a good supply of ropes to hang all who have gone over to the enemy.

[A Soldier.]

General, we are defeated.

Defeated! Why man the war is just begun.

Our party is in flight.

Tell them I have provided for every one of them to get a title if they will only turn back.

[Hem *with* Soldiers.]

Rajen, you are our prisoner.

Hands off man! You forget yourself. I am your King.

You have forfeited your right to be a king. The people have pronounced their judgment against you, and I must carry it out.

No, not while I am alive.

[Crowd]

Down with Rajen the Unjust!

General, you let these wretches insult their sovereign!

Sire, I am powerless.

My Chief Justice, why don't you punish these miscreants?

Because justice is on their side and also the whole army. I think it will be a better move for you to lay down your crown peacefully and take up the role of an ordinary person.

But if fighting is of no avail can't I argue my case in the law court? I will engage my court orator to justify my policy.

The orator is haranguing the people already.

I was sure he would. He is true to his salt and I will reward him when the time comes.

He is arguing that merely deposing you would not satisfy justice and even hanging would be too mild a punishment. The hearts of the populace are deeply stirred by his passionate speeches.

Indeed! Then it is time for me to take my departure May I ask what my court poet is doing?

He is engaged in writing an ode in commemoration of the people's victory.

My dear, Hem, allow me to congratulate you on your brilliant success. But take my parting advice—abolish the post of the court orator and honour the court poet by hanging him with the rope that I specially reserved for yourself. Delay will be dangerous. Good bye gentlemen.

[*Court Scene.*]

King. My Kingdom is great, but I do all the work of the state and hear all complaints, so, my dear subjects, rest assured that you will always have justice Minister, what business awaits us today? Be quick, for I shall have to go to the review of the army you know.

Minister. Yes, your majesty, I am acquainted with your desire. We have only two cases today—one instituted by Bhola, and the other is in which Gopen is the accused.

King. What does Bhola complain of? Bhola, come forward and tell us what you complain of. Who is your counsel?

Bhola. I have no counsel. My complaint is, your majesty, that Ranjit slapped me so hard on my cheek that the marks of his fingers are still visible.

King. Yes, I see them I am sorry for you, Bhola, but where is Ranjit? Policeman, did you arrest him?

Policeman. Yes, your majesty,—here he is.

King. What have you to say for yourself?

Ranjit. Bhola ate a rosogolla from my share, your majesty, and I had none this evening.

King. Why did you eat his rosogolla, Bhola?

Ranjit.[1] 'May it please your majesty, I ate the rosogolla. I plead guilty, but I crave your majesty's indulgence—I could not help it, for my mouth was watering at the sight of that rosogolla.

King. Why, you had yours, I suppose?

Ranjit.[1] Yes, your majesty, I had mine, to be sure, but that was the reason why the temptation was so great,—it tasted so sweet. Your majesty would have done the same thing under similar circumstance.

King. That is not for you to judge. This is contempt of the court. Is it not so, minister?

Minister. Yes, your majesty, and this offence calls for capital punishment.

King. Bhola, I am sorry for you. I sentence you to go without sweets this evening, and there will be no story class for you, and considering your tender age, these sentences are to run concurrently.

Now, Ranjit, why did you take the law in your own hands? Why did you inflict those five finger marks on poor Bhola's cheek without our permission?

Ranjit. May it please your majesty, the provocation was great. It was beyond human powers to refrain from doing it.

---

1. Slip of pen. Read 'Bhola'.

King. Yes, the provocation was great, I would have done the same thing under similar circumstance. Policeman, the prisoner is discharged. Let us proceed to the next case. Who is the complainant, and who the accused?

Minister. I am the complainant, your majesty, for this case is one King vs. Gopen. The Government counsel will argue the case.

Counsel. Whereas Gopen had the audacity of sneezing twice while his majesty was passing by, he is called upon to show cause why he shall not be proceeded against in the court of his Most Exalted Majesty.

King. Indeed, this case has no parallel in the history of our realm.

Counsel. Your Majesty, it was atrocious, with no parallel except that a few months ago when your most august Majesty sneezed Harish actually forgot to snap his fingers.

King. What have you to say, Gopen?—you have been charged with an offence which cannot go unpunished.

Gopen. I plead guilty, your majesty. But your majesty will kindly consider that I could not possibly help it, as I was suffering from cold which was so distressing that I had to sneeze every minute that day, and believe me, your majesty, my ears which were already red on account of the cold were made redder still by my friends who pulled at them at every sneeze I gave. I tried to avoid your majesty but you appeared suddenly and in your august presence I sneezed. Your majesty will, I pray, pardon me my fault, as your majesty will remember your own most august sneeze at which Harish forgot to snap his fingers.

King. Yes, yes, I remember. It was no fault of yours to sneeze. When one gets cold one must sneeze as even we did. Policeman, the prisoner is discharged.

STORIES

The Victory

She was the Princess Ajita. And the court poet of King Narayan had never seen her. On the day he recited a new poem to the king he would raise his voice just to that pitch which could be heard by unseen hearers in the screened balcony high above the hall. He sent up his song towards the star-land out of his reach, where, circled with light, the planet who ruled his destiny shone unknown and out of ken.

He would espy some shadow moving behind the veil. A tinkling sound would come to his ear from afar, and would set him dreaming of the ankles whose tiny golden bells sang at each step. Ah, the rosy red tender feet that walked the dust of the earth like God's mercy on the fallen! The poet had placed them on the altar of his heart, where he wove his songs to the tune of those golden bells. Doubt never arose in his mind as to whose shadow it was that moved behind the screen, and whose anklets they were that sang to the time of his beating heart.

Manjari, the maid of the princess, passed by the poet's house on her way to the river, and she never missed a day to have a few words with him on the sly. When she found the road deserted, and the shadow of dusk on the land, she would boldly enter his room, and sit at the corner of his carpet. There was a suspicion of an added care in the choice of the colour of her veil, in the setting of the flower in her hair.

People smiled and whispered at this, and they were not to blame. For Shekhar the poet never took the trouble to hide the fact that these meetings were a pure joy to him.

The meaning of her name was the *spray of flowers*. One must confess that for an ordinary mortal it was sufficient in its sweetness. But Shekhar made his own addition to this name, and called her the Spray of Spring Flowers. And ordinary mortals shook their heads and said, Ah, me!

In the spring songs that the poet sang the praise of the spray of spring flowers was conspicuously reiterated; and the king winked and smiled at him when he heard it, and the poet smiled in answer.

The king would put him the question: 'Is it the business of the bee merely to hum in the court of the spring?'

The poet would answer: 'No, but also to sip the honey of the spray of spring flowers.'

And they all laughed in the king's hall. And it was rumoured that the Princess Ajita also laughed at her maid's accepting the poet's name for her, and Manjari felt glad in her heart.

Thus truth and falsehood mingle in life—and to what God builds man adds his own decoration.

Only those were pure truths which were sung by the poet. The theme was Krishna, the lover god, and Radha, the beloved, the Eternal Man and the Eternal Woman, the sorrow that comes from the beginning of time, and the joy without end. The truth of these songs was tested in his inmost heart by everybody from the beggar to the king himself. The poet's songs were on the lips of all. At the merest glimmer of the moon and the faintest whisper of the summer breeze his songs would break forth in the land from windows and courtyards, from sailing-boats, from shadows of the wayside trees, in numberless voices.

Thus passed the days happily. The poet recited, the king listened, the hearers applauded. Manjari passed and repassed by the poet's room on her way to the river—the shadow flitted behind the screened balcony, and the tiny golden bells tinkled from afar.

Just then set forth from his home in the south a poet on his path of conquest. He came to King Narayan, in the kingdom of Amarapur. He stood before the throne, and uttered averse in praise of the king. He had challenged all the court poets on his way, and his career of victory had been unbroken.

The king received him with honour, and said: 'Poet, I offer you welcome.'

Pundarik, the poet, proudly replied: 'Sire, I ask for war.'

Shekhar, the court poet of the king did not know how the battle of the Muse was to be waged. He had no sleep at night. The mighty figure of the famous Pundarik, his sharp nose curved like a scimitar, and his proud head tilted on one side, haunted the poet's vision in the dark.

With a trembling heart Shekhar entered the arena in the morning. The theatre was filled with the crowd.

The poet greeted his rival with a smile and a bow. Pundarik returned it with a slight toss of his head, and turned his face towards his circle of adoring followers with a meaning smile.

Shekhar cast his glance towards the screened balcony high above, and saluted his lady in his mind, saying: 'If I am the winner at the combat today, my lady, thy victorious name shall be glorified.'

The trumpet sounded. The great crowd stood up, shouting victory to the king. The king, dressed in an ample robe of white, slowly came into the hall like a floating cloud of autumn, and sat on his throne.

Pundarik stood up, and the vast hall became still. With his head raised high and chest expanded, he began in his thundering voice to recite the praise of King Narayan. His words burst upon the walls of the hall like breakers of the sea, and seemed to rattle against the ribs of the listening crowd. The skill with which he gave varied meanings to the name Narayan, and wove each letter of it through the web of his verses in all manner of combinations, took away the breath of his amazed hearers.

For some minutes after he took his seat his voice continued to vibrate among the numberless pillars of the king's court and in thousands of speechless hearts. The learned professors who had come from distant lands raised their right hands, and cried, Bravo!

The king threw a glance on Shekhar's face, and Shekhar in answer raised for a moment his eyes full of pain towards his master, and then stood up like a stricken deer at bay. His face was pale, his bashfulness was almost that of a woman, his slight youthful figure, delicate in its outline, seemed like a tensely strung *vina* ready to break out in music at the least touch.

His head was bent, his voice was low, when he began. The first few verses were almost inaudible. Then he slowly raised his head, and his clear sweet voice rose into the sky like a quivering flame of fire. He began with the ancient legend of the kingly line lost in the haze of the past, and brought it down through its long course of heroism and matchless generosity to the present age. He fixed his gaze on the king's face, and all the vast and unexpressed love of the people for the royal house rose like incense in his song, and enwreathed the throne on all sides. These were his last words when, trembling, he took his seat: 'My master, I may be beaten in play of words, but not in my love for thee.'

Tears filled the eyes of the hearers, and the stone walls shook with cries of victory.

Mocking this popular outburst of feeling, with an august shake of his head and a contemptuous sneer, Pundarik stood up, and flung this question to the assembly: 'What is there superior to words?' In a moment the hall lapsed into silence again.

Then with a marvellous display of learning, he proved that the Word was in the beginning, that the Word was God. He piled up quotations from scriptures, and built a high altar for the Word to be seated above all that there is in heaven and in earth. He repeated that question in his mighty voice: 'What is there superior to words?'

Proudly he looked around him. None dared to accept his challenge, and he slowly took his seat like a lion who had just made a full meal of its victim. The pandits shouted, Bravo!

The king remained silent with wonder, and the poet Shekhar felt himself of no account by the side of this stupendous learning. The assembly broke up for that day.

Next day Shekhar began his song. It was of that day when the pipings of love's flute startled for the first time the hushed air of the Vrinda forest. The shepherd women did not know who was the player or whence came the music. Sometimes it seemed to come from the heart of the south, wind, and sometimes from the straying clouds of the hill-tops. It came with a message of tryst from the land of the sunrise, and it floated from the verge of sunset with its sigh of sorrow. The stars seemed to be the stops of the instrument that flooded the dreams of the night with melody. The music seemed to burst all at once from all sides, from fields and groves, from the shady lanes and lonely roads, from the melting blue of the sky, from the shimmering green of the grass. They neither knew its meaning nor could they find words to give utterance to the desire of their hearts. Tears filled their eyes, and their life seemed to long for a death that would be its consummation.

Shekhar forgot his audience, forgot the trial of his strength with a rival. He stood alone amid his thoughts that rustled and quivered round him like leaves in summer breeze, and sang the Song of the Flute. He had in his mind the vision of an image that had taken its shape from a shadow, and the echo of a faint tinkling sound of a distant footstep.

He took his seat. His hearers trembled with the sadness of an indefinable delight, immense and vague, and they forgot to applaud him. As this feeling died away Pundarik stood up before the throne and challenged his rival to define who was this Lover and who was the Beloved. He arrogantly looked around him, he smiled at his followers and then put the question again: 'Who is Krishna, the lover, and who is Radha, the beloved?'

Then he began to analyse the roots of those names—and various interpretations of their meanings. He brought before the bewildered audience all the intricacies of the different schools of metaphysics with consummate skill. Each letter of those names he divided from its fellow, and then pursued them with a relentless logic till they fell to the dust in confusion, to be caught up again and restored to a meaning never before imagined by the subtlest of wordmongers.

The pandits were in ecstasy; they applauded vociferously; and the crowd followed them, deluded into the certainty that they had witnessed, that day, the last shred of the curtains of Truth torn to pieces before their eyes by a prodigy of intellect. The performance of his tremendous feat so delighted them that they forgot to ask themselves if there was any truth behind it after all.

The king's mind was overwhelmed with wonder. The atmosphere was completely cleared of all illusion of music, and the vision of the world around seemed to be changed from its freshness of tender green to the solidity of a high road levelled and made hard with crushed stones.

To the people assembled their own poet appeared a mere boy in comparison with this giant, who walked with such ease, knocking down difficulties at each step in the world of words and thoughts. It became evident to them for the first time that the poems Shekhar wrote were absurdly simple, and it must be a mere accident that they did not write them themselves. They were neither new, nor difficult, nor instructive, nor necessary.

The king tried to goad his poet with keen glances, silently inciting him to make a final effort. But Shekhar took no notice, and remained fixed to his seat.

The king in anger came down from his throne—took off his pearl chain and put it on Pundarik's head. Everybody in the hall cheered. From the upper balcony came a slight sound of the movements of rustling robes and waist-chains hung with golden bells. Shekhar rose from his seat and left the hall.

It was a dark night of waning moon. The poet Shekhar took down his MSS from his shelves and heaped them on the floor. Some of them contained his earliest writings, which he had almost forgotten. He turned over the pages, reading passages here and there. They all seemed to him poor and trivial—mere words and childish rhymes!

One by one he tore his books to fragments, and threw them into a vessel containing fire, and said: 'To thee, to thee, O my beauty, my fire! Thou hast been burning in my heart all these futile years. If my life were a piece of gold it would come out of its trial brighter, but it is a trodden turf of grass, and nothing remains of it but this handful of ashes.'

The night wore on. Shekhar opened wide his windows. He spread upon his bed the white flowers that he loved, the jasmines, tuberoses and chrysanthemums, and brought into his bedroom all the lamps he had in his house and lighted them. Then mixing with honey the juice of some poisonous root, he drank it and lay down on his bed.

Golden anklets tinkled in the passage outside the door, and a subtle perfume came into the room with the breeze.

The poet, with his eyes shut, said: 'My lady, have you taken pity upon your servant at last and come to see him?'

The answer came in a sweet voice: 'My poet, I have come.'

Shekhar opened his eyes—and saw before his bed the figure of a woman.

His sight was dim and blurred. And it seemed to him that the image made of a shadow that he had ever kept throned in the secret shrine of his heart had come into the outer world in his last moment to gaze upon his face.

The woman said: 'I am the Princess Ajita.'

The poet with a great effort sat up on his bed.

The princess whispered into his ear: 'The king has not done you justice. It was you who won at the combat, my poet, and I have come to crown you with the crown of victory.'

She took the garland of flowers from her own neck, and put it on his hair, and the poet fell down upon his bed stricken by death.

Giribala

Giribala is overflowing with exuberance of youth that seems spilling over in spray all around her,—in the folds of her soft dress, the turning of her neck, the motion of her hands, in the rhythm of her steps, now quick now languid, in her tinkling anklets and ringing laughter, in her voice and glances. She would often been seen, wrapt in a blue silk, walking on her terrace, in an impulse of unaccountable restlessness. Her limbs seem eager to dance to the time of an inner music unceasing and unheard. She takes pleasure in merely moving her body, causing ripples to break out in the flood of her young life. She would suddenly pluck a leaf from a plant in the flower-pot and throw it up in the sky, and her bangles would give a sudden tinkle, and the careless grace of her hand, like a bird freed from its cage, would fly unseen in the air. With her swift fingers she would brush away from her dress a mere nothing; standing on tiptoe she would peep over her terrace walls for no cause whatever, and then with a rapid motion turn round to go to another direction, swinging her bunch of keys tied to a corner of her garment. She would loosen her hair in an untimely caprice, sitting before her mirror to do it up again, and then in a fit of laziness would fling herself upon her bed, like a line of stray moonlight slipping through some opening of the leaves, idling in the shadow.

She has no children and, having been married in a wealthy family, has very little work to do. Thus she seems to be daily accumulating her own self without expenditure, till the vessel is brimming over with the seething surplus. She has her husband, but not under her control. She has grown up from a girl into a woman, yet escaping, through familiarity, her husband's notice.

When she was newly married and her husband, Gopinath, was attending his college, he would often play the truant and under cover of the midday siesta of his elders secretly come to make love to Giribala. Though they lived under the same roof, he would create occasions to send her letters on tinted paper perfumed with rosewater, and would even gloat upon some exaggerated grievances of imaginary neglect of love.

Just then his father died and he became the sole owner of his property. Like an unseasoned piece of timber, the immature youth of Gopinath attracted parasites which began to bore into his substance. From now his movements took the course that led him in a contrary direction from his wife.

There is a dangerous fascination to be leaders of men, to which many strong minds have succumbed. To be accepted as the leader of a small circle of sycophants, in his own parlour, has the same fearful attraction for a man who suffers from a scarcity of brains and character. Gopinath assumed the part of a hero among his friends and acquaintances, and tried daily to invent new wonders in all manner of extravagance. He won a reputation among his followers for his audacity of excesses, which goaded him not only to keep up his fame, but to surpass himself at all costs.

In the meanwhile, Giribala, in the seclusion of her lonely youth, felt like a queen who had her throne, but no subjects. She knew she had the power in her hand which could make the world of men her captive; only that world itself was wanting.

Giribala has a maidservant whose name is Sudha. She can sing and dance and improvise verses, and she freely gives expression to her regret that such a beauty as that of her mistress should be dedicated to a fool who forgets to enjoy what he owns. Giribala is never tired of hearing from her the details of her charms, while at the same time contradicting her, calling her a liar and a flatterer, exciting her to swear by all that is sacred that she is earnest in her admiration, which statement, even without the accompaniment of a solemn oath, is not difficult for Giribala to believe.

Sudha used to sing to her a song beginning with the line, 'Let me write myself a slave upon the soles of thy feet,' and Giribala in her imagination could feel that her beautiful feet were fully worthy of bearing inscriptions of everlasting slavery from conquered hearts, if only they could be free in their career of conquest.

But the woman to whom her husband Gopinath has surrendered himself as a slave is Lavanga, the actress, who has the reputation of playing to perfection the part of a maiden languishing in hopeless love and swooning on the stage with an exquisite naturalness. When her husband had not altogether vanished from her sphere of influence, Giribala had often heard from him about the wonderful histrionic powers of this woman and in her jealous curiosity had greatly desired to see Lavanga on the stage. But she could not secure her husband's consent, because Gopinath was firm in his opinion that the theatre was a place not fit for any decent woman to visit.

At last she paid for a seat and sent Sudha to see this famous actress in one of her best parts. The account that she received from her on her return was far from flattering to Lavanga, both as to her personal appearance and her stage accomplishments. As, for obvious reasons, she had great faith in Sudha's power of appreciation, where it was due, Giribala did not hesitate to believe her in her description of Lavanga, which was accompanied by a mimicry of a ludicrous mannerism.

When at last her husband deserted her in his infatuation for this woman, she began to feel qualms of doubt. But as Sudha repeatedly asserted her former opinion with ever greater vehemence, comparing Lavanga to a piece of burnt log dressed up in a woman's clothes, Giribala determined secretly to go to the theatre herself and settle this question for good.

And she *did* go there one night with all the excitement of a forbidden entry. Her very trepidation of heart lent a special charm to what she saw. She gazed at the faces of the spectators, lit up with an unnatural shine of lamplight; and, with the magic of its music and the painted canvas of its scenery, the theatre seemed to her like a world where society was suddenly freed from its law of gravitation.

Coming from her walled up terrace and joyless home, she had entered a region where dreams and reality had clasped their hands in friendship, over the wine cup of art.

The bell rang, the orchestra music stopped, the audience sat still in their seats, the stage-lights shone brighter, and the curtain was drawn up. Suddenly appeared in the light, from the mystery of the unseen, the shepherd girls of the Vrinda forest, and with the accompaniment of songs commenced their dance, punctuated with the uproarious applause of the audience. The blood began to throb all over Giribala's body, and she forgot for the moment that her life was limited to the circumstances and that she was not free in a world where all laws had melted in music.

Sudha came occasionally to interrupt her with her anxious whispers urging her to hasten back home for the fear of being detected. But she paid no heed to her warning, for her sense of fear had gone.

The play goes on. Krishna has given offence to his beloved Radha and she in her wounded pride refuses to recognize him. He is entreating her, abasing himself at her feet, but in vain. Giribala's heart seems to swell. She imagines herself as offended Radha; and feels that she also has in her this woman's power to vindicate her pride. She had heard what a force was woman's beauty in the world but to-night it became to her palpable.

At last the curtain dropped, the light grew dim, the audience got ready to leave the theatre, but Giribala sat still like one in a dream. The thought that she would have to go home had vanished from her mind. She waited for the curtain to rise again and the eternal theme of Krishna's humiliation at the feet of Radha to continue. But Sudha came to remind her that the play had ended and the lamps would soon be put out.

It was late when Giribala came back home. A kerosene lamp was dimly burning in the melancholy solitude and silence of her room. Near the window upon her lonely bed a mosquito curtain was gently moving in the breeze. Her world seemed to her distasteful and mean like a rotten fruit swept into the dustbin.

From now she regularly visited the theatre every Saturday. The fascination of her first sight of it lost much of its glamour. The painted vulgarity of the actresses and the falseness of their affectation became more and more evident, yet the habit grew upon her. Every time the curtain rose the window of her life's prison-house seemed to open before her and the stage, bordered off from the world of reality by its gilded frame and scenic display, by its array of lights and even its flimsiness of conventionalism, appeared to her like a fairyland where it was not impossible for herself to occupy the throne of the fairy queen.

When for the first time she saw her husband among the audience shouting his drunken admiration for a certain actress she felt an intense disgust and prayed in her mind that a day might come when she might have an opportunity to spurn him away with her contempt. But the opportunity became rarer every day, for Gopinath was hardly ever to be seen at his home now, being carried away, one knew not where, in the centre of a dust-storm of dissipation.

One evening in the month of March, in the light of the full moon, Giribala was sitting on her terrace dressed in her cream-coloured robe. It was her habit daily to deck herself with jewellery as if for some festive occasion. For these costly gems were like wine to her—they sent heightened consciousness of beauty to her limbs; she felt like a plant in spring tingling with the impulse of flowers in all its branches. She wore a pair of diamond bracelets on her arms, a necklace of rubies and pearls on her neck, and a ring with a big sapphire on the little finger of her left hand. Sudha was sitting near her bare feet admiringly touching them with her hand and expressing her wish that she were a man privileged to offer her life as homage to such a pair of feet.

Sudha gently hummed a lovesong to her and the evening wore on to night. Every body in the household had finished their evening meal, and gone to sleep. When suddenly Gopinath appeared reeking with scent and liquor, and Sudha drawing for cloth-end over her face, hastily ran away from the terrace.

Giribala thought for a moment that her day had come at last. She turned away her face and sat silent.

But the curtain in her stage did not rise and no song of entreaty came from her hero, with the words—'Listen to the pleading of the moon-light, my love, and hide not thy face.'

In his dry unmusical voice Gopinath said, 'Give me your keys.'

A gust of south wind like a sigh of the insulted romance of the poetic world scattered all over the terrace the smell of the night-blooming jasmines and loosened some wisp of hair on Giribala's cheek. She let go her pride, and got up and said, 'You shall have your keys if you listen to what I have to say.'

Gopinath said, 'I cannot delay. Give me your keys.'

Giribala said, 'I will give you the keys and everything that is in the safe, but you must not leave me.'

Gopinath said, 'That cannot be. I have urgent business.'

'Then you shan't have the keys,' said Giribala.

Gopinath began to search for them. He opened the drawers of the dressing table, broke open the lid of the box that contained Giribala's toilet requisites, smashed the glass panes of her almirah, groped under the pillows and mattress of the bed, but the keys he could not find. Giribala stood near the door stiff and silent like a marble image gazing at vacancy. Trembling with rage Gopinath came to her and said with an angry growl, 'Give me your keys or you will repent.'

Giribala did not answer and Gopinath, pinning her to the wall, snatched away by force her bracelets, necklace and ring, and, giving her a parting kick, went away.

Nobody in the house woke up from his sleep, none in the neighbourhood knew of this outrage, the moonlight remained placid and the peace of the night undisturbed. Hearts can be rent never to heal again amidst such serene silence.

The next morning Giribala said she was going to see her father and left home. As Gopinath's present destination was not known and she was not responsible to anybody else in the house her absence was not noticed.

2

The new play of 'Manorama' was on rehearsal in the theatre where Gopinath was a constant visitor. Lavanga was practising for the part of the heroine Manorama, and Gopinath, sitting in the front seat with his rabble of followers, would vociferously encourage his favourite actress with his approbation. This greatly disturbed the rehearsal but the proprietors of the theatre did not dare to annoy their patron of whose vindictiveness they were afraid. But one day he went so far as to molest an actress in the greenroom and he had to be turned away by the aid of the police.

Gopinath determined to take his revenge,—and when, after a great deal of preparation and shrieking advertisements, the new play 'Manorama' was about to be produced, Gopinath took away the principal actress Lavanga with him and disappeared. It was a great shock to the manager, who had to postpone the opening night, and, getting hold of a new actress, taught her the part, and brought out the play before the public with considerable misgivings in his mind.

But the success was as unexpected as it was unprecedented. When its news reached Gopinath he could not resist his curiosity to come and see the performance.

The play opens with Manorama living in her husband's house neglected and hardly noticed. Near the end of the drama her husband deserts her and concealing his first marriage manages to marry a millionaire's daughter. When the wedding ceremony is over and the bridal veil is raised from her face she is discovered to be the same Manorama, only no longer the former drudge, but queenly in her beauty and splendour of dress and ornaments. In her infancy she had been brought up in a poor home being kidnapped from the house of her rich father, who having traced her to her husband's home, has brought her back to him and celebrates her marriage once again in a fitting manner.

In the concluding scene, when the husband is going through his period of penitence and humiliation, as is fit in a play which has its moral, a sudden disturbance arose among the audience. So long as Manorama appeared obscured in her position of drudgery Gopinath showed no sign of perturbation. But when after the wedding ceremony she came out dressed in her red bridal robe and took her veil off, when with a majestic pride of her overwhelming beauty she turned her face towards the audience and, slightly bending her neck, shot a fiery glance of exultation at Gopinath, applause broke out in wave after wave and the enthusiasm of the spectators became unbounded.

Suddenly Gopinath cried out in a thick voice, 'Giribala', and like a madman tried to rush upon the stage. The audience shouted, 'Turn him out,' the police came to drag him away and he struggled and screamed, 'I will kill her,' while the curtain dropped.

The Patriot

I am sure, that Chitragupta, who keeps strict record at the gate of Death, must have noted down in big letters accusations against me, which had escaped my attention altogether. On the other hand many of my sins, that have passed unnoticed by others, loom large in my own memory. The story of my transgression, that I am going to relate, belongs to the latter kind, and I hope that a frank confession of it, before it is finally entered in the Book of Doom, may lessen its culpability.

It all happened yesterday afternoon, on a day of festival for the Jains in our neighbourhood. I was going out with my wife, Kalika, to tea at the house of my friend Nayanmohan.

My wife's name means literally a 'bud'. It was given by my father-in-law, who is thus solely responsible for any discrepancy between its implication and the reality to which it is attached. There is not the least tremor of hesitancy in my wife's nature; her opinions on most subjects have reached their terminus. Once, when she had been vigorously engaged in picketing against British cloth in Burrabazar, the awe-struck members of her party in a fit of excessive admiration gave her the name, *Dhruva-vrata,* the woman of unwavering vows.

My name is Girindra, the Lord of the Rocks, so common among my countrymen, whose character generally fails to act up to it. Kalika's admirers simply know me as the husband of my wife and pay no heed to my name. By good luck inherited from my ancestors I have, however, some kind of significance, which is considered to be convenient by her followers at the time of collecting subscriptions.

There is a greater chance of harmony between husband and wife, when they are different in character, like the shower of rain and the dry earth, than when they are of a uniform constitution. I am somewhat slipshod by nature, having no grip over things, while my wife has a tenacity of mind which never allows her to let go the thing which it has in its clutches. This very dissimilarity helps to preserve peace in our household.

But there is one point of difference between us, regarding which no adjustment has yet become possible. Kalika believes that I am unpatriotic.

This is very disconcerting, because according to her, truth is what she proclaims to be true. She has numerous internal evidences of my love for my country; but as it disdains to don the livery of the brand of nationalism, professed by her own party, she fiercely refuses to acknowledge it.

From my younger days, I have continued to be a confirmed book-lover: indeed, I am hopelessly addicted to buying books. Even my enemies would not dare to deny that I read them; and my friends know only too well how fond I am of discussing their contents. This had the effect of eliminating most of my friends, till I have left to me Banbihari, the sole companion of my lonely debates. We have just passed through a period, when our police authorities, on the one hand, have associated the worst form of sedition with the presence of the Gita in our possession; and our patriots, on their side, have found it impossible to reconcile appreciation of foreign literature with devotion to one's Motherland. Our traditional Goddess of culture, Saraswati, because of her white complexion, has come to be regarded with suspicion by our young nationalists. It was openly declared, when the students shunned their College lectures, that the water of the divine lake, on which Saraswati had her white lotus seat, had no efficacy in extinguishing the fire of ill-fortune that has been raging for centuries round the throne of our Mother, Bharat-Lakshmi. In any case, intellectual culture was considered to be a superfluity in the proper growth of our political life.

In spite of my wife's excellent example and powerful urgings I do not wear Khaddar,—not because there is anything wrong in it, nor because I am too fastidious in the choice of my wardrobe. On the contrary, among those of my traits, which are not in perfect consonance with our own national habits, I cannot include a scrupulous care as to how I dress. Once upon a time, before Kalika had her modern transformation, I used to wear broad-toed shoes from Chinese shops and forgot to have them polished. I had a dread of putting on socks: I preferred *Punjabis* to English shirts, and overlooked their accidental deficiency in buttons. These habits of mine constantly produced domestic cataclysms, threatening our permanent separation. Kalika declared that she felt ashamed to appear before the public in my company. I readily absolved her from the wifely duty of accompanying me to those parties where my presence would be discordant.

The times have changed, but my evil fortune persists. Kalika still has the habit of repeating: 'I am ashamed to go out with you.' Formerly, I hesitated to adopt the uniform of her set, when she belonged to the pre-nationalist age; and I still feel reluctant to adopt the uniform of the present regime, to which she owns her allegiance.

The fault lies deep in my own nature. I shrink from all conscious display of sectarian marks about my person. This shyness on my part leads to incessant verbal explosions in our domestic world, because of the inherent incapacity of Kalika to accept as final any natural difference, which her partner in life may possess. Her mind is like a mountain stream, that boisterously goes round and round a rock, pushing against it in a vain effort to make it flow with its own current. Her contact with a different point of view from her own seems to exercise an irresistible reflex action upon her nerves, throwing her into involuntary convulsions.

While getting ready to go out yesterday, the tone with which Kalika protested against my non-Khaddar dress was anything but sweet. Unfortunately, I had my inveterate pride of intellect, that forced me into a discussion with my wife. It was unpleasant, and what more, futile.

'Women find it convenient,' I said to her, 'to veil their eyes and walk tied to the leading strings of authority. They feel safe when they deprive their thoughts of all freedom, and confine them in the strict Zenana of conformity. Our ladies today have easily developed their devotion to Khaddar, because it has added to the over-burdened list of our outward criterion's of propriety, which seem to comfort them.'

Kalika replied with almost fanatical fury: 'It will be a great day for my country, when the sanctity of wearing Khaddar is as blindly believed in as a dip in the holy water of the Ganges. Reason crystallised becomes custom. Free thoughts are like ghosts, which find their bodies in convention. Then alone they have their solid work, and no longer float about in a thin atmosphere of vacillation.'

I could see that these were the wise sayings of Nayanmohan, with the quotation marks worn out; Kalika found no difficulty in imagining that they were her own.

The man who invented the proverb, 'The silent silence all antagonist', must have been unmarried. It made my wife all the more furious, when I offered her no answer. 'Your protest against caste', she explained, 'is only confined to your mouth. We, on the contrary, carry it out in practice by imposing a uniformly white cover over all colour distinctions.'

I was about to reply, that my protest against caste did truly have its origin in my mouth, whenever I accepted with relish the excellent food cooked by a Muhammadan. It was certainly oral, but not verbal; and its movements were truly inward. An external cover hides distinctions, but does not remove them.

I am sure my argument deserved utterance, but being a helpless male, I timidly sought safety in a speechless neutrality; for, I knew, from repeated experience, that such discussions, started in our domestic seclusion, are invariably carried by my wife, like soiled linen, to her friendly circle to be ruthlessly beaten and mangled. She has the unpleasant habit of collecting counter-arguments from the mouth of Professor Nayanmohan, exultantly flinging them in my face, and then rushing away from the arena without waiting for my answer.

I was perfectly certain about what was in store for me at the Professor's tea-table. There would be some abstruse dissertation on the relative position in Hindu culture of tradition and free thought, the inherited experience of ages and reason which is volatile, inconclusive, and colourlessly universal. In the meanwhile, the vision floated before my mind's eye of the newly-brought books, redolent of Morocco leather, mysteriously veiled in a brown paper cover, waiting for me by my cushions, with their shy virginity of uncut pages. All the same, I was compelled to keep my engagement by the dread of words, uttered and unuttered, and gestures suggestive of trouble.

We had travelled only a short distance from our house. Passing by the street-hydrant, we had reached the tiled hut occupied by an up-country shopkeeper, who was giving various forms to indigestibility in his cauldron of boiling mustard oil, when we were obstructed by a fearful uproar.

The Marwaris, proceeding to their temple, carrying their costly paraphernalia of worship, had suddenly stopped at this place. There were angry shouts, mingled with the sound of thrashing, and I thought that the crowd were dealing with some pickpocket, enjoying the vigour of their own indignation, which gave them the delightful freedom to be merciless towards one of their own fellow beings. When, by dint of impatient tooting of horn, our motor car reached the centre of the excited crowd, we found that the old municipal sweeper of our district was being beaten. He had just taken his afternoon bath and was carrying a bucket of clean water in his right hand with a broom under his arm. Dressed in a check-patterned vest, with carefully combed hair still wet, he was walking home, holding his seven-year-old grandson by his left hand, when accidentally he came in contact with somebody, or something, which gave rise to this violent outburst. The boy was piteously imploring everybody not to hurt his grandfather; and the old man himself with joined hands uplifted, was asking forgiveness for his unintentional offence. Tears were streaming from his frightened eyes, and blood was smeared across his grey beard.

The sight was intolerable to me. I decided at once to take up the sweeper into my car and thereby demonstrate to the pious party, that I was not of their cult.

Noticing my restlessness, Kalika guessed what was in my mind. Griping my arm, she whispered: 'What are you doing? Don't you see he is a sweeper?'

'He may be a sweeper,' said I, 'but those people have no right to beat him in this brutal manner.'

'It's his own fault.' Kalika answered, 'Would it have hurt his dignity, if he had avoided the middle of the road?'

'I don't know', I said impatiently. 'Anyhow, I am going to take him into my car.'

'Then I leave your car this moment,' said Kalika angrily. 'I refuse to travel with a sweeper.'

'Can't you see,' I argued, 'that he was just bathed, and his clothes are clean,—in fact, much cleaner than those of the people who are beating him?'

"He's a sweeper!" She said decisively. Then she called to the chauffeur, 'Gangadin, drive on'.

I was defeated. It was my cowardice.

Nayanmohan, I am told, brought out some very profound sociological arguments, at the tea-table, specially dealing with the inevitable inequality imposed upon men by their profession and the natural humiliation which is inherent in the scheme of things. But his words did not reach my ears, and I sat silent all through the evening.

The Parrot's Training

Once upon a time there was a bird. It was ignorant. It sang all right, but never recited scriptures. It hopped pretty frequently, but lacked manners.

Said the Raja to himself: 'Ignorance is costly in the long run. For fools consume as much food as their betters, and yet give nothing in return.'

He called his nephews to his presence and told them that the bird must have a sound schooling.

The pundits were summoned, and at once went to the root of the matter. They decided that the ignorance of birds was due to their natural habit of living in poor nests. Therefore, according to the pundits, the first thing necessary for this bird's education was a suitable cage.

The pundits had their rewards and went home happy.

A golden cage was built with gorgeous decorations. Crowds came to see it from all parts of the world. 'Culture, captured and caged!' exclaimed some, in a rapture of ecstasy, and burst into tears. Others remarked: 'Even if culture be missed, the cage will remain, to the end, a substantial fact. How fortunate for the bird!'

The goldsmith filled his bag with money and lost no time in sailing homewards.

The pundit sat down to educate the bird. With proper deliberation he took his pinch of snuff, as he said: 'Text-books can never be too many for our purpose!'

The nephews brought together an enormous crowd of scribes. They copied from books, and copied from copies, till the manuscripts were piled up to an unreachable height. Men murmured in amazement: 'Oh, the tower of culture, egregiously high! The end of it lost in the clouds!'

The scribes, with light hearts, hurried home, their pockets heavily laden.

The nephews were furiously busy keeping the cage in proper trim. As their constant scrubbing and polishing went on, the people said with satisfaction: 'This is progress indeed!'

Men were employed in large numbers, and supervisors were still more numerous. These, with their cousins of all different degrees of distance, built a palace for themselves and lived there happily ever after.

Whatever may be its other deficiencies, the world is never in want of faultfinders; and they went about saying that every creature remotely connected with the cage flourished beyond words, excepting only the bird.

When this remark reached the Raja's ears, he summoned his nephews before him and said: 'My dear nephews, what is this that we hear?'

The nephews said in answer: 'Sire, let the testimony of the goldsmiths and the pundits, the scribes and the supervisors, be taken, if the truth is to be known. Food is scarce with the fault-finders, and that is why their tongues have gained in sharpness.'

The explanation was so luminously satisfactory that the Raja decorated each one of his nephews with his own rare jewels.

The Raja at length, being desirous of seeing with his own eyes how his Education Department busied itself with the little bird, made his appearance one day at the great Hall of Learning.

From the gate rose the sounds of conch-shells and gongs, horns, bugles and trumpets, cymbals, drums and kettle-drums, tomtoms, tambourines, flutes, fifes, barrel-organs and bagpipes. The pundits began chanting *mantras* with their topmost voices, while the goldsmiths, scribes, supervisors, and their numberless cousins of all different degrees of distance, loudly raised a round of cheers.

The nephews smiled and said: 'Sire, what do you think of it all?'

The Raja said: 'It does seem so fearfully like a sound principle of Education!'

Mightily pleased, the Raja was about to remount his elephant, when the fault-finder, from behind some bush, cried out: 'Maharaja, have you seen the bird?'

'Indeed, I have not!' exclaimed the Raja, 'I completely forgot about the bird.'

Turning back, he asked the pundits about the method they followed in instructing the bird. It was shown to him. He was immensely impressed. The method was so stupendous that the bird looked ridiculously unimportant in comparison. The Raja was satisfied that there was no flaw in the arrangements. As for any complaint from the bird itself, that simply could not be expected. Its throat was so completely choked with the leaves from the books that it could neither whistle nor whisper. It sent a thrill through one's body to watch the process.

This time, while remounting his elephant, the Raja ordered his State ear-puller to give a thorough good pull at both the ears of the fault-finder.

The bird thus crawled on, duly and properly, to the safest verge of inanity. In fact, its progress was satisfactory in the extreme. Nevertheless, nature occasionally triumphed over training, and when the morning light peeped into the bird's cage it sometimes fluttered its wings in a reprehensible manner. And, though it is hard to believe, it pitifully pecked at its bars with its feeble beak.

'What impertinence!' growled the kotwal.

The blacksmith, with his forge and hammer, took his place in the Raja's Department of Education. Oh, what resounding blows! The iron chain was soon completed, and the bird's wings were clipped.

The Raja's brothers-in-law looked black, and shook their heads, saying: 'These birds not only lack good sense, but also gratitude!'

With text-book in one hand and baton in the other, the pundits gave the poor bird what may fitly be called lessons!

The kotwal was honoured with a title for his watchfulness, and the blacksmith for his skill in forging chains.

The bird died.

Nobody had the least notion how long ago this had happened. The faultfinder was the first man to spread the rumour.

The Raja called his nephews and asked them. 'My dear nephews, what is this that we hear?'

The nephews said: 'Sire, the bird's education has been completed.'

'Does it hop?' the Raja enquired.

'Never!' said the nephews.

'Does it fly?'

'No.'

'Bring me the bird,' said the Raja.

The bird was brought to him, guarded by the kotwal and the sepoys and the sowars. The Raja poked its body with his finger. Only its inner stuffing of book-leaves rustled.

Outside the window, the murmur of the spring breeze amongst the newly budded *asoka* leaves made the April morning wistful.